SIXTYFIVE ROSES

SIXTYFIVE ROSES

A SISTER'S MEMOIR

HEATHER SUMMERHAYES CARIOU

Foreword by Céline Dion

McArthur & Company
Toronto

First published in Canada in 2006 by
McArthur & Company
322 King St. West, Suite 402
Toronto, Ontario
M5V 1J2
www.mcarthur-co.com

Library and Archives Canada Cataloguing in Publication

Summerhayes Cariou, Heather
Sixty-five roses : a sister's memoir / Heather Summerhayes Cariou.

ISBN 1-55278-611-0

1. Cystic fibrosis--Patients—Canada—Biography. 2. Canadian Cystic
Fibrosis Foundation—History. I. Title.

RC858.C95S94 2006   362.196'3720092C2006-903858-9

Printed in Canada by Friesesns

The publisher would like to acknowledge the financial support of the
Government of Canada through the Book Publishing Industry Development
Program (BPIDP) and the Canada Council for our publishing activities. The
publisher further wishes to acknowledge the financial support of the Ontario
Arts Council for our publishing program.

10 9 8 7 6 5 4 3 2 1

For Pam

I am pleased that Heather Cariou is donating a portion of the proceeds from this book to the Canadian Cystic Fibrosis Foundation. This is a moving account of her family's refusal to give up when faced with the devastating news that her sister had Cystic Fibrosis (CF).

Known today as the most common, fatal genetic disease affecting young persons throughout North America, CF attacks both breathing and digestion. And although research, funded by donations, has made it possible for children and adults with CF to live longer and healthier lives, a cure, so far, has eluded us.

Cystic Fibrosis has touched Heather Cariou, and it has touched my family, in a very personal way. Heather's cherished sister, Pamela, died of complications related to CF at the age of twenty-six, and my beloved niece, Karine, lost her battle with CF at the age of sixteen. Like Heather, I remain committed to doing all I can to help defeat this devastating disease, which is still stealing the future from so many young people.

On behalf of the Canadian Cystic Fibrosis Foundation, and the families who battle CF bravely every day, I would like to thank Heather Cariou for supporting the cause we share, through this inspirational book. With her generous encouragement, and the contributions of many others, I remain confident that together we will beat cystic fibrosis, once and for all.

Céline Dion
Celebrity Patron
Canadian Cystic Fibrosis Foundation

I live where the river meets the sea.

I live where the waters of the Hudson end their cold journey to the Atlantic. My windows open to the East, the direction Native Americans believe one must face to ask blessings for a new beginning. The morning sun glances off the water strongly enough to blind you. Late afternoon turns the entire West side of Manhattan to flame. At night the rising moon hangs above the jeweled horizon like the Eye of God. The river flows by me, and flows through me. Memory flows through me.

I live where the river meets the sea, where push comes to shove, where love and anguish, blame and forgiveness, laughter and sorrow converge on the way to understanding.

My sister tries to breathe. Her lungs make crackling sounds as she takes quick, shallow gasps, her chest heaving in short bursts followed by long-drawn-out moments of utter stillness, each one longer than the last. My heart jumps before she breathes again. Her lips are blue. They flutter almost imperceptibly beneath the plastic of her oxygen mask. Her eyes are closed.

My own breath comes hard against the pain of losing her. I hold her hand, sitting next to her bed in the room where she once dreamed her teenage dreams. Gray light bleeds through curtains drawn against a late summer storm. We are cocooned by death and the sound of heavy rain.

As children, we loved to watch it storm—the wind flailing the trees, the lightning stabbing the sky, the rain thrashing its way toward earth. We stood together in the open doorway breathing in the dank sweet air, squealing, clutching each other with fear and glee at every clap of thunder. The mixing bowls, pots, and pans we placed in the driveway spilled over with soft rainwater. After the storm died, we stood together at the kitchen sink using the rain we'd saved to wash each other's hair.

But that was long ago, when rain was clean and hope was still a blessing.

She stirs, yanking the mask from her face, slowly focusing her eyes.

"Where's Mom?"

"Making tea. I'll get her."

We three are alone in the house. My brothers and sister-in-law have not arrived yet. My father is out at the pharmacy picking up morphine to mix with Pam's favorite peach brandy. "Bromptman's Cocktail" it is called, a drink prescribed for death, to ease the pain.

Quickly I fetch my mother from the kitchen, but linger in the hallway while she ministers to Pam. Our baby pictures hang along the wall. There I am, the proud big sister, not quite three, with Pam nestled up beside me, almost a year old. She has just learned to sit. There we are again, our infant brother Gregg propped between us, leaning on my sheltering arm. I am six and Pam is four. She grins triumphantly, having just pulled a bow from her hair. I remember her annoyance at that bow the moment before the shot was taken. I remember her chesty cough, and the way she matter-of-factly explained it to the photographer. "I have Sixtyfive Roses." She couldn't pronounce the name of her disease. Cystic Fibrosis.

"Heather," my mother whispers behind me, "Pam wants to see you."

I go in and stand at the foot of her bed. My stomach lurches as I realize that when she speaks, her words will be the last we share. She sits upright, propped by pillows, her fragile arms stretched forward up and over a hospital table to create more space for air in lungs filling relentlessly with blood and mucus, lungs punctured and scarred, frothing, folding in on themselves like wet plastic bags.

She wheezes, the humidity of August a granite slab weighing on her chest. Her words come hard, slowly, one by one, punctuated by long, trembling, tortuous breaths that she draws from the center of the earth. Her hazel eyes bore into me. Her bony fingers, clubbed and purple at the tips, clench the sides of the table as she struggles to speak.

"Write...our...story," she commands.

My sister's voice is not her own.

"Tell...what we...lived through...together."

A great energy washes through the room, as if a veil between worlds has been lifted. My skin prickles with the sensation.

"Yes," I whisper. "I will."

She reaches out, fiercely grasping my hand. "PROMISE ME."
"I promise."
She releases her grip and falls back. A soft roar fills my ears; the hiss of the rain, maybe, the whirr of my own blood racing, the cold hush of swift black water as my sister begins to drown and I am swept alone downstream.

HEADWATERS

Oh very young, what will you leave us this time?
You're only dancing on this earth for a short while...

And though you want to last forever,
You know you never will
(You know you never will)
And the goodbye makes the journey harder still...

— CAT STEVENS

CHAPTER ONE

"The real voyage of discovery consists not in seeking new landscapes, but in having new eyes." — MARCEL PROUST

There are promises that can't be broken. Mustn't be.

On pain of death. Or, as I have learned, on pain of life.

There are moments that can't be forgotten. Mustn't be.

I used to tell myself. Remember everything, because her life will be so short.

Yet underneath, there's this forgetting: how paper airplanes fly from the hands of a dying child, how the knife pierces flesh between the ribs and how the chest tube inflates the lung, though only briefly. Like people, memories can't always be saved.

There are words that can't be spoken. Mustn't be.

Or even thought.

But the words pile up inside, pressing against my heart.

Pam said, tell our story. Mother says, tell the truth. My truth, but perhaps a truth in which others may find their own, both shattering and uplifting.

The truth about our lives is hard to see, much less face. Except perhaps from a distance.

I have distance now I never wanted. Years of a life shared with my sister only in spirit or memory. Yet in that distance, in that time and space, has come perspective. Life and love have brought me to a new landscape from which, inevitably, I go to revisit the old.

Each time I return to my small, Canadian hometown I look, and look again, driving slowly through the familiar streets, following my life all the way back, thinking everything through once more from beginning to end, as if in wrenching the memories around, revisiting and reshaping them, I could change their outcome if only by a few degrees. I could perhaps discover how to assuage the sorrow that still lingers, or heal the wounds that still open at the slightest touch. I might learn how to lift the heart of my youngest brother, distant and melancholy, or open the heart of my other brother, tightly wound and closed-off. I could dispel the wounded bewilderment that has found a home in the fine crevasses of my father's face. I could bless the light that shines through the window of my mother's heart, broken, and broken again, and again.

Invariably, I make the trek through Brantford's north end, past each of the five houses we grew up in and the sixth where Pam died, past our schools and the good old General Hospital where we were born and where Pam spent part of her childhood, past Thorpes Brothers Funeral Home and First Baptist Church, and on down Brant Avenue, now bereft of elm trees, its stately nineteenth-century homes turned into 7-Elevens and video stores. As I turn right at the old Armory and cross the Lorne Bridge over the Grand River, I feel a faint tug in my chest, not quite grief, but a longing. Finally, I reach Farringdon Hill, and the laneway that rises behind the church where my parents were married, and the cemetery where my sister rests.

We planted her here as if we were gardeners burying early autumn bulbs, in a box made of rosewood, beneath a tree, atop a hill, on a warm September day after the rain, when the earth was heavy and smelled of grief. We planted her like a seed, a dead girl who would grow memories, the fruit of her short life ripening on our own branches.

On that day, the fields around the cemetery rustled with dry cornstalks and green, purple-tasseled tobacco. We tossed white sweetheart roses on her casket, comforted by the murmur of wind through the maples, the soft whisper of clouds passing overhead, and the cry of bagpipes coming up the hill, a surprise she had arranged for us, "Amazing Grace."

The piper was unsteady and his tune errant. This was exactly the kind of irony that would have made my sister and me both giggle in sweet union. We would have tried desperately to contain ourselves, biting our lips, clutching each other, avoiding each other's eyes to prevent a total breakdown of decorum. It would have been no use. Laughter would have defeated us, and we would have opened our mouths howling, the sound finally rising up into the sweet blue sky loud enough to wake the dead.

I turned, half-expecting to find her there beside me. Then I remembered: it was Pam who was dead, and if I had any laughter left in me, it would not rouse her.

We used to laugh at just about anything. It didn't take much to get us started. We had a secret, unspoken signal. All Pam had to do was look at me, and I was gone, we were both gone. The sound she made was infectious, a bubbling spring, a sound I couldn't get enough of. I did everything I could to amuse her, especially when times were bad. I danced, sang off-key, made faces, did impressions, told jokes and stories, the sillier the better, until her lips curled up along the edges, until her eyes sparkled, until she erupted with such joy that we were both reeling, clasping our sides and batting each other away, laughing so hard she had to cough, and I had to pound her back to help her stop.

I was her jester. She was my audience of one. Her laughter was a standing ovation.

Memory begins with Pam, and the day she entered my life. My mother called from the foot of the stairs in our first, tiny house on Willow Drive, urging me to get up from my nap, telling me she had brought home a surprise. I descended the stairs carefully, step by step, clinging to the banister, bleary-eyed from sleep. My mother stood in silhouette, a halo of sunlight blazing through the picture window behind her, and the fields beyond, once farmed by my father's parents, white with a late spring snow.

"Look," she smiled, "I've brought you a new baby sister." She held Pam out to me in her arms as if my sister was a special gift just for me.

My Pammy.

Pam and I were "baby boomers," born into the post-war era smack in the middle of the twentieth century. Our hometown of Brantford, population thirty thousand then, was an industrial farm town nestled on the banks of the Grand River in southwestern Ontario. Visitors were welcomed by a simple blue-and-white signpost planted in the ditch that ran alongside the King George Road proclaiming the city as the "Birthplace of the Telephone." If Pam and I were told once, we were told a hundred times, how Alexander Graham Bell draped wires along the farmers' fences from Tutela Heights all the way to Paris, Ontario, to make the first long-distance phone call.

We were the great-granddaughters of Scottish, English, and German pioneers possessed of stout hearts, stiff backs, strong hands, swift tempers, and stoic demeanors.

I was the oldest sister by twenty-two months, but Pam liked to insist that she was the oldest because her birthday fell in March, before mine, which came in May. Whenever I told her she was wrong, she got mad.

In 1957 Elvis was king, Diefenbaker was prime minister, Eisenhower was president, and life was good even though we were in a Cold War. Frank Sinatra crooned "Love and Marriage" from the radio, and my parents danced together in the kitchen as Pam and I perched on the kitchen counter, watching. They were delighted with their girls, and with their fresh, anything-was-possible life.

They captured that life in the eye of a camera. These pictures, small, glossy, black-and-whites on stiff paper, now curl with age at their serrated edges. Me at five years old, a chubby-cheeked, curly-haired cherub, already an actress, saying "cheese" so hard it looks painful, performing in Grandma's backyard atop a tall, round table that is my stage. My sister at age three, a tiny, white, china doll with a Dutch-boy haircut, gazing soberly from the saddle of a pinto horse on our front lawn. We had already survived our first disaster, hiding from Hurricane Hazel down in the basement with my mother, a candle flickering in the dark.

Before we left the house on Willow Drive, and the pear tree in the backyard, my father nearly died of jaundice, I hit my only friend, Kathy Duke, over the head with my toy shovel after she bit me, and Pam had pneumonia at least three times.

We traded up for a bigger house in Greenbrier, a newly con-structed subdivision built by my grandfather's company, Summerhayes Lumber. Lush farmland sprawled to the horizons north, east, and west.

Our new house was one of the three-bedroom bungalows advertised on a huge billboard that towered over the White Rose Gas Station at the turnoff from Highway 24. Built of red brick and set on a double lot landscaped with lush green sod, rimmed with poplar and pine trees, ours was a 1950s middle-class dream home. There was plenty of room for a swing-set, a sandbox, and the painted red playhouse our father built for us. On fine spring days my sister and I played in the dirt, pretending to help our mother plant red geraniums and a rainbow of petunias around the perimeter of the house.

We roamed at liberty, ranging across our new territory as far as our short legs would carry us. The sun shone. Milkweed pods exploded around us and their fluffy seeds floated lazily in the sweet-smelling air. We grabbed them with eager hands, made wishes, and let them fly.

"Look!" Pam gasped one day, pointing at a large chunk of pink granite half-embedded in mud, hidden by a tangle of weeds. The way it sparkled in the sun as we tore away its curtain of goldenrod and Queen Anne's lace, we just knew the rock was MAGIC.

"Daddy, Daddy," we raced home shouting. "Wait 'til you see what we found! Please, can we bring it home?"

Our father drove the forklift over from Grandpa Bill's lumberyard, ferried the rock down the street, and dumped it ceremoniously at our feet, at the edge of our lawn at the end of our driveway. Thrilled with our find, Pam and I washed it down with the garden hose until its rough, rosy complexion glowed. It became our special place to think, and dream. The rock was just big enough to accommodate our two skinny little bottoms, if we scrunched close and put an arm around each other. At night we sat on our Wishing Rock beneath the moon, shouting wishes to the twilight sky and laughing, trying to out-wish one another.

"Star light, star bright, first star I've seen tonight, wish I may, wish I might have the wish I wish tonight."

"I wish for a red bicycle!"

"I wish for new skates and not stupid old used ones!"

"A nurse's uniform for Christmas!"

"The blue chiffon dress from the Tog Shoppe!"

Pam and I couldn't have been more different, in looks or temperament. She was terrifyingly small for her age, with fairy arms and legs. My mother cut her flaxen, stick-straight hair short, "to frame her face." Her hazel eyes were bright saucers, and when she smiled, her pug nose crinkled and freckles danced across her alabaster cheeks. Everyone oohed and aahed over her.

People often remarked that I was "the spitting image" of my mother, tall and agile, with her corkscrew brown hair and blue, blue eyes.

I slept in the same room as my sister. We awoke and dressed in tandem, ate our Shreddies side by side in the kitchen, ran outdoors to greet the day hand in hand.

The walls of our room were papered with ballerinas in pink tutus that swirled and danced around us. Since I was allowed to choose it, Pammy went into a four-day snit where she wouldn't speak to anyone. My father said she took after Grandma Birdsell that way.

I guessed that made me more like Eva Rene, which was what my dad called his mother when he took her name in vain after one of their weekly fights, though we grandchildren called her by her dead husband's given name, Grandma Bill. Mom said that my father and his mother didn't consider it a good week unless they'd had a healthy go at one another. I guessed Grandma Bill had a temper, though I'd never seen it. My dad claimed he didn't have a temper, though I'd seen what passed for one plenty of times. To hear him tell it, he never yelled at anyone unless he was provoked and he never spanked me unless I deserved it, but I thought he was easily provoked, and I found myself "deserving it" a lot, which he said was on account of my bad temper. He rarely spanked Pam.

Pam and I fought about as often as two sisters might who were twenty-two months apart and shared the same room. Our different temperaments showed in our styles of combat. I was a volcano that erupted in magnificent explosion, all flying rocks and a flowing lava of tears. Pam was a slow burn, a fire smoldering through peat moss flaring up here and there in tiny vicious licks of flame. We took our fights for granted, as children do, and quickly turned our energy over to inventing games.

We loved to run and slide in the hall in our stocking feet

after my mother had waxed and polished the cork tile floor. When tiring of this, we closed all the doors, turned off the lights, and felt our way along to opposite ends of the hall. Then Pam ran toward me in the pitch dark while I listened for, or rather tried to sense, her approaching presence. I bent my knees and held out my arms while Pam, taking a complete leap of faith, jumped into the air, where nine times out of ten I caught her. Of course it was the tenth time that made the game worth playing, when our antennae didn't work and she just smashed into me or toppled blindly on top of me, and we fell to the floor in a tangled heap, rubbing our bruised knees and elbows, crying "ouch, ouch," squealing and giggling.

Our favorite pastime was something we called The Rescue Game.

We designated our beds, placed end-to-end along one wall, The Land, and pretended that the swirl-patterned pink-and-blue linoleum floor was The Ocean, and our closet, which ran the length of the room opposite our beds, The Boat.

We threw open the closet doors, stood on tiptoe at the edge of our beds, and jumped back and forth to and from The Boat, trying not to fall in The Ocean, scoring points for every safe landing.

Pam was too small to jump far enough, so she almost always fell in, and then lay squirming and gasping on the floor, floundering in The Ocean.

"Help, help, I'm drownding!" she cried out to me.

"Don't worry, I'll save you!"

I jumped down to grab her, and together we pretended to struggle against the roiling tide while I dragged her to safety.

Once securely back on The Land we hollered in unison, "Hooray, yay!" cheering the rescue, gleefully bouncing up and down on the beds.

"Look, I can almost touch the ceiling!"

"How many times do I have to tell you girls not to do that? You'll fall and hurt yourselves! You'll wreck the box springs!" our mother called out from the kitchen.

We dropped to the bed breathless and laughing, laughing so hard that Pam started to cough, a spiky, rumbling, terrible cough that made her whole body shake.

"Stop laughing," I demanded, still giggling, slapping her back to help dislodge the strange gobs of mucus that frothed up from her lungs.

"I can't," she said, and coughed and laughed and laughed and coughed until she turned pale blue. I gave her a couple more hard whacks on the back, and she spit up gray-green phlegm into a Kleenex from a box on the dresser.

"Let's do it again!" she exclaimed. "Only this time you have to fall in."

So we jumped again, and I fell into The Ocean so she could rescue me, too.

My sister never let her mysterious cough keep us from exploring the streets and alleys of Greenbrier by bicycle or on foot. The world of our earliest childhood was safe and sweet, bounded at one end of the street by a brand-new four-room schoolhouse and at the other by the Big Woods. Less than a mile to the north, past Consolidated Trucking, was McClures' farm. The big Summerhayes Lumberyard sat right across Highway 24 from the McClures, and adjacent to it, our grandmother's house.

Alone together, or in the company of neighborhood pals like Jan and Molly McGregor, we played hopscotch, tag, hide and seek, wore out the swings in the schoolyard, and picnicked with peanut butter sandwiches and orange Kool-Aid in the nearby woods.

Pam tired easily.

"Stop and rest," I scolded her.

"No," she retorted, panting. "I want to keep up."

We swarmed Stan's convenience store with our friends, crowding around the *Archie* and *Millie the Model* comic books, squeezing our allowance of dimes or quarters in sweaty fists, jostling to get close to the array of Pez, Lik-M-Aid, Sweet Tarts, and licorice. Clouds of cold vapor billowed from the huge freezer where our greedy hands searched for Good Humor Popsicles and Chocolate Drumsticks.

We built tree forts in a large grove of pine trees we called the Big Woods, ran laughing through McClures' cornfield, searched the grass for four-leaf clovers, and armed with empty jam jars, hunted caterpillars and tadpoles. The skeletons of half-built houses made excellent castles with cool basement dungeons and open-air throne rooms steeped in the sweet scents of fresh poured St. Lawrence cement and raw lumber cut from Northern Ontario forests.

On rainy days we pulled sheets and blankets from the closet, grabbed wooden clothes pegs and safety pins from the wicker laundry basket, and turned the entire family room into a giant tent. We dragged our dolls and jam sandwiches inside, giggling with delight at the private world we'd created, too small for grownups to fit. Our mother indulged our loud pleas to leave the tent in place for days at a time, after we promised, "cross our hearts and hope to die," to leave Dad's chair free so he had a place to sit and read the paper.

My voice rises up out of the geography from which I sprang. It is born of broad-leaved tobacco fields rolling as far as the eye can see, and gravel roads lined with rows of peak-roofed green drying kilns. It rises out of corn and cows and red-brick Victorian farmhouses with wide, white gingerbread porches, out of late summer thunderstorms and scattered patches of thick forest, out of deep snow, and damp cold, and the sweet, dank smell of mud and manure in spring pastures. It rises from the old assembly line at Massey-Ferguson, from the now-vanished, open-air farmer's market in the city square, from sun-baked enclaves of squat, pastel-painted wartime tract housing, and from the elm trees that used to shade the elegant nineteenth-century homes along Brant Avenue.

My voice rises out of the broad, brown Grand River, winding slowly through places with Mohawk names like Cayuga and Onondaga. As a child I was enchanted by the heritage that went with those names, and the oft-repeated stories of the tribes of the Six Nations. I wished I was part Indian like E. Pauline Johnson, a poet and local heroine, daughter of a Mohawk chief and his English wife, who became famous in vaudeville for staging her works in full native regalia. I wanted to grow up like her, to write poetry and perform, to be famous, and to have my home become a shrine like Chiefswood, crowded with glass cases full of relics. I loved spending time alone in the Big Woods at the end of our street, where I sat beneath "A fir tree rocking its lullaby," as if I were a young, modern Pauline, writing my own verse.

My voice rises out of the poems I brought home to my mother, and out of her eyes, blue as a clean morning sky after a night of rain. It rises from her ample bosom and ripe hips. She was a full-blown woman at sixteen when my father brought her to hear Glen Miller records and jive at Teen Town, a community club where young people gathered for entertainment.

Photographs from the cardboard box in my parents' closet show my mother's teenage face shining with sweetness and intelligence. She was a creamy-skinned girl with a shy but dazzling smile, wearing her kinky, chestnut hair swept back simply off her high forehead. Crimson lipstick and neatly arched eyebrows were her only bow to vanity. Sitting in a modest cheesecake pose high in the branches of a tree, wearing white shorts and saddle shoes, she beamed down at the camera, coyly modeling her great set of gams. Horsing around in front of the lens with a couple of girlfriends, she grinned playfully, clamping a cigar between her teeth, showing off all five-foot-seven of her statuesque charm in a clinging sweater set and pants.

When I first discovered these photos at about age ten, they seemed shocking to me, for by that time most of the coy mischief so apparent in the young Donna Birdsell had disappeared under the weight of caring for my sister. The pictures left me longing to know more of my mother's playful side, and I began to anticipate those moments when the sun showed itself through the clouds that by then had already come to darken her face.

It floored me to learn that my mother could ace a time-step, slam dunk a basketball, and do algebra in her head. Behind her skills, she warned me sternly, were hours of dedicated preparation, discipline, and practice.

Pam and I supposed our mother, so modest and intense, was too straight-laced for shenanigans. We collapsed in embarrassment the day my father winked and told us that when he first saw Mom dancing at Teen Town, her sparkling laugh, and the way her hips moved when she jived, gave him hints of a wilder spirit.

My father ran Teen Town. Mother told us, with a loving smirk, that was because he owned the records and the phonograph. Being a Summerhayes, she said, he could afford them. At age nineteen he was a skinny sapling rising six feet, beardless and soft-skinned, so pale his friends called him "Whitey." All gangly arms and legs draped in expensive clothes from Ludlow's, he wore his wavy brown hair fashionably slicked back off his forehead. His fine wool pants were crisply pressed, his jackets hand stitched, his brown-and-white spectator shoes polished to a gloss. He was fond of jingling the change in his pockets. Spectacles did not hide the curiosity in his eyes, blue as the larkspurs in his mother's garden, set in a slender face that lied about his age, as it still does. His guileless nature and desire to please made folks take him for an easy mark, someone to tease or take advantage of. Yet he was not as naive as some people imagined, and he was certainly no fool.

Fond of romance as I am, I wish I could say that when my parents looked at each other for the first time love hit like a two-by-four, but I can't. When they met, according to my mother, my father was a randy youth capable of driving off the road while gazing at a woman who was "stacked"—or even better, a good stack of lumber. She initially thought him a jerk: on at least two early dates they emerged from Teen Town into the snowy cold to find that my father had left the car lights on, killing the battery. She then had to help push the car down the lane while my father sat behind the wheel, shouting to her out the window, "Keep pushing, the engine's going to turn any minute!"

This turned out to be classic Doug Summerhayes, denying that anything frozen and dead couldn't be brought back to life through the forces of sheer will and optimism. By my estimate, this story has proved a metaphor for their entire marriage: my mother has served as the driving force, while my father has tried to steer their life with parts of it disabled.

Still, it was this intrepid attitude that my mother found part of his charm. Besides, my father was a Summerhayes.

"You're a Summerhayes. You must be rich."

Kids in the schoolyard jeered at us and their parents passed comment when we visited their homes to play, as if by being a Summerhayes we were guilty of some crime. I never understood this for it did not appear to me that we were any better off than most of our neighbors. Still, I grew up ashamed of who I was, and found myself defending the Summerhayes name while longing to disassociate myself from it. People assumed we were wealthy because my late paternal grandfather had prospered, working his way from country farmer to C.E.O. of his own thriving lumber business.

At family gatherings I overheard a lot of talk about "The Estate," spoken in a hushed but inflated rhetoric. His fiduciary legacy was, I guess, substantial for its place and time. We did not realize as much benefit from it as many people might have imagined, due to the way the estate was structured, and because the costs of caring for a sick child quickly devoured our share.

My father was his father's third son. It upset Pam and me to realize that he felt overshadowed by his two older brothers and undermined by his two younger sisters, who seemed to consider him something of a ne'er-do-well. He saw himself as the family scapegoat, and there were times when that was likely true. My father's family was fractious, and the estate's administration was the subject of a number of family rows. This ongoing contention hung over our lives like a threatening sky.

Even so, Pam and I adored going to the lumberyard with our dad, playing hide and seek between the stacks of lumber, rolling in the sawdust of the Big Shed, or fooling around with Formica samples and typewriters in the office showroom. I loved the musty odor of the linoleum floors in the office, the sweet air that filled the cool, cavernous dark of the Big Shed, and the spicy, green fragrance of fresh-cut lumber.

We clapped our hands with glee, laughing as we watched our father ride high atop the forklift truck, whipping in and around between the stacks of lumber, shifting the gears like he was at the wheel of a Formula One racing car. Or when he was on-site building a house, loping around the roof with his tall, spare frame, shouting directions at his crew, kneeling down beside them, banging away with his hammer beneath the hot sun, yowling "Jeez Murphy!" if he hit his thumb. His canvas apron, heavy with tape measures and tools, sagged down below his skinny waist around slim, blue-jeaned hips. His arms were long and sinewy; his chest hairless and sunburned. He'd nurse his injured thumb in his mouth, smiling with what the other workmen might call a "shit-eating grin," and it was clear to us that he was happier than the father we saw most of the time going back and forth to the office in a suit and tie.

We could not help sensing how deeply he felt compelled to live up to the name Summerhayes, how much he wanted the esteem he thought would come only from wearing that suit and sitting at the mahogany desk in the air-conditioned front office. He dreamed of making a million before he was forty, hoping that would finally gain him the respect of his mother and older brothers. He invested a great deal of himself in that dream, and lost a great deal of himself chasing it, but in the process he demonstrated to us how much big dreams can cost, and why some are still worth pursuing.

Prior to meeting Doug Summerhayes, my mother had been accepted at Nursing School and asked to join the first Canadian women's professional basketball team. She was strong tea in a porcelain cup, a sweet-natured, industrious soul who, as a young wife and mother, was bent on keeping her life and her house in order. So determined was she to fulfill her role that her efforts sometimes threatened to diminish her joy. She came by this honestly, having learned as a child how to be well organized, how to make the most out of very little, whether love or money, how to keep busy to avoid feeling lonely or sad, and the importance of being "well turned out."

Unlike my father, she was raised in a one-bedroom cottage with a pot-belly stove and no indoor plumbing, a fact that both astonished and appalled me, my own Aboriginal fantasies notwithstanding. Her mother worked as a practical nurse, "wiping old people's bottoms," while her father eked out a living as a truck mechanic.

"Your grampa and me come from nothing, *nothing*!" Grandma loved to cry, her voice sharp with pride and resentment.

At the age of three, my mother was "boarded out" for several months while her parents separated during a patch of marital discord. She saw her own mother for only an hour once a week, and her custodians, a childless couple from the neighborhood, were Victorian in their notions. If she didn't eat everything on her plate, my mother was forced to sit alone in the empty dining room for hours, her cold food still in front of her. This is only a small sample of the mistreatment she endured. The trauma of that early experience was deeply wounding, branding her with a lifelong fear of abandonment, and a sense of raw vulnerability.

She began mothering at the age of nine when her brother, my Uncle Doug, was born. He was left largely in her care while my grandmother returned to work.

My mother often told us that no matter how poor they were, my grandmother always set a "lovely" table. There was always a white lace tablecloth and decent china, she wanted Pam and me to know. I was a grown woman before I fully came to understand how much of my mother's young life was lost to pressing those tablecloths, washing that china, and preparing the food eaten at that lovely table—a girl not yet in puberty left with little supervision or praise, burdened with the care of her baby brother and running the house while her parents worked to make ends meet.

Dreams of pro basketball and nursing shattered like cheap glass when I was conceived in the haste of young love, Teen Town swing music in my veins. Hearing the news, Grandma Birdsell said she knew someone who did abortions, but my parents said, "No, thanks."

I didn't give a thought to the circumstances of my conception until I was sixteen. While planning a surprise anniversary party for my parents, I subtracted May from October, and went crying to my sister.

"I'm responsible for them being together, and if it wasn't for me, Mom would have gone ahead and been a nurse like she wanted instead of marrying Dad, and none of us would have been born, and then you and Jeff wouldn't have CF…it's all my fault."

"Don't be silly," Pam smirked.

I confronted my parents, accusing them of not wanting me in the first place, crying that I was just a big mistake.

"You don't really love me, you just put up with me because you have to."

My father's face turned to ash.

"That's not true." He began to weep. "Your mother and I wanted you very much. That's why we got married. Because we wanted you. We loved you from the moment we found out about you."

My mother wed two months before her eighteenth birthday. Her dress was made of fine French silk velvet, sewn on someone's kitchen table and paid for with a case of beer. Grinning broadly, she and my father, who was barely twenty-one, were paraded out of Farringdon Hill Church, past the cemetery where their second child would someday rest, and on through town, borne by a streamer-festooned horse and buggy.

"We were ready to take on the world," my mother chuckles ruefully as she looks back with me, and take it on they did, though not in the way they might have imagined on that radiant October day.

My voice rises out of my mother's need for affection and security and my father's fear of failure, out of their integrity, their compassion, and their dogged determination. It rises too from my sister's laughter, the courage I witnessed in her, her wisdom, and her faith. Most profoundly, my voice rises up from the grave where memory stands, the river where it flows.

Pam said tell our story. Mother says tell the truth.

The story I tell lies somewhere between truth and memory. Pam survives through the telling.

So do I.

CHAPTER TWO

"The child who tastes salty will soon die."
— OLD GERMAN SAYING

In memory, it's a short trip back to the house at 16 Brier Crescent, to the poplar trees and my mother's petunias and the room with the ballerina wallpaper. It's been a longer journey coming to terms with how our lives changed there.

Like the television shows of the time, the world of my early childhood was so *Leave It to Beaver* and *Father Knows Best*, so clean and ordered and promising, my parents' dreams for the future so fresh and sweet, it was impossible to believe anything sinister was already insidiously in our midst. Perhaps that was why it took so long for anyone to acknowledge that the signs of trouble that appeared weren't merely worrisome, they were ominous. Even so, there was always the hope, the bedrock belief, that whatever it was, once identified, could be made right.

The first sign was that my sister delivered at only four pounds, three ounces, slipping out of my mother like a wet fish, her blue-marbled skin translucent as onion paper. Judging from her appearance, the doctors told my mother that Pam was four weeks premature, and she believed them in spite of her doubts, because it was 1954, and she was only twenty-one, and doctors were Gods.

Later, of course, we would realize that Pam was likely full-term, that the odds had been against her virtually from conception, a tiny struggling creature with malformed pancreas and lungs, tucked up in my mother's womb, kicking with clubbed feet. Once born, she suffered from the condition every new mother fears, "failure to thrive," barely growing and gaining little weight. Initially this was explained by the fact that she spent her first weeks of life immobilized by casts to correct the foot deformity. Once the casts were removed, however, she continued to languish, wheezing and coughing, eating but not flourishing.

Every week, my mother loaded my baby sister and me into her little beige Hillman roadster to go see Dr. Hutton. I didn't like going there. It was a small warren of dim rooms that reeked of Mercurochrome and danger. I didn't like the thin broadloom in the vestibule, or the cold linoleum in the examining rooms. I didn't like the strange instruments made of rubber and steel, or the long needles that seemed to appear from the same drawers as the cherry lollipops. Dr. Hutton lifted Pam onto the scale, shook his head, and sighed. I didn't like how he listened to her chest through his black snake of a stethoscope, a grave stillness always settling into the features of his mustached, hound-dog face.

"What can it be?" my mother asked, every week.

I didn't like that he never gave her a straight answer: colic, celiac disease, bronchitis, asthma, any or all of the above.

"Fine then, what should I do?" Her neck flushed red as she fought back tears.

"I've told you. Don't let her drink cow's milk, don't let her wear wool, and be careful to keep the house free from dust."

"It's an odd thing you know, she tastes very salty when I kiss her."

Dr. Hutton always harrumphed when my mother said this, and I didn't like that either.

By the time Pam was four she had suffered through several nasty bouts of "pneumonia" and been tested for everything Dr. Hutton could think of. Her malingering cough had grown to the size of a small explosion. At bedtime my father rigged a sheet over Pam's bed to catch the steam from a nearly boiling kettle, hoping the hot mist would help her breathe.

"What's wrong with my Pammy?" I asked every night as he tucked us in.

"I don't know," he said, his voice reedy and hollow, "but Mommy and I are trying to find out."

Pam's terrifying, volcanic cough woke me in the middle of the night. I lay paralyzed in the dark, swallowed up by the sound. Her breath was wet with infection, a shuddering, crackling wheeze that labored against a tide of mucus thick as the minty white glue in my Kindergarten.

I felt her struggle from across the room. I listened, and I watched, and I breathed with her, in and out.

My sister was not a whiner. Right from the word go, she never complained. "Stoic," my father called her. When she was in pain, she pressed her lips tight and her face turned whiter than white. Her eyes became cold steel. You could feel the barometric pressure drop in the room, but she wouldn't let go a peep.

I knew she hurt badly the night my parents brought her home from the umpteenth round of allergy tests, because she winced loudly as Mom undressed her for bed. I looked up from putting on my own pajamas to see vicious red needle marks covering her entire emaciated body, running up and down her arms and legs, patterned neatly across her back. I felt an anger I had never known before, as if it had happened to me, as if every swollen pinprick pierced my heart.

"How can you let them hurt her?" I cried out, thrashing myself on the floor, sobbing. "You can't let them do that to her anymore!"

"Heather, sweetheart, calm down." My mother tried to pick me up in her arms and calm me with a patient explanation about the tests, but I would have none of it. I wriggled away from her back to the floor where I knelt weeping, pounding my fists on my bed while Pam stood half undressed by the closet, staring wide-eyed, silent and still.

"It's bad enough we have one child who's sick," cried my mother, "now we have one who is hysterical. It's the last straw, Doug. Heather is right. We can't let them put Pam through any more of this. We have to find out what's wrong with her once and for all."

The last straw was really Grandma Bill, who brought my mother to tears berating her to "Get that child to a specialist!"

Dr. Hutton finally referred Pam to T. Emmett Cleary, a soft-spoken young pediatrician. Dr. Cleary, in turn, sent my sister for assessment to the Hospital for Sick Children in Toronto. The purpose of these tests served merely to rule out everything except what he suspected from the moment he first laid eyes on Pam.

As we waited at home for the results, my mother washed dishes, made beds, ironed hankies. The simple tasks of every day swelled in size and importance to fill the time. My parents spoke softly. The clock ticked loudly. The whole house held its breath. Each time the telephone rang, we leapt out of our skin. Hours became days, days grew into a week.

One afternoon, my mother made a cup of tea, curled up in a quiet spot alone in the living room, and tried to read a magazine. She came across an article about children who tasted salty when they were kissed, who had terrible coughs and repeated chest infections, and who ate voraciously but did not grow or gain weight. These children had something called Cystic Fibrosis. These children died.

Another week later, on a warm day in May of 1958, two months after Pam's fourth birthday and twelve days after I turned six, the telephone rang and my parents made the long, silent drive to Toronto.

As the story goes, they entered the cavernous front lobby of the Hospital for Sick Children and listened to their hearts pound in the carpeted, heavily draped silence, waiting to be called upstairs. Life-sized oil portraits of famous doctors stared down at them benignly. Finally they rode a slow elevator to a stark white floor and searched their way through a maze of florescent-lit, windowless corridors. They were invited to sit again, in a cramped, airless cubicle. They held hands, waiting. Waiting. Waiting. Finally the doctor appeared, brusque, perfunctory, sorry to have kept them, the measure of authority and the picture of bad news. He found it hard to look my parents in the eye.

Where is God? My mother asked herself when they heard their worst fears confirmed. *Is God the doctor? He speaks as though he is.* My mother swallowed hard. My father sighed through pursed lips, slowly.

"There is no treatment," the doctor-god said. "There is no cure. All you can do is take her home and make her comfortable."

"How long does she have?" my father stuttered.

"Most children with Cystic Fibrosis are diagnosed in infancy, usually at autopsy, so we can't say for sure. Six weeks, six months maybe. If you're lucky and watch her closely, you might get six years."

The next afternoon my mother came into our bedroom, gathered us up onto our pink chenille bedspreads, put her arms around us, and took a deep breath.

"Pammy has been very sick, as you know. We found out she has something called Cystic Fibrosis. It is something you were born with, Pam. Now listen to me very carefully. The doctors say that you might always have to feel sick, but your daddy and I are going to do everything we can to find a way to make you better. We will never give up hope. We will never stop trying."

My mother's neck turned red and blotchy. She swallowed hard and went on.

"Now girls, some children die of this sickness. I'm not sure you understand what this means, but everybody has to die some time; even Mommy and Daddy will die some day. It's part of life. This means we stop living here with each other and go to Heaven to live with God."

I tried hard to make sense of this. Somehow I knew that life would never open up before me, for instead it had opened beneath me, and I felt as if I were falling.

My mother continued to speak. "The time you die is decided by God, but that time is a long way off for all of us I'm sure, so in the meantime it is important for you to remember that we love you, and God loves you, and we'll just keep asking Him to help us find a way to make Pammy better."

The room began to spin and I couldn't make it stop. I could barely breathe. I was drowning in my mother's words, flailing, trying to stay afloat.

"Do you have any questions?" she asked, her voice raw but gentle.

"Will I get Cystic Fibrosis?"

"No," she answered, "you have to be born with it like Pammy was."

"That's not fair. Why didn't I get it too?"

"I don't know, Heather," my mother sighed, "I guess it's just the way God meant it to be."

I knew I shouldn't be mad at God, but I was. My heart pounded furiously at the betrayal. How dare He make my sister die without me?

Pam began to weep, burying herself in my mother's bosom.

"There, there," whispered my mother holding Pam close, rocking her back and forth. Her tears fell into my sister's baby-fine hair. My mother's arms had always been open to both of us, but now the space filled up between them and I did not fit.

I ran to the bathroom. The color of terror was green. Green tiles, green Formica countertops, green chenille scatter rugs, green linoleum, green towels, all swirled dizzily around me. My stomach backed up into my throat; I choked on the burning acid and spit up into the toilet.

I closed my eyes and tried to imagine what it felt like to be dead. I opened one eye a speck so I could see in the mirror what it might look like. My heart jumped against the pain in my chest. I opened my mouth and screamed, but no sound came out. Tears fell suddenly, and hard. I whimpered to myself, pulling with stubby fingers at my wet eyes.

The bedroom door creaked. My mother's footsteps sounded in the hall as she left our room and fled to her own. I willed myself to stop crying and ran cold water over a facecloth. It stung my hot cheeks. I took a deep breath and crept back to where my Pammy lay curled alone on her bed, tearfully sucking her thumb. I climbed up and lay down behind her, enfolding her in my arms, holding her close.

"Are you okay?" I whispered.

Yes, she nodded, though she trembled like the baby sparrow we found once, fallen from its nest in our backyard. Her heart beat right through my rib cage, in rhythm with my own, as if we were two bodies with one heart.

"I have Sixtyfive Roses."

"I know, but I promise you won't have to die alone. I will be your Protector, and we will die together."

CHAPTER THREE

"Light the fires
And close the door
To the old homes
To the loved shore
The far-farers
Return no more."
— ROBERT LOUIS STEVENSON

What is it like to wake the morning after diagnosis?

My parents drifted from troubled sleep into a terrible new consciousness, the sound of giggling children down the hall bittersweet.

I sprang from my pillow at the sound of my sister's laugh, forgetting, then suddenly, like a physical blow to the head, remembering.

My sister was going to die.

For a long moment I couldn't breathe. My throat hurt. Tears rose and sorrow swept through me. My breath came back to me in great heaving sobs, face down on my pillow. Then, just as suddenly, the tide of grief receded and I was calm again, believing, as children do, that I had the power to change things.

I dressed quickly and went outside to sit on the Wishing Rock. I looked up into the sky, hurting and bewildered, wishing and praying with all my might.

"God," I begged. "Please don't let Pammy die."

I asked as much for my own sake as Pam's. I was thinking of the promise I had made, to die with her. I didn't want to die, but I didn't want to live without my sister. Still, a promise was a promise. I couldn't take it back. So I cried to the heavens, "I'll do anything, anything…just please God, don't make Pammy die."

My life was tied to Pam's now, beyond being sisters. I knew that I was willing to give up my life, sacrifice a part of me, as much of me as I could bear, if only God would let her live in return. Where was He in the sky? What could I do to make Him listen? How could I get Him to answer my prayer?

"Heather," I heard my mother's voice calling. "What are you doing out there?"

I turned around. My mother peered through the open kitchen window, waving me inside for breakfast. The air was sugary with spring and the scent of poplar trees bursting with sticky green leaves. The robin's-egg sky yawning over my head, the neat houses lining our street, the barking dogs on the emerald front lawns, all appeared to be just as they had been the day before, but appearances were deceiving. That morning, I knew the world had changed and would not ever be the same.

God looked down, silent. Soon it would be time to plant petunias.

With the advent of my sister's diagnosis, it was as if my family had crossed the waters to a foreign land. We became immigrants in our own lives, leaving behind our identities and relationships as we had known them, losing the future we might otherwise have imagined for ourselves. Swept miserably onto this far shore, ignorant of language or custom, bereft of compass or map, we quickly learned that Cystic Fibrosis was uncharted and hostile territory. The doctors behaved like border officials to a country engaged in civil war, sternly warning of the chaos and certain death that awaited us in the landscape beyond, as if we had a choice whether to enter or turn back.

The world of chronic-terminal illness is, in many ways, akin to the world of war. It exists as a parallel universe to what might be termed "the real world." This so-called real world lies outside the door, down the street, across the river, beyond the boundaries of the battlefield. A world that presumes to be the definition of normal, where folks get up and go and do and be as they please, unfettered by the obligations of disease, or the assiduous anticipation of death. A world that carries on without you as you fight, one you long for, have a relationship with, even get leave to visit, but a world from which you must always return to face a harsher reality.

It was this double life we were called to lead. Under siege, our home became the frontline from which the battle to save Pam's life would be waged. Pam herself became contested territory. Like soldiers under fire, my parents went on permanent alert. Overwhelmed with fear and uncertainty, their fight or flight responses became geared for the worst. They slept poorly, startled readily, frustrated easily. Life wasn't simply life anymore. It was life and death, every moment of it, every reaction to it. I picked up on my parents' signals, copied their rhythms, and mimicked their responses.

Extended family and friends questioned whether we were "overreacting."

Faced with my sister's life-threatening diagnosis, the term "overreacting" was not part of our lexicon. We were caught up in a cataclysm. Fear was the undercurrent on which our days and nights flowed. Each new medical crisis reaped fresh emotional trauma, and the chain response of catastrophe couldn't help but ripple through the small and ordinary moments of our lives. The implications of Pam's illness assaulted us practically, emotionally, and psychologically. Our regular routines were immediately and thoroughly thrown into disarray. Our coping mechanisms, patience, humor, and logic, grew thin. Some days there was little calm or discernment to spare. Insignificant problems suddenly seemed too big to manage. If we ran out of milk, all hell could break loose.

My parents were hurt, scared, and constantly tired. They had moments of panic. Sometimes my father shouted. We wept bitterly, all of us, behind closed doors. In spite of it all, my father tried to remain outwardly optimistic and philosophical, while my mother was determined to appear cheerful and strong.

No one on the outside could grasp the complexity of our new circumstances. Nor could we, yet we expected so much from ourselves. Little did we know this was just the beginning of a chronic sorrow that even now still pulses in our blood.

What is it like to wake the morning after diagnosis? I'll tell you. It is like waking up after a night of storm to find that the river has flooded its banks, sucked your house off its foundation, swept it along on a wild black torrent, and dashed it back to shore in pieces, miles from what you recognize as Home.

No one came to keep us company. No aunts or girlfriends to sit with my mother and hold her hand. No uncles or cohorts to stand with my father in the driveway, in awkward silence. At least not that I remember.

Were they afraid of our tears? Afraid we'd ask more than they had to give? Embarrassed by a sense of futility?

A phone call. A greeting card. A casserole. It's the small things that people in crisis need. Comfort is easier to give than most people imagine. Our neighbor Ivy Johnson knew this as few others did. Ivy, with her British cheer and war-toughened grit, looked in, and brought comfort.

"You'll get through this," she would chirp in her Cockney accent, patting my mother on the back with one hand and offering pansies from her garden with the other. "Just like all of us in London made it through the Blitz. I'll look in on you later. Remember I'm right across the street if you need anything, a cuppa tea or a shoulder to cry on."

The Blitz. Ivy understood.

Our house reeked of onion and mustard plasters. Grandma Birdsell helped Mom make them. They stood together in the hot kitchen, slicing onions and mixing bowls of goose grease with mustard. Carefully, they spread the onion and goose-grease mixture onto big flannel squares cut from my father's old pajamas. The squares baked in the oven. Every so often my mother put on her fat oven mitts and carried one of the foul-smelling squares into our bedroom.

"Don't hover like that in the doorway," she scolded me.

Pam laid on the bed at her end of our room, gulping air through purple lips.

"Let me fold back your jammy-top," my mother whispered, and tenderly slipped the steaming mustard plaster onto my sister's bare chest. Pammy moaned. My mother glanced at me. "I thought I told you not to stand there like that. Now go play in the den and do it quietly."

I did as I was told, trying to hold my breath, suffocated by the sharp, pungent odor. I dressed and undressed my Betsy Wetsy. I read my *Pierre the Bear* book. I fetched our baby brother from his crib.

Gregg was eighteen months old. I was six going on ancient. I rocked him in the squeaky wicker rocking chair and fed him his bottle, or bounced him on my knees and sang "Ponyboy" like I'd seen my mother do.

Grandma whistled to herself in the kitchen. "Oh dear, oh dear," she sighed. The oven door squeaked as she opened it to check on the fresh mustard plasters.

The grownups bustled back and forth between the kitchen and sick room for days on end. Threads of muted adult conversations carried on in far corners and behind closed doors. The air was thick with sighs, whispers, and muffled sobs, suffocating me in a cloud of loneliness. Dark circles blossomed beneath my mother's watery blue eyes. She and my father stood together in the hallway. He reached out to hold her but she struggled with him, unwilling to be consoled.

"I feel so guilty."

"Donna, you mustn't blame yourself. It's not your fault. It's not anybody's fault."

"That's not what other people think."

My mother placed great importance on what other people thought. In spite of the diagnosis, there was hardly anyone who hadn't phoned to offer an opinion about what was wrong with Pam, and why.

"Everyone says she's sick because of something we have or haven't done, that either we are or aren't supposed to do. Both your mother and mine say the same thing—there's never been anything like this in either of our families before! They think it's our fault that Pammy's sick!"

"Oh, Donna, they're not blaming us."

"Aren't they? Shouldn't we have gone to someone else besides Dr. Hutton long before now? And who else should they blame? If anything happens to that girl in there it's going to be our fault for not taking good enough care of her."

At night my father paced the floor, crying out softly in the family room after he thought we were asleep. "I don't believe that nothing can be done! I can't believe there is no cure, no treatment!"

Dr. Cleary came and went at odd hours, carrying his stethoscope and a black leather bag. He was a small man with red hair and a kind voice.

"He's a good doctor," my mother murmured to no one in particular.

He took Pam's temperature. Gently, he folded back her nightie, slowly moving his stethoscope over her emaciated chest and across her bony white back. I wondered if it felt cold. He held her wrist and looked at his watch, counting her pulse, the beats of her heart. He smiled benignly as I waited at his side, watching, and he patted me on the head. He sighed as he stood to leave the room to confer with my parents.

My mother and father cared for Gregg and me with earnest love and affection, though it came at a premium, for they were preoccupied not only by my sister's care but by their own desolation. My sense of abandonment was keen, and their sorrow weighed heavily on my small shoulders. How was I to comfort them? What was I to make of my mother's emotional turmoil and my father's helplessness? The specter of my sister's illness overwhelmed me with its hidden terrors, but how could I share my fears with parents already overburdened by their own? Who was I to be in that house, and what was I to do to make things right?

I woke in the night as Pam convulsed with her shattering cough. I called out to my mother. She raced barefoot down the hall, my father close at her heels. They flipped on the light, flying to Pam's side. Holding my sister upright, they smacked their hands on her back as mucus exploded from her mouth. When the episode had passed, my mother picked up the thermometer from the bedside dresser, stuck it in Pam's mouth, felt her cheeks and forehead, checked the thermometer and replaced it on the dresser, opened the familiar bottle of cherry-flavored cough medicine, and spooned the sticky syrup down her throat. How much good it would do was anybody's guess, but there was nothing else to offer. My sister tucked herself back into bed. My father turned out the light. My mother sat with Pam in the dark, patting her back, singing.

"Away in a manger, no crib for a bed..."

When Pammy finally settled down, my mother crossed the room to where I sat up in bed, eyes still wide, knees hugged tightly to my chest. Gently, she guided me back under the covers, stroking my hair, crooning another song.

"Close your wee eyes now, close your wee eyes now..."

Soon my own breathing calmed.

She left the door open just enough so she could hear if Pam started coughing again, just enough so I could hear her weeping in the kitchen, hear my father sighing deeply, hear the kettle boiling for another pot of tea.

We had to explain Pam to others when we went out. Her cough turned heads and raised eyebrows. One day Pam and I tagged along with Dad to Parson's appliance store to help pick out a new washing machine. Ours was always overflowing. Dad immediately began talking with a man he recognized. Our father simply had to chat for at least half an hour with everyone he knew, and apparently he knew everyone. Deep in conversation, the two men leaned against a pair of refrigerators while Pam and I amused each other playing Hide and Go Seek between the freezers, ovens, washers, and dryers. The store was dusty, and after running up and down the aisles for a few minutes, Pam began to cough.

"My," said the man as Pam dashed by, "that's quite a big cough for such a little girl." His remark was no surprise to either of us. Pam shot him a look worthy of Bette Davis. He smiled sheepishly.

"Ready or not, here I come!" she shouted.

"She has Cystic Fibrosis," my father explained.

I was crouched nearby, hiding from my sister down on the dirty wooden floor, wedged between two General Electric stoves. My father's voice sounded sad, but brave, as always. I had heard several versions of this conversation by now, enough to be both bored and irritated by it. People either looked annoyed or questioned my father when they heard Pam cough, so he felt compelled to tell the whole story whether anyone wanted to hear it or not.

"Sis, uh, Six, uh,...is that the one with the muscles?"

"No. Cys-tic Fi-bro-sis. It's a disease of the lungs and the pancreas."

My father was launched. Graphically, he explained how Pam's lungs filled up with mucus like with pneumonia, and that there was no way to get rid of it, which was why she coughed so badly. He said her pancreas wouldn't secrete the enzymes necessary to absorb the nutrients from food, so no matter how much she ate, she starved, so her immune system couldn't get strong enough to fight her lung infections, and it became a vicious cycle.

Pam stuck her head around a corner of the stove and found me.

"Boo!" she squealed, and ran. I chased her down past the vacuum cleaners. "Let me hide now," she begged, "I have to catch my breath."

I walked back up near my dad and held my hands over my eyes, counting long enough to give Pam a chance to conceal herself.

"So," the man said, "even if she just catches a cold, there can be hell to pay."

"Oh, heck yeah."

My father went on to explain all that was known about Cystic Fibrosis in 1958.

It was the most common fatal hereditary disease of infants and children. It was incurable. It was caused by a recessive gene that both parents carried. The odds were one in four with each pregnancy that the child would have CF, one in two that it would be a carrier, and one in four that it would neither be a carrier, nor have CF. There was no way to know if you were a carrier until you had a CF child, because carriers had no symptoms, and because the gene, being recessive, skipped generations. It was estimated that one in every twenty persons was a carrier. The disease had only recently been isolated by Dr. Dorothy Anderson, a pathologist at New York Presbyterian Babies and Children's Hospital, who did a study of autopsies performed on infants killed by respiratory illness. Symptoms of the disease included a constant cough producing thick mucus, excessive appetite but loss of weight, frequent, large, foul-smelling bowel movements, an excessive salty taste to the skin, and repeated, prolonged bouts of pneumonia. CF affected the body's exocrine glands, which secrete tears, sweat, saliva, and mucus. It was often misdiagnosed as asthma, bronchitis, allergies, or celiac disease. Doctors referred to it as *The Great Masquerader* or *The Pied Piper*.

Dad, I always wanted to shout when I heard these facts reeled off, *nobody cares*. As young as I was, not quite seven, I could have given the speech myself, having heard it so many times.

The man's face glazed over politely.

"Ready or not, here I come!" I called. Fed up with my father, I went in earnest to search for my sister, and found her gazing fondly at sewing machines at the back of the store.

"C'mon, let's go see if we can get Dad to stop talking and start looking at washing machines. He hasn't even found a salesman yet. He's still blabbing to that man about CF."

We walked back and stood on each side of my father, staring up at the two men.

"So, you and Donna didn't know you had this uh...gene?"

"No. There's no way of knowing until you have a child with CF, like we did."

"And there wasn't any kind of test they can give you to find out?"

"Nope," my father sighed, "nope."

"We had a Sweat Test," I volunteered.

The man looked at me quizzically, then back to Dad.

Instantly I was sorry I opened my mouth. Now my father had to explain how doctors used the Sweat Test to help make a diagnosis, collecting samples of sweat and measuring it for its salt chloride content. If it was high, it was a pretty good indicator, along with other symptoms, that CF was likely. One of the first things they noticed about Pam, he always told people, was how salty she tasted when they kissed her.

"I see. Well, I'm sorry to hear all that about little Pammy. Will she be able to go to school and everything?"

"She's not retarded," I piped up.

"Heather," said my father, chagrined, "that's not what the man meant."

"Daddy, can we go now?" my sister begged.

"We'll go in a few minutes. You girls just be patient."

Pam coughed vigorously, hoping to deter the man and snag my father's attention. When that failed, she frowned at me in disgust. Her frail shoulders slumped beneath the weight of her wool coat.

"Take that off," I instructed, "you're getting too hot."

I bundled Pam's coat between my arms along with my own as we went to inspect the toasters on sale. Glancing over my shoulder, I saw the man shake his head while my father carried on, telling the part about CF being fatal, that the average life expectancy was five years but he and Mom weren't buying that, and how lucky we were that Pam was diagnosed in time. *In time for what?* I always wondered. The man gestured toward us and whispered something to my father.

"Oh yes," my father's voice echoed around the room, "yes, the kids know everything. Donna and I feel it's best to be up front about this so we've been very frank with them. We've told them in a way we feel they'll understand and we answer all their questions."

"Well, Doug, I'm sorry to hear all that."

"Oh hey, that's okay, thanks. Donna and I are determined not to let this affect us. We're just gonna carry on and...(sigh)...well, our lives are going to be normal, that's all, just as normal as we can make them..."

It was hard for me to know what my father meant by the word "normal." Maybe he didn't really know either. Was it that he would try not to let Pam's diagnosis change anything, our beliefs, our routines, our dreams for the future? As I grew, I came to view this as a kind of naïveté, which angered me, for it was clear that Pam's illness had changed everything. But I was naïve too. For many years, I held both parents in contempt for their efforts to be normal. While they were being staunch and cheerful, always looking for the silver lining, I perceived them as rigid and overly demanding. I didn't understand that the need to be normal was in fact completely normal, that their effort to create normalcy was a healthy, and necessary, coping mechanism. It was a Herculean task, protecting whatever scraps of normalcy were left to us. A kind of exactitude was undoubtedly part of the price they had to pay.

"What else were we supposed to do?" my father has since asked me. "Throw our hands up in resignation, or collapse, devastated, to the ground?"

In families with seriously ill children, there is always the question of how much to tell, to whom, and when, all in service of the need to keep things "normal." There is always a debate concerning how much should be let on about the elephant coughing in the middle of the room.

For the rest of Pam's life, we would walk a fine line between fearing her prognosis and maintaining hope. We would try to protect her, yet pray for the faith it would take to allow her both the risks and pleasures of an ordinary childhood and adolescence. We would balance a potent cocktail of emotions with the practical demands of our day-to-day functioning. We would be asked to trust the doctors even as we confronted the limitations of the care offered at any given time. Hardest of all would be detaching enough to prepare for Pam's death, while still working tirelessly to keep her alive. Under these circumstances, the need to create a "normal" environment would be paramount. Yet, the effort to do so, however necessary or well intentioned, would require a healthy dose of denial, which in itself would eat up enormous reserves of energy and beg a number of questions.

Could such denial fail to serve its purpose at some point, and become unhealthy? What might we have to expect of ourselves during those times when we were too tired, or the situation became too dire, to deny the truth? Once a crisis passed, how would we get back to normal? How were we to respond when friends and family applied pressure, directly or indirectly, to conform to their definitions of normal? For in the end, no matter how we wished, how much we vowed, or how hard we tried to fit the convention, our normal could only be the constant ebb and flow of uncertainty, and the anxiety it fostered.

My parents believed in an honest sharing of facts, and disclosed them to my sister and me with appropriate discretion. While I was grateful for their candor, the facts as I understood them vied with my parents' insistence on a "normal" life, repeatedly forcing me to swim the gap between expectation and reality. This left me floundering emotionally, unable to live up to their expectations, if indeed I could ever grasp what those were.

But I clearly grasped that reality was, well, reality. It was Pam's brutal cough in the middle of the night, her bones fleshless beneath powder white skin, her lips and fingernails tinged with blue.

The definition of normal is different for everyone, but insofar as my parents understood it, they tried to create as normal a life for us as possible. I learned from them, in spite of my own naïveté and belligerence, that when the river is sucking you down, if the effort to be normal is the one thing that will keep you afloat, then you hang onto it. If you were my mother and father, you tried to manufacture it with diligence and love.

Knowing there were rough waters ahead, when we woke the morning after Pam's diagnosis, and every morning after, my parents threw normalcy on us like a life preserver, the one precious gift they hoped might save us all from drowning.

CHAPTER FOUR

"In each family a story is playing itself out, and each family's story embodies its hope and despair." — AUGUSTE NAPIER

My mother sent me to a sleepover at Grandma Birdsell's place most weekends.

"It's a chance for Heather to feel normal," she said to Dad.

I was happy to get away from home, where the anguish and the smell of mustard plasters overwhelmed me, and where I felt all but invisible. Unabated pleasure awaited me in my grandmother's tiny kitchen. I loved the hanging lamp of beaten copper fringed with dangling glass "diamonds," the yellow wall clock that chimed the happy hours, and the claw-foot walnut table neatly set with crisp pressed linens for unexpected guests. A big picture window looked out over a sweeping backyard, all the way down to a rickety green shanty stuffed with all kinds of old furniture, shaded by the giant elm tree my mother planted as a sapling, when she was six, like me. Grandma kept a drawer full of string and pipe-cleaners, buttons, gumdrops, glass doorknobs and souvenirs from Niagara Falls. She whipped up crispy bacon, fresh squeezed lemonade, hot chocolate with marshmallows, root-beer floats, buttered popcorn, and Orange Crush. She offered me roast beef, elderberry pie with fresh cream, strong tea, and undivided attention.

I got to stay up late with my Uncle Doug watching vampire movies on TV. He was my mother's brother, nine years younger than she, and nine years older than I was. He was very tall, with a goofy grin and ears that stuck out just enough to make perfect mantles for his eyeglasses. He made me laugh by rolling his eyes, making silly faces, and singing "It Ain't Gonna Rain No More, No More," and "Lulu Had a Steamboat." He tossed me up and down in a blanket, or swung me around by an arm and a leg in the backyard until I got so dizzy my stomach did flip-flops. He owned a brand-new tape-recording machine and let me listen, *quietly*, while he recorded Buddy Holly and the Big Bopper off the radio.

My grandmother was, as my grandfather always said, "a piece of work" all by herself. A resolute, red-haired woman who had known nothing but hard work and hard times, she carried herself like Lady Eaton, even when mowing the lawn in a pair of cut-offs. Throughout my childhood she worked for a succession of wealthy widows, referring to each of them as "Madam." For many years I labored under the false impression that they were all one and the same person, living to an astonishing age.

I liked going with Grandma down to the dry dump by the river, to pick through other people's cast-off furniture. When she found what she thought was a gem—a small cherry side table or a walnut settee, she badgered Grandpa and Uncle Doug to get a wagon and haul it back home, where it sat out in the shanty until she had saved up enough spare change to have it recovered or refinished. She crowded her tiny house with these treasures and viewed them as extensions of herself, to be valued by us as such.

Appearances were very important to my grandma. When she could afford it, she did herself over like the furniture, perming and dying her hair, clothing herself smartly, out of spite for the "rich people."

"Ma," Grandpa teased her, "what are you doing all dressed up to the nines?"

"What's the matter? Don't you like the way I look? How else do you expect me to keep up with Donna's in-laws?"

She had her own wounds left over from childhood, losses she would only allude to, but which clearly had left her feeling impoverished. Grandma needed to show the world she was worth something in the only way she knew how.

Grandpa Birdsell was a simple man, an armchair philosopher clad in work pants and a sleeveless undershirt, with a penchant for Navy tobacco and Red Cap Ale. I thought he looked like Burt Lancaster, one of my favorite movie stars.

I knew Grandpa loved me because he called me "Het," took me for rides in the country in his black Chevy, and treated me to ice cream cones at the gas station. He mixed bread and milk with brown sugar in tall glasses, like he ate when he was little, and we would sit together at the kitchen table, talking. He said I was a little "musscat" and teased me that if I didn't behave, I'd end up in "The Hooscow." He imagined out loud what the world would be like in the future, his own science fiction.

"Someday, Het," he'd say, "you'll be able to call up someone on your wristwatch, just like Dick Tracy. Wish I could be here to see that." He'd light a cigarette, the matchstick crackling to life in flame, perfuming the air with sulphur. I'd sit quietly in the blue smoke of my grandfather's longing, wondering how he lost the little finger on his left hand. We stared together through the picture window, watching Grandma run in and out of the shanty.

Grandpa was at home with himself, but there was something about Grandma that kept everyone on their toes. She could be both generous and spiteful in the extreme. Although he waxed poetic about meeting "the red-haired girl of his dreams" at a dance, Grandpa also observed that "if you don't dance to Grandma's tune, she can cut you cold." It was true that when I visited, I often heard about some poor soul she was no longer speaking to. She worried all the time about what other people thought, but couldn't stand it when they told her. She took things far too much to heart, and usually the wrong way.

"People think we're trash," she'd lament. I wondered if anyone had really said that to her. "Those Summerhayeses, up there in their big houses, they think we're nothing, nothing."

It hurt to hear her talk about the other side of my family that way, yet secretly, I often felt the same.

Grandma Bill lived in a big house, with a big kitchen, a big formal dining room, a big billiard room, and a bathroom with a pink marble floor. I can hardly ever remember her coming to our house. We saw her only at church, or at her house on Sunday afternoons, or when we were at the lumberyard with my father.

Grandma's sister Great Aunt Elsie, or Dad's baby sister Auntie Ruth, sometimes came over to babysit. If we were lucky, we got invited to my cousin's pool to swim on a hot summer day. Otherwise, we rarely saw or heard from my father's family, except at church on Sunday, or when one of my uncles called to discuss the family business and tell my father what he was doing wrong. They didn't show up on our doorstep with groceries and jars of goose grease for Pam's mustard plasters the way Grandma Birdsell did.

A few weeks before Christmas, my father climbed a thirty-foot ladder to hang a huge lighted star on our rooftop TV antenna, and another on the tallest pine tree in Grandma Bill's front yard. He swayed high in the wind while our mother stood with her hands over her eyes.

"Doug, you're going to fall and kill yourself if you're not careful!"

Pam and I loved that everyone could see the stars shining in the dark from far away, like the one that guided the Wise Men to Bethlehem.

My mother baked shortbread cookies into stars that gleamed in our mouths like buttered gold. She collected pinecones from our yard and frosted them with glitter to make a centerpiece. She enlisted us girls to cut snowflakes out of white paper to tape on the windows. With cotton balls, glue and more glitter, we fashioned milk bottles into snowmen to decorate the fireplace mantle.

We wrote letters to Santa Claus, care of Hengerer's Department Store in Buffalo, New York, hoping Forgetful the Elf would read them on channel 7 TV. We waited eagerly for the first snow, each morning standing on tiptoe on our beds, craning our faces up to the window, anxious for the frosty miracle to occur. Finally our impatience was rewarded, for one morning the grass in our yard looked as if it had been sprinkled with icing sugar. We raced in our pajamas to the front door and flung it open, leaping as our bare feet burned on the frozen cement stoop.

"Snow! Snow! Snow!" Our breath hung in the cold air like frozen lace.

"What are you two thinking? Do you want Pam to get sick?" my mother cautioned, hurrying to whisk us inside, smiling in spite of her concern.

On Christmas morning we had to cut short our own celebrations to get over to Grandma Bill's. Uncle Frank, dressed in a red sports jacket and green felt holly bow tie, scotch in hand, drew my father aside in the corner of Grandma's big kitchen.

"How's Pammy?" he asked, sounding more officious than concerned.

Auntie Barb called out from the dining room, instructing our cousins, "Don't let her cough all over you!"

All of our cousins had been sweat-tested, but none had Cystic Fibrosis.

"You've got germs!" some of them taunted, racing around the den.

"You can't catch CF!" I shouted.

"Pipe down in there!" barked Uncle Lloyd.

"Don't pay any attention to them," Pam whispered, grabbing my hand to calm me down. "They don't know anything."

"We're going to Disneyland!" I bragged loudly to anyone within earshot. "We're going to be Mouseketeers!"

My cousins laughed. I couldn't explain to them, in front of Pam, why we were going to Disneyland, *why* I hoped we could be Mouseketeers. I had heard my mother talking to Grandma Birdsell on the phone, saying she wanted Pam to see as much of the world and experience as much joy as possible before she died.

I followed my cousins into the rec room. Grandma Bill had a large black eight ball, a novelty they took turns playing with. You could ask the eight ball a question, shake it between your hands, and the answer (yes, no, maybe, ask again) would appear floating in water behind a tiny glass window.

My cousins asked the ball if there would be skis or new clothes under Grandma's Christmas tree. I anxiously waited my turn. When they tired of the game and wandered elsewhere, I took the eight ball in my own eager hands.

"Leave me alone," I instructed Pam. She looked at me skeptically, pursed her lips, and slunk out of the room.

"Will Pammy die soon?" I asked the eight ball. *Ask again.* I shook the ball harder. "Will they find a cure for CF?" I whispered in case my sister was eavesdropping around the corner. *Maybe.* Again and again I shook the ball, panic rising in my chest until I got the answers I wanted.

Later, the families congregated around the tree in the front parlor.

My cousins sat on the other side of the room whispering to each other behind their hands, rolling their eyes, laughing. Were they mocking us, or was I just imagining? Why did their laughter pierce my heart? Were they simply reflecting the scorn their fathers had for mine, or did they see something in me, an irresistible soft spot that demanded ridicule? Or was it Pam, and her Cystic Fibrosis? Aching, I searched the faces of my aunts and uncles for answers. They were smiling and pink, oblivious with Christmas Cheer. How could everybody be so happy while I felt so sad?

Pam saw me close to tears. She told me not to mind. I couldn't help it. Holly didn't have to go home and wonder if her sister Nancy would be dead next Christmas, next month, or even next week.

Back at our house later in the afternoon, Grandma and Grandpa Birdsell came with Uncle Doug to join us for Christmas dinner.

This is the family I can count on, I thought.

In the soft buttery light of the kitchen, my grandmother mashed potatoes. Next to her, my mother made the gravy. My father chatted with Grandpa in the den, talking mechanics, talking Buicks and V-8 engines.

This is the safe, warm place.

Uncle Doug frolicked with Pam and Gregg and me in the living room, singing "Darling Clementine" to a tangerine, making us laugh.

We were called to the table. We sat down together and bowed our heads for grace.

This is the sturdy basket in which I'll put all my eggs.

A week later Grandma Birdsell showed up at our door to return my mother's gift to her. When she left, my mother wept at the kitchen table. I didn't understand.

There was a lot I didn't understand.

Year after year, the holidays tangled the chain of emotions around my family. Festivities took on extraordinary importance, underscored by the unspoken fear that each Christmas might be Pam's last. Our joy was always bittersweet. There was always the dread of going to Grandma Bill's, and the nauseating sensation that my family and I existed only on the margins while everyone pretended it wasn't so. New Year's Eve heralded both hope and misgiving, wondering if Pam would live to see the next. And Grandma Birdsell, perennially returning my mother's gifts, or calling a few days later to find fault with the way Christmas had been orchestrated. My mother's birthday, which fell the day after Christmas, would always be lost in the shuffle of trying to please both families, and failing to do so.

Some things, I finally understand, are not to be understood: that behind her smiles and cups of tea, my Grandma Birdsell kept a secret list of hurts and slights, cherishing her grudges, silently building a vast reservoir of subterranean rage. That my Uncle Doug would grow up to disown us. That at the end of her days my grandmother would follow suit, cutting my mother out of her heart, her life, and her Will, for reasons that remained her secret. In the end, my mother's family turned out not to be the safe place after all.

Most of the Summerhayes cousins would suffer the loss of each other's friendship, falling prey to negative kitchen table chat about each other's families. We were bound to take up the swords of our parents' sibling rivalries, and carry banners that weren't really ours.

The estrangements that evolved on both sides of my family were no doubt aggravated by the consequences of Pam's protracted and devastating illness. They magnified the loneliness, making our nights darker, our fears deeper, and our losses more profound.

I know now that our experience was not exclusive. Many families encountering catastrophic disease find themselves splintering in ways they could not have imagined.

We want so much from our families, regardless of illness or other provocative circumstance. We want to be heard by them, supported, accepted, and embraced. We want them to meet our expectations of what a family should be, expectations likely based more on our own ideals than on the individuals themselves.

We don't want to forgive our loved ones their flaws and shortcomings, and God forbid we should account for our own. We make unforgiving decisions about each other, or carry fears and doubts based on lack of information, unrealistic expectations, and false assumptions.

"There's this dream you have," a dying friend once confided to me, "that your family is going to rally around you. And then you find out who everyone really is. You get to see their true colors."

Just at the time your defenses are at their lowest, and your energy is needed to fight the illness, you are forced to stop and deal with the difficult realization that many of your family members, and indeed your friends, are not who you hoped they were. You discover that few people are ever completely up to the task of giving the kind of support demanded by catastrophe, especially over the long haul. They are frightened, like you, and frightened by you. They feel inadequate, so turn away and do nothing. Or they simply have their own agendas and hide in them, ignorant of the pain you are suffering, or of the way their awkward indifference contributes to that pain. Your world has changed, but everyone else gets to go on with their routines, finding safety and comfort in them. You begin to learn not to ask for help, because the answer might just as often be no, or worse, silence. You find it hard not to blame others for what they do not have to give.

The resulting isolation can be devastating, and asks each of us to confront the fear that we may not only continue to live in that isolation, we may die in it. Many AIDS patients have certainly discovered this.

I know there are families who do pull together in the face of illness or tragedy, who take the night shift and hold each other's hands and wipe each other's tears inexhaustibly. There are blessed friends who rally round. But I also know there are those who abandon the sinking ship, and I know that happens far more often than any of us would like to think.

Wanting to believe that "family always comes through for each other in the end," my parents and I continued to long for help and understanding long after we knew it wasn't coming. We could not relinquish that expectation, for it was too entwined with the hope we so desperately needed.

Pam had made her peace with this by the end of her life. I have tried to follow her example. It's a waste of heart and energy to be angry with people for what they are simply unable to give. I have built a family of friends that sustains me and renews my faith in this world, and the people in it, every day, as do my parents, and my husband's family.

I have renewed ties with two of my cousins.

Gail, from whom I'd been estranged for twenty years, hugged me unexpectedly at Great Aunt Elsie's funeral, and held me while I cried. Moved by this act of kindness, I wrote to ask her if we could meet and get to know each other woman to woman, leaving family history outside the door. Our first meeting at Tim Hortons turned one hour into four. That was several years ago. She has since offered me a place in her heart and in her life that I never anticipated. And she has a place in mine.

I also wrote to Nancy, who invited me to sit down in her kitchen with a glass of wine one summer afternoon, and talk. We continue to visit like that on occasion, cautious with our words, but mutual in our longing to find a place in our hearts where we can connect.

Essentially, my family was alone when we began our journey through the war zone of catastrophic illness. In many ways, and for many reasons, we have continued so throughout the years. Our hearts might have grown hard but for the way our losses broke them open. Living with a broken heart, and the pain that isolation breeds, I've learned that bitterness weakens the soul. It's compassion that makes you strong. And with compassion, forgiveness and love are always possible. They have to be, for they are the only physic that can truly heal.

CHAPTER FIVE

*"I have had dreams and I have had nightmares. I overcame
the nightmares because of the dreams."* — Jonas Salk

Just prior to the New Year of 1959 we packed Gregg off to
Grandma and Grandpa Birdsell's, and the four of us boarded a
plane for Pam's Dream Trip to Disneyland. We arrived at our first
stop, the Camelback Inn in Phoenix, Arizona, in darkness, but
when we woke the next morning, our hearts lifted at the sight of
foothills and palm trees silhouetted against a vast, bright southwestern sky. Before we went down to breakfast, my father perused
a list of local community services, looking for a Baptist church.

"Geez Murphy! Donna, look at this. It's a phone number for
the National Cystic Fibrosis Research Foundation!"

"Call them, call them!" Pam and I shouted, jumping up and
down on the hotel beds.

My mother's face flushed with hope as my father dialed the
number and spoke briefly with the representative. We held our
breath, never taking our eyes off our grinning Dad.

The N.C.F.R.F. turned out to be a group of doctors and parents trying to do *something* about CF. Barely a couple of years old,
the organization was setting up chapters all across the U.S. to raise
money for clinics and research. My father took down the number
of one of the founders, Dr. Wynne Sharples of Philadelphia.

"Let's call her right now," said my father, so excited he was vibrating.

"We'll call her when we get back home," mother argued affectionately. "First we'll have our vacation." Still, tears of hope glittered in her blue eyes.

"Yaaaay, yaaaay, yaaaay!" Pam and I squealed ecstatically as we bounced again on the beds.

The days that followed were all Dude Ranch and Disneyland, trail rides and teepees, cotton candy and the Mad Hatter's flying teacups. We laughed and played with abandon, eating ravenously and sleeping deeply, as if something lost had been found and we had indeed become the normal, happy young family of my parents' dreams, our future filled with hope and promise.

The night we returned home, my father didn't even unload the suitcases from the car before he was in the house and on the phone to Dr. Sharples, asking questions and jotting down information. By the time my mother got us into our pajamas and made a pot of tea, Dad was stuttering excitedly over the phone to Dr. Irene Uchida, a prominent geneticist he had met when Pam was first diagnosed.

"Irene? Doug Summerhayes here. Listen, remember when I brought Heather and Gregg up to be sweat-tested and you and I went out for coffee? Remember I told you how angry I feel when people say there is nothing we can do for Pam? Oh, I'm sorry...am I shouting?"

It never mattered to my father where he was when he raised his voice. Whether he was eager or angry you heard about it, and so did everyone within earshot.

"Well," he chuckled, "I guess I am a little excited. But remember what I asked you? Instead of just saying it's hopeless, why doesn't someone do something to help these kids? And remember what you said? That's right! You smiled at me and said, *Why don't you?* Well, that's why I'm calling. I'm going to do something and I need your help."

Next he called Dr. Cleary.

"How did it go with Emmett?" my mother asked when Dad got off the phone.

"I told him that Irene said I'm nuts, and he said she's right, but I'm *his* kind of nuts. He's going to get together with Irene to set up a meeting with Dr. Chute, the Chief of Medical Staff at the Hospital for Sick Children in Toronto."

It took several weeks and a number of phone calls to convince Dr. Chute of the need for such a meeting, and to pin everyone down to a date. What followed next passed into legend in our home. I heard the story so many times, I could vividly imagine it.

On a damp March afternoon, my parents gathered with a group of doctors in the hospital cafeteria. Dr. Chute, a stiff-upper-lipped Brit, sat at the head of a long table with all the arrogance of the medical profession stuffed into his starched white lab coat. Small, dark-haired and olive-skinned, Dr. Uchida sat with my parents at the opposite end, offering gentle encouragement. Dr. Douglas Crozier, a harried-looking, prematurely balding young man with deep bags beneath his eyes, sat chain-smoking between the two factions. He had done his internship at Presbyterian Babies Hospital in New York under the aegis of Dr. Dorothy Anderson, the pathologist credited with first isolating Cystic Fibrosis. Now he ran a general family practice with a special interest in CF babies.

My parents nervously presented their ideas for starting a Canadian Cystic Fibrosis Foundation.

"I don't understand what's driving you to do this," Dr. Chute responded in his cold, clipped English accent. "There's nothing that can be done for children with Cystic Fibrosis. I hate to be so blunt, but it would be better for all concerned if you'd just accept that. Why do you insist in pursuing a path that can only lead to heartbreak? You're just going to end up getting kicked in the teeth."

My mother sat dumbfounded and embarrassed. She has told

me her face and neck blushed red. Her eyes welled up with tears, but she found her resolve along with her voice.

"Do you think my heart isn't broken already? Do you think it will break any less if I just sit by and watch my daughter and others like her die? How can Doug and I live with ourselves if we don't try to do something?"

Her words hung in the stuffy air. Everyone stared down into their half-empty coffee cups. She rummaged through her purse looking for the Kleenex she used to blot her lipstick in the car on the way there, and blew her nose without apology.

My father flipped his paper napkin onto his tray, shrugged his shoulders, and leaned back in his chair.

"Well," he said, gruffly clearing the emotion from his throat, "if you won't help us, we'll do it without you." He pulled a rumpled white linen hankie from his back pants pocket and wiped his nose from side to side, his characteristic nervous gesture.

Dr. Uchida exchanged glances with Dr. Crozier. Both stared down the table toward Dr. Chute, who sighed deeply and asked grudgingly, "What do you want?"

"We want to hold a meeting of parents. Donna and I would like to write a personal letter of invitation to each family, so we'd like you to provide a list of their names."

"I can do no such thing," Dr. Chute erupted. "It's unethical!"

"Sitting by and doing nothing while these children die in front of our eyes is unethical," replied my father quietly, not about to back down. Everyone froze.

"All we want is their names so that we can write the letters," he continued. "We don't need their addresses. We'll turn the letters back to you, and you take it from there."

"It's against my better judgment," Dr. Chute argued, but in the end, with all those faces staring at him expectantly, he relented. That very evening, my parents sat down to draft their letter at the kitchen table. We had orders not to disturb them. My mother didn't wash the dinner dishes but put them to soak, a sign that the letter was important. The TV buzzed in the background, but the June Taylor Dancers found no audience in our home. Pam curled up next to me on the couch in the den, sucking her thumb as we watched Mom and Dad labor over their writing pads.

"Let me run this by Emmett," my mother said, and read the letter to Dr. Cleary over the phone. My father rose and made a fresh pot of tea. I noticed that my mother's telephone voice was different from her Mommy voice. My parents sat down again to rewrite.

"What's going on?" Pammy asked me.

"They're starting a foundation," I replied proudly. "They're going to find a cure for Cystic Fibrosis."

"C'mon girls, Gregg's in bed and you should be too," said my father, yawning.

I followed him as he carried Pam to our bedroom. He tucked us both in with a kiss.

"How many letters do you have to send, Daddy?"

"Oh, about three hundred."

"Then what happens?"

"Well, we'll cross our fingers and see who shows up for the meeting."

"When is the meeting?"

"In a few weeks, near the end of May."

"When in May?"

"Why is it so important?" he asked impatiently.

"When in May?"

"May twenty-third."

"That's my birthday. How come you picked my birthday to have the meeting?"

"Damn," he said, and flipped off the light.

On May 23rd, 1959, I turned seven, and the Canadian Cystic Fibrosis Foundation was born. I didn't care what I got for my birthday because the foundation was my real present. I knew the foundation would save Pam.

My mother emerged from her bedroom dressed to attend the meeting. Her looks matched her telephone voice, mature and forthright. After three pregnancies her figure was still shapely, stunning in a fitted red wool-crepe sheath dress and jacket ensemble, likely bought at Nyman's, the elite salon where Grandma Bill had entrée. Her thick, fuzzy hair had been cut short and tortured into stylish waves, and her lips were bee stung with Elizabeth Arden red. As she bent down to kiss me good-bye, teetering in her high heels, the scent of Blue Grass perfume made me sneeze.

My father whistled appreciatively.

"Oh Doug, stop it," she blushed.

We three children stood in the doorway with Auntie Elsie, waving several rounds of good-byes as my father breathlessly made trips back into the house for things he'd forgotten while my mother shouted at him from the car: his speech ("Doug, I've got it right here in my purse!"); his car keys ("Doug, they're right here in the ignition!"); someone he forgot to call ("Doug, I've already spoken to them! Let's just go!").

The moon had risen and Auntie Elsie had bribed us to bed with promises of stories about the chipmunks in her backyard when Pam and I heard the crunch of gravel in the driveway. We dove out from beneath our covers and raced barefoot to the side door as Mom and Dad burst in the house. The very air rushing in behind them smelled fresh with excitement.

"There were over a hundred parents," my mother exclaimed, breathless and on the verge of tears. "Many of them came from hundreds of miles away, carrying their sick children in their arms."

"Wait, wait, I'll put on the kettle," laughed Auntie Elsie amid a flurry of hugs and kisses.

In a few minutes we were crowded around the kitchen table, listening as the best bedtime story ever unfolded.

"One man stood up and asked, 'Are you really going to do something to help us?' like he just couldn't believe it," marveled my father.

"He probably couldn't. I was hoping that new suit and tie I put on your father would make him look older, but I guess it didn't. No one would believe he's twenty-eight. They all gasped when he took the podium to introduce himself."

My father's speech had ended with this declaration:

There are many obstacles to overcome, but Donna and I don't see them as immovable. And, yes, we have our fears, but our greatest fear is that our daughter, and others like her, will die if we don't do something. That is what drives us.

By the end of the meeting, my parents told us, the newly formed membership and Board of Directors had named our father founding president of the Canadian Cystic Fibrosis Foundation. The Board pledged to seek a charter from the Canadian government to incorporate on a non-profit basis to raise funds for research. A preliminary Medical Advisory Board had been set up, along with a Financial Advisory Board.

Our parents documented this to us as if we were part of it. My father confided that he felt an instant bond with a gentleman named Bob Ivey, who was elected as foundation treasurer. Bob's daughter, Karna, was my age and every bit as sick as Pam.

"Bob asked what we were going to do about headquarters while we're establishing our funding and working out our budget. I told him not to worry, we'll just use our house for the time being," my father chuckled. "And I told him the budget will just have to come out of the pockets of the executive board!" He pulled his empty pants pockets inside out and grinned.

"Your father thinks he's Don Quixote." My mother laughed her beautiful silvery laugh, and I knew that what they had brought home for my birthday was a wonderful, perhaps not impossible, dream.

Dreams don't always come true the way your heart wishes they would.

With the birth of the Canadian Cystic Fibrosis Foundation, the focus of our life at home became as much welded to the foundation as fractured by it, as if there were another child in the house vying for my mother's attention and my father's time.

My father was away from home more often than he was there. He juggled work at the lumberyard with trips across Canada, giving speeches on Cystic Fibrosis and setting up new chapters for the foundation. Montreal, Halifax, Moncton, St. John's. Thunder Bay, Winnipeg, Calgary, Edmonton. Rouen and Medicine Hat on bush planes. Vancouver. Many times, my mother went with him while Aunt Elsie babysat. They spoke to crowds of strangers, though they didn't consider them so, for the crowds were made up of fathers and mothers just like themselves.

They wrote letters on stationery printed with green letterhead that read:

CYSTIC FIBROSIS FOUNDATION
16 Brier Crescent, Brantford, Ontario

Our mother was late planting the petunias because she had begun a new project: a newsletter for the foundation that she called "Candid Facts." She spent hours at the kitchen table, under our watchful eyes, writing and rewriting the monthly issues in longhand on thick legal pads. The finished drafts were whisked off in my father's briefcase to the lumberyard office where his secretary typed them onto a stencil and ran off copies on a hand-cranked Gestetner. When the stack of newsletters returned home, still damp and sweet smelling, we piled them on the kitchen table.

"You girls can help fold and stuff these," my mother instructed. We happily obliged.

When Pam and I wanted to get away from foundation business, we closed the door at the top of the basement stairs and ran down to the cool, damp rec room. Pressed-wood paneling adorned the walls, and linoleum squares covered the concrete floor.

Pam ignored the old couch and worn overstuffed chairs that Dad cursed about hauling down the stairs, preferring to sit on the floor in the corner by the record player.

"You're not supposed to do that," I counseled her. "Mom said I'm not supposed to let you catch cold." Pam mimicked my words back to me and stuck out her tongue.

"All right then, sit on this," I demanded, dragging a huge brown cushion off a chair and onto the floor for her.

Together we sifted through our small collection of pressed-wax 45s.

"Let's start with the green one!"

Pam laughed as I danced a jig and sang along to the music. *"Oh me name is MacNamara, I'm the leader of the band..."*

We sang "How Much Is That Doggie in the Window?" as a duet. Pam took the part of the dog, sending me into fits of laughter with her "ruff, ruff."

Done with that, we turned to our Uncle Doug's records. Mom let her teenage brother throw parties in our basement, and some of his 45s had been inadvertently left behind.

Using our toy sand shovels, we mimed the action, giggling and singing, *"Ya load sixteen tons, and whadya' get? Another day older and deeper in debt..."* Later we fished our plastic telephones from the toy box and crooned, *"Put your sweet lips a little closer to the phone…let's pretend that we're together all alone…"* By this time we were laughing so hard we could hardly sing.

"C'mon girls, it's time to come up for bed," Mom called down the stairs.

"Just one more…" we pleaded.

We could not finish without singing our special song, on the yellow record that was our souvenir from Disneyland. I lifted the arm of the record player and placed the needle delicately at the edge of the disc so as not to scratch it. Orchestral strains and dreamy voices wafted from the tinny speaker as Pam and I whirled gently around the room, singing along.

> *"A dream is a wish your heart makes*
> *When you're fast asleep*
> *In dreams you will lose your heartache*
> *Whatever you wish for you keep*
> *Have faith in your dreams and someday*
> *Your rainbow will come shining through*
> *No matter how your heart is grieving*
> *If you keep on believing*
> *The dream that you wish will come true…"*

CHAPTER SIX

"Pull thy oar, all hands, pull thy oar, 'til thou be stiff
and red and sore..." — DR. SYDNEY DANGELL

We had a wicker rocking chair that squeaked softly, to and fro.

My mother rocked my baby brother Gregg when he needed to go down for his nap. My mother rocked Pam when she was not feeling well, which was nearly every day. My mother rocked me only when I begged her to, close to tears, because she said I was too big for that now. When she gave in, and I crawled up on her lap trying to make myself as small as possible, I closed my eyes, and the swaying back and forth felt like we were in a boat riding gentle swells on a river. The steady squeak, rhythmic, hypnotic, was the oar turning in the lock. The sky was blue in my mind, serene. In those rare moments I fell into heaven, my mother and I together, floating far away from a life that felt more and more like a hard row upstream.

My parents and Dr. Cleary returned home from a pediatrics conference in Montreal with news of a "mistogen tent," a controversial new treatment for Cystics.

"You can't make me sleep in a tent!" Pam insisted, tears spilling down her chalky, freckled cheeks.

They explained to her that if she slept in this tent, the mist would help thin out the mucus in her lungs, making it easier for her to breathe. It worked like an oxygen tent, except the nebulizers spewed a misty solution of distilled water and propylene glycol instead of oxygen.

"I don't care," my sister cried, "I won't do it!"

My sisters' protests were in vain, for the contraption had already been ordered and was on its way.

"Oh come on now," Dad teased when the tent arrived, "it came all the way from California. Hollywood!" He tore open the big cardboard box, and with Dr. Cleary's and Dr. Crozier's help, pulled out pieces of metal tubing and thick shiny bundles of plastic stamped with red letters that said No Smoking. They spread the parts out before us on Pam's bed.

"Pammy," I gushed, "isn't this exciting? You have something no one else in the whole country has." However wary I may have been of this apparatus invading our bedroom, I was still keen on the drama it embodied. The tent was the first of its kind in Canada and Pam was its guinea pig. If it worked for her, the foundation would purchase more for other CF kids.

"Now, Pamela," cautioned Dr. Cleary, "you understand you will have to sleep in this every single night for the rest of your life."

A large, noisy air compressor was stowed down in the basement and wired upstairs to our room to run the tent. Once the whole thing was assembled, after a lot of "damns" and "Jeez Murphys" on my father's part, it hulked over the top half of my sister's bed looking like a gelatinous creature from outer space, its shiny plastic skin drooping down from silver tentacles. The twin nebulizers, a pair of Mason jars, the kind you put homemade pickles or jam into, perched together inside like the flaring nostrils of an alien, more likely to suffocate you than breathe life into your body. We all crowded around to see what it would do when Dad turned it on. The compressor boomed loudly, echoing through the empty basement, coming to life with the rattling roar of a savage beast. The ferocious noise traveled upstairs, vibrating sharply through the floor vents as a white mist hissed menacingly from the nebulizers.

I held Pam's hand while we both stared, mortified. Here was cold proof, the embodiment of abnormality. Clearly this meant there would be no slumber parties with girlfriends in this house.

In time, the presence of the tent would become normal, my first lesson that you can get used to just about anything. Eventually, Pam would expect her friends to be as blasé about it as she would also become, but standing there in that moment, such a time was unimaginable.

"Go on, Pam," said my father, "get in and try it out."

"It's going to eat me," she cried, clutching me. "I'm not getting in. You can't make me."

We stood collectively staring at the tent and at each other, wondering how we would get Pam inside, short of picking her up and pitching her in, something the grownups seemed reluctant to do.

Peeling myself away from Pam, I climbed up on the bed and crawled into the tent. The mist was cool, choking, and bitter. I tried to hold my breath.

"C'mon, Pam," I said finally, lifting the front flap and waving, "climb in here with me. It's okay. It's sort of like the tents we build in the den."

Pam crawled in beside me and we held onto each other as the tent filled with mist. The wet whiteness swirled around us until we could barely make out the grownups gawking at us from the other side of the plastic.

"All right, Heather," my mother said, "you come on out here and let Pammy try it for a bit on her own."

"I won't leave you if you don't want me to," I whispered. "Will you be okay?" My sister's hazel eyes shifted subtly, but she set her jaw and nodded yes. I crawled out, landing damp and guilty at the edge of her bed, glad it wasn't me who had to sleep in the thing.

When Pam woke the next morning, the mist had drenched her from head to toe, along with the sheets, pillows, and blankets.

"It doesn't feel as yucky as it looks," she lied.

My mother had to strip the bed, air the mattress, wash the sheets, wipe out the tent, sterilize the nebulizers, and put the whole thing back together again, clean and dry.

Every day.

"Heather, would you come and set the table please while I get dinner ready?"

"I'm reading. Why can't Pammy do it?"

"I shouldn't have to explain this to you. Pammy's been sick and needs her rest. I want her to take a nap before dinner."

"It's not fair. I have to do everything. You love Pammy more than me or Gregg!"

My mother's face pinched as she drew in her breath.

"That's not true and you know it," she said, bending down to speak with me eye to eye. "You and Gregg are both very important to me and to Daddy. We both love you very much, but you know Pammy is sick and needs a lot of extra attention. You're a big girl now. I know you can understand."

"I don't understand!"

"No, you don't want to understand." My mother stood up and raised her voice. "You're not helping things by arguing with me."

"I'm not arguing. I just don't see why I have to do everything and Pam doesn't have to do anything."

"Listen, when Pam is older and stronger, I'll get her to do the few chores she can handle, but for now you're the strong and healthy one and you're also the oldest, so it's up to you to help me. Why, when I wasn't much older than you my mother was already working for Madam and I had to do all the cooking and cleaning myself and take care of your Uncle Dougie. Now get cracking. Your father will be home for dinner soon and I want everything ready when he comes in the door."

"Pam doesn't even care," I whined. "She's glad she's sick and doesn't have to help. It's like I'm a slave or something."

"That's it! Go to your room and not another word. I don't have time for this and I won't have you saying things that make your sister feel worse than she already does!"

"It's not fair."

"Listen, young lady, if you don't do as I say I'll tell your father when he gets home and you'll get The Belt." When Dad was *really* mad he whipped the belt off his pants, doubled it up, and spanked me.

Pouting, I turned on my heels and headed for the room I shared with Pam. She lay on her bed, eyelids fluttering, pretending to be asleep. I bet she'd heard everything.

I climbed up on my bed, hugged my doll to my chest, and sulked, scowling at my sister.

"Pam," I whispered, "Pammy?"

She lay motionless. I tiptoed to the door and peeked out to see if the coast was clear.

"Are you all right?" Pam's voice behind me made me jump.

"What makes you think I'm not?"

"I heard you and Mom fighting."

"I thought you were supposed to be asleep."

"I don't want you and Mom to fight about me."

Pam sat up in her bed. Her cheek was damp and the pillow had creased her soft, flushed face. She probably had a fever.

"C'mon," she said, "I'll help you set the table."

"You stay put. I'm supposed to be helping Mom and you're supposed to be resting. I'm bigger than you, so you do as I say."

Pam's saucer-shaped eyes grew sullen as she kicked her legs against the side of the bed.

"I'll come back and wake you when dinner's ready." I pulled the covers back and motioned for her to get under them. "C'mon…"

She sighed deeply, folding her skinny white limbs into the sheets. I kissed her forehead and stroked her fine, straight hair.

"Don't worry, everything's going to be all right." Pam put her thumb in her mouth, looked at me doubtfully, and closed her eyes. I pulled myself up straight, mustered my courage, and marched back to the kitchen.

I set the table carefully for dinner, counting the knives, forks, and spoons one by one under my breath, remembering, imagining, what it was like in the old house before Pammy came…*Mommy and I waiting for Daddy to come home from work…Mommy all dressed up, me too…she parks me on the kitchen counter and we play Peek-a-Boo…she sings "I'm a Little Teapot" to me while she makes dinner, keeping an eye on the clock that hangs over the fridge…a man on the radio sings "Love and marriage, love and marriage…Go together like a horse and carriage…" Suddenly, the door bursts open and my father rushes in, coattails flying, arms wide…he drops his briefcase on the floor and swoops my mother into his arms, covering her with kisses…he scoops me up too, twirls me around and tosses me in the air…" How are my two beautiful girls?" he exults…he smells like fresh-cut lumber, his cheeks are cool, his hair is sprinkled with sawdust, and we all laugh and clap…*

Dr. Cleary gave Pam enzymes to make up for the ones her pancreas wouldn't produce. They came in big jars and looked like birdseed. Mom and Dad called them her "granules."

The first time Pam tried them, Mom sprinkled them on her morning oatmeal, but my sister dawdled over her breakfast and the granules began to digest the oats right in the bowl. At various times Mom tried mixing them with orange juice, ice cream, applesauce, even Pam's favorite, Junket pudding—an immediate disaster.

"Tonight we're trying them in the mashed potatoes," my mother said brightly one evening.

"Yuck," cried Pam. "I'm not eating that stuff."

"Oh yes you are, young lady," said my mother, "I'm at the end of my rope."

"I DON'T WANT IT," shouted my sister, clamping her jaw shut.

We went through this with Pam every time we ate. Once or twice my mother tried force-feeding spoonfuls of enzyme-treated food into Pam's mouth, but it wasn't worth the tears and the spitting that went on.

Knowing that the granules might help save her life, I ate granule-treated food several times, hoping Pam would follow my example. This time I dove into Pam's potatoes.

"It's not so bad. Look, I'm eating it," I said, gagging on the sticky concoction. "C'mon, Pam, eat it, it will help you get better. It will get rid of your awful stomach cramps."

Pam crossed her arms over her chest, squared her jaw, and shot me a filthy look.

"Why do I have to eat this junk?" she pouted.

"Pam," said my father gently, "for the umpteenth time, you have to eat your granules. It's the only way you can digest your food."

Tears rolled down her pasty cheeks. "Is it because of my Sixtyfive Roses?"

"CYS-TIC FI-BRO-SIS," I corrected her, exasperated. "She can never say it right."

"You stay out of this, Miss Smarty-pants," my father retorted. He took Pam's hand and explained gently, "Yes, it's because of your Sixtyfive...uh, Cystic Fibrosis."

"Do I always have to take them?"

"Yes, I'm afraid so."

"But they're awful."

"I know, honey," said my mother, "but maybe someday something better will come along that will be easier for you. In the meantime, we have to find a way for you to take these so you'll be well and ready for whatever comes next. I know," she suggested, her voice brighter than ever, "how about I mix some granules in chocolate milk and we'll have a game? I'll time you and see how fast you can drink it down. Then I'll throw out those old potatoes and give you some new ones."

The potatoes were now goo on Pam's plate. We all stared at them. Gregg pointed from his high chair and giggled.

"Can I have some chocolate milk too?" I begged.

"No, it's just for Pam so she can take her granules."

"It's not fair. Pam gets to have chocolate milk and I don't."

"Heather, I'm not doing this to be unfair. We've got to find a way to get your sister to take these. Now let me do this and let's not have another word."

Mom carefully poured a tablespoon of Nestlé's Quick and a tablespoon of granules into a tall glass, added the milk, and gave it a good stir.

"There, how fast can you drink that down?"

My mother looked at her watch while Pam tipped her head back and made polite gulping sounds as the chocolate milk slid down her throat. Her Adam's apple bobbed up and down. She finished the whole thing in seconds then grinned at us, a brown milk mustache gleaming under her nose. My mother inspected the bottom of the glass for traces of granules. There were none.

"Well I'll be. Now why didn't I just think of that in the first place?"

We all cheered.

The granules were only the beginning. Soon I was learning to pronounce words like Tobermycin, Tetracycline, Neomycin, Staphcillin, Streptomycin, and Chloromycetin. Dr. Cleary switched Pam on and off of these antibiotics, back and forth, in a vain attempt to keep her lungs infection-free.

None of this came cheap. While children on the playground taunted me about being a rich Summerhayes, my father was spending half his yearly income to keep Pam alive. The tent cost four hundred dollars, the granules several hundred, the antibiotics several thousand. This didn't include incidental expenses for propylene glycol, cough syrup, and aspirin.

The darkness that cloaked my bed came alive with night sounds, the hiss of Pam's tent, the hum of the highway beyond the backyard, the tense voices of my parents discussing our finances. The long-distance charges were killing them, but they had to make calls setting up foundation meetings in other parts of the country. My mother spent hours on the phone, counseling parents of newly diagnosed children across Canada. As she told my father, "Most of these folks are half out of their minds, Doug. You remember what we were like." Like my parents, many of them felt they were without the complete support or understanding of family and friends. These people came to my parents for help and advice, and my parents felt bound to render it.

One couple, with Jewish and Catholic backgrounds, had been disowned by both their families, on the belief that their CF child was God's punishment for marrying outside of their faith. When my mother heard that, it just about did her in.

Running the tent raised our electric bill, regular chest x-rays for Pam were an absolute but expensive necessity. We owed Emmett Cleary for house calls. When my father flew somewhere to set up a new chapter, he paid for his own airfare out of pocket, refusing to use foundation money that might go toward research. At times they had to make a choice between paying the bills or the mortgage, and my mother's sobbing, soft and low, permeated the night like a mourning dove.

"Aw honey, don't cry," my father sighed. "I'll find a way."

He took Bob Ivey with him to meet with the secretary of state. They petitioned for a charter, otherwise known as a Federal Letters Patent, for the Cystic Fibrosis Foundation. The charter was necessary to operate as a non-profit organization, and they began the task of raising money. The secretary of state passed them off to the deputy minister of national health, Dr. Cameron, who turned them down flat.

"Goddammit!" my father shouted at the walls when he came home, and pounded his fist on the kitchen table. He slumped in his easy chair, but looked up to see Pam and me peering out at him from around the corner.

"Aw girls, I'm a cockeyed optimist in a world full of goddamn cynics!" he chuckled, and we ran to his open arms.

A few days later he and Bob took my mother and Bob's wife, Marty, to a CF conference in Philadelphia, and returned fired up to obtain federal sanction for the Canadian foundation.

"You should have seen us," Dad laughed. "We bought a bottle of scotch and a bottle of rye and opened a hospitality suite in Mr. Ivey's room for the other CF parents. Your mother and Mrs. Ivey made sandwiches for anyone who dropped by. We all laughed and cried together, showed each other photographs of our kids, told stories. And, there were some doctors, heavens, that were arguing eyeball to eyeball about the best way to treat CF! The best thing was," he went on, "we met a doctor from Rainbow Children's Hospital in Cleveland who's got a reputation for keeping CF kids alive. Cleveland's not too far from here, you know, just a few hours' drive."

The mortality rate at Dr. Lee Matthews' clinic was the lowest anywhere. Bob Ivey was taking his daughter Karna there right away.

"Are you taking Pammy?"

"Well, we're going to think about it."

What was there to think about? Cleveland was suddenly the Land of Oz. I went to sleep dreaming of a Great Wizard at a hospital in The Emerald City, and a cure for Pam.

⌐

Hoping publicity might spur government support to gain the charter, my parents arranged for a reporter from the *Brantford Expositor* to visit our house, do a story on the foundation, and take a picture of Pam in her tent.

Pam posed awkwardly on the edge of her bed, wearing a red jumper, grinning shyly at the photographer while I stood by listening to my mother answer questions about CF and what it was like to "live with this disease." He asked Pammy how it felt to sleep in the tent and take granules and antibiotics, but she got tongue-tied and would only say, "It's all right...

Ask me, ask me, I thought as hard as I could, sidling over next to Pam.

"This is our other daughter, Heather," my mother said sweetly. The reporter nodded, but asked me to step back out of the way.

"Maybe a picture of the two girls together," my mother suggested when she saw my face fall.

The reporter agreed, but I knew from the perfunctory manner with which he complied that my picture would not appear in the paper.

"We saw Pammy in the paper," Jane Wilson and Janice McGregor squealed when the article appeared.

"How come you're all excited about Pam?" I pouted. "I thought you were supposed to be my friends."

"That was a nice write-up in the paper about your sister," said my teacher, "I'm sure you're very proud of her."

"Wasn't that a caution," Grandma Birdsell gushed, "that picture of Pammy in the paper? I called all my friends and told them to look it up."

Our phone rang non-stop for a couple of days with neighbors and relatives calling to offer congratulations.

"You know," my mother said over and over into the receiver, "we weren't sure whether to have Pammy sit for that photograph, but it's got a tremendous response and turned out to be good publicity for the foundation."

I raced off alone to the Big Woods and wandered through the pines, wishing I could just build myself a fort there and never go home.

My sister's newfound notoriety intruded again later that week when Pam and I went downtown with Grandma Birdsell.

"I'm just going to run and put some money in the parking meter," Grandma told us, "I'll just be a minute. Here, you girls can buy yourselves some French fries over there in the market square while I'm gone."

Pam and I grabbed our quarters and ran to get in line at the chip wagon. A woman fell in behind us and stared at Pam intently. After a few seconds she tapped me on the shoulder, nodded at Pam, and said, "Isn't that the little girl whose picture was in the paper the other day?"

I blushed and stammered. "What paper?"

"The *Brantford Expositor*. Isn't she the little one who is so sick?"

"Yes," I mumbled. Pam turned around, gave the lady a filthy look, and pointedly reminded me that we were not supposed to speak to strangers.

I stood on tiptoe and ordered our fries.

"Here," said the lady, "I'll buy those for the little girls. This one's sick to death ya' know. It's all in the paper."

Horrified, I declined the offer and threw our quarters up

onto the counter. We took our vinegar-soaked boxes of steamy potatoes and retreated to the street corner, looking up and down for Grandma.

"I'm going to get into trouble," said Pam, "eating these without my granules. That lady is still staring."

"Ignore her."

We turned away. I felt another tap on my shoulder. Pam and I looked up at the lady and back again at each other.

"What is it she has?" asked the lady loudly, shoving French fries into her mouth.

"I have Sixtyfive Roses," snapped Pam, "so I cough a lot and sleep in a tent at night and take lots of pills. I thought you said you read it all in the paper."

My sister looked at me and giggled, startled by her own temerity.

"Tsk, tsk," said the lady, shaking her head as she walked away, "it's a shame really, just tragic."

"Tsk, tsk, just tragic," Pam mimicked the lady, and then murmured softly, "I hate being pitied."

My mother looked stricken when I told her what happened at the French Fry Wagon.

"Oh Doug," she cried, "maybe we've made a mistake using our own situation for publicity. The girls shouldn't have to go through that kind of thing."

My father was sympathetic, but argued that they couldn't ignore how phone calls and contributions had increased since the article appeared.

"How can we be effective spokesmen for the foundation if we don't publicize our own story?" he asked. "And I've had a call from the secretary of health."

"Just the same, I'm not doing it again without asking Pam's permission."

With the rare exception of being treated as an object of pity, my sister was otherwise ambivalent, in fact nonchalant, about being put in the spotlight. She didn't mind the attention as long as it didn't detract from more important things in her life, like playing dolls or Hide and Go Seek. Her attitude was remarkably sanguine for a six year old. My parents' debate about using Pam for publicity continued, but so did the newspaper articles. With each one that appeared, I grew angrier. Pam got enough attention as it was. To my way of seeing things, the publicity put her up on a pedestal. I aimed to knock her down. I started to pick fights with her, pushing her roughly and on occasion, hitting her.

"Don't be mad at your sister," my parents warned repeatedly, "it's not her fault." Pouting furiously, I ran off to the Big Woods and ranted to an audience of pine trees and birds.

It was growing harder to keep a lid on my feelings. Pam got away with so much. She got to play with my toys without asking, yet I couldn't play with hers. She got to eat candy when I had to worry about cavities. She got to snooze on my mother's lap in the rocking chair when I had to go nap alone in our room. When she got a write-up in the paper and everyone started referring to her as "Poor Pammy," it all just made me want to scream.

Other times though, when her cough raised goosebumps on my neck, or when she was curled up with her blankie, sucking her thumb and looking fragile and pale, my heart went out to her, and I felt bad about my feelings without having to be told. I knew she got to do things I didn't because she was going to die.

Winter was hard on Pam. She got skin-and-bones cold even if Mom bundled her up good and heavy. Her lips turned blue as soon as she stepped out into the snow. The sharp air made her cough.

"It doesn't matter," she insisted. "I'm playing outside with the rest of you."

She went to kindergarten half-days. In the afternoon, she slept. I woke her when I got home from school and we had a snack together. She liked pink Junket, or Borden's Eagle Brand condensed milk right out of the can. It was supposed to fatten her up. It never did.

Gregg napped a lot, not because he was tired but because my mother was always putting him down for a nap so she would have more time to do housework, or complete an issue of "Candid Facts," or make phone calls for the foundation, or shop for groceries and bake hermit bars for tea. When these tasks were done, she hoisted Gregg from his crib to brush his woolly hair, trying in vain to bring it under control. My mother's life was a study in trying to bring things under control.

Our lives had to be very organized so my parents had time for foundation work. We all had to do what we were told and do it right the first time. Time was very important.

It's time to get up it's time to clean your room it's time for Pam's treatment it's time you behaved it's time to set the table it's time to eat it's time to pick up the babysitter it's time I left for the meeting I'm going to be late. Life is too short there's no time to waste...

"Be quiet, I'm on the phone." My parents said this ten times a day.

"Hello, this is Donna Summerhayes calling. I wonder if you could help me. I'm trying to persuade the YM/YWCA to donate gym time to the Brantford chapter of the Cystic Fibrosis Foundation so that parents can bring their CF children together for play and exercise..."

"Hello there, Doug Summerhayes calling. I wonder if you can help me. I'm trying to negotiate with some of the local pharmacies to sell antibiotics to local CF families at a discount. Yes, that's right, and I also want to try to get compressors and tents shipped from the U.S. duty-free..."

"Hi, it's Donna Summerhayes. I'm calling to order a new copy of the film *The Mask of the Pied Piper*. Yes, (laughter), we've shown it so many times I'm afraid we've worn it out."

Several nights a month, my mother or father spoke about CF at community service clubs like the Jaycees, the Lions, the Kinsmen, the Knights of Columbus, or the Rotary club, and showed the film produced by the American CF Foundation. My father bought the Dale Carnegie book on public speaking. At night, after we were in bed, he and Mom took turns practicing in the den. I fell to sleep listening to their speeches, and dreamt.

I am swimming, alone, in a vast, calm ocean. Suddenly, three giant brains foam up out of the water on the heads of pins. The brains silently speed through the water toward me. They surround me, smothering me, pushing me beneath the surface.

I woke gasping for air. The house was silent, save for the hiss of Pam's tent. I lay in the dark, and softly wept.

When summer arrived, I was grateful. Nightmares turned to daydreams as I leapt into each morning and ran to the Woods. Wandering there among the pines and poplars, the sumac and Queen Anne's lace, blessed by the sweet symphony of birds, I found refuge and strength.

July. The sweet, clean fragrance of fresh-mown grass. Fluffy clouds like giants stalking the sky. Bedsheets snapping in the warm breeze on the clothesline in the backyard. Party sandwiches made with cream cheese and maraschino cherries. Lemonade. Hula Hoops.

I was eight years old and Pam was six. Remember everything, I kept telling myself. How we loved to roll together down grass-covered hills, the world tumbling about us. Flashes of sky, sun, cloud, landscape, glimpses of blue, white, yellow, green; the tickling grass brushing our nostrils, the sweet pungency of the soil, the hard lumpiness of the earth as it passed beneath our revolving shoulder blades, elbows, knees, the dull thump of our bodies as we rolled; the random noise of the world around us, and the cacophony of our own squealing laughter! Then at the bottom of the hill, dizzy and breathless, staggering to our feet, our hearts flying with joy, our grins unstoppable, dragging each other back up to do it again.

Playing Hide and Go Seek in-between the woodpiles at the lumberyard, and playing secretary on the typewriters in the musty office while we waited for Dad to make a few extra phone calls and lock up. Constructing our elaborate tents in the family room out of blankets, sheets, and TV tables. Tying our legs together with skipping rope, standing up with one arm around each other, and practicing for the three-legged race at the Summerhayes Lumber picnic. Falling down, getting up, and falling down again, howling with laughter. Waiting up at night for the tooth fairy, seeing a light dance around our bedroom walls and ceiling, certain it was Tinkerbell. Sunday afternoon drives in the back seat of my father's Studebaker, holding hands, staring through the window at the shining bars of sunlight streaking out from behind the clouds. We thought it was God sitting up there, and we called the light "God's Glory."

What I couldn't see to remember, I had to imagine. The seven-year-old boy who was swept over Niagara Falls in a rowboat that summer, and survived. My mother in a black lace party dress with three-quarter sleeves and a full skirt. The swish of taffeta. She needed no jewelry, for her eyes sparkled like sapphires, and her smile shone. My father in a tux, his grin almost goofy, shaking hands and accepting congratulations. They were in Toronto at the King Eddie, in the grand old Victorian ballroom, eating fancy hors d'oeuvres, making speeches, and toasting with champagne. I was dying to be there with them. It was the 15th of July, 1960, and the Federal Letters Patent for the Canadian Cystic Fibrosis Foundation was being awarded to my father at a gala banquet. With five chapters officially incorporated, we could finally launch a full-scale campaign to raise money for research.

I decided to believe in miracles.

Through the weeks that followed, my parents, Bob Ivey, and the Board began work to assemble a Medical Education Advisory Board, a Scientific Advisory Board, and to draft a set of by-laws. A library of pamphlets and slides ordered from the American Foundation filled several drawers in our den.

"We'll soon be printing our own literature," my father exclaimed, "with our own logo!" He showed us the proofs, a drawing of a child's face superimposed on a maple leaf, next to the letters CF. Beneath it was written the motto, "Give a child the breath of life."

Meetings of the CF Board of Directors took place in our living room every six weeks or so. In the few days before each one, it got crazy around the house.

My mother fussed and cleaned, juggling the vacuum cleaner and dust rag with her telephone and a notepad. She did extra grocery shopping, polished the silver tea service borrowed from Grandma Bill, pored over her notes for the meeting, made sandwiches and canapés from the latest recipes in *Chatelaine* magazine, washed the dust from the good china cups, set up the forty-cup electric coffee urn borrowed from the Imperial Order of the Daughters of the Empire, and on the night, made us eat dinner early in our pajamas.

Close to six-thirty, my mother jumped into the tub.

"I'll only be five minutes. You girls look after Gregg, and behave yourselves."

As soon as the bathroom door closed we sprang into action, pilfering my mother's lipstick from her bedroom, and clambering into costume for the entertainment I had planned. CF Board meetings, I discovered, were marvelous opportunities for me to grab attention, and I spent the weeks between meetings like Florenz Ziegfeld, dreaming up new skits to perform.

On the day in question, while my mother set up for the meeting, I held my sister and brother hostage in the basement, rehearsing them. Then, while my mother was getting ready, I attended to the final details.

"You can wear Mom's old squirrel collar from high school," I instructed Pam, "and maybe a little lipstick," fussing with the costumes as if I were Edith Head. I chose my mother's honeymoon negligee, set off with the detachable mink collar from her good winter suit. In case it should escape notice that I was the star, I crowned myself with her fake rhinestone tiara.

I wrestled my brother to the ground to put him in a dress.

"C'mon, Gregg, hold still. I have to do this because we need an extra girl or we can't do the Lennon Sisters! We're still two short as it is."

My three-year-old brother made faces and yanked his head from side to side as I smeared my mother's red lipstick on him. A couple of times I made a cape for him out of a bath towel and allowed him to be Superman, but that ended after he hurt himself trying to fly from the back of an armchair.

During the meeting, the three of us hung around in the hall near the doorway to the living room, waiting for a lull in the proceedings. As soon as the opportunity presented itself, I launched Pam into the middle of the room to announce my act.

"Ladies and gentlemen," Pam gestured toward the hallway, pursing her smiling lips in an effort not to guffaw, "Marilyn Monroe!"

I swished in, fluttering my mother's mink collar as if it were a stole, struck a pose, and began in a breathy voice, "Mary had a little lamb...(breath, breath)...her fleece was white as snow...(breath, breath)..."

The grownups laughed and clapped while my mother blushed in the kitchen doorway. "All right now, that's enough, Heather."

"No, wait, we have to do the Lennon Sisters."

Pam dragged Gregg into the lineup while I pretended to be

Lawrence Welk. "And a one a, and a two a..." We sang to more polite applause. This encouraged me sufficiently to offer a recitation of a poem I had written.

"Heather, that's enough now, really."

"Nooooo!"

"Now, Heather, you're not going to have a tantrum in front of all these nice people are you?"

You bet. Exit stage left, strong-armed by my mother, screeching all the way.

I was only eight years old, but I knew what was going on in the news. My mother made us pay attention to current events.

Chubby Checker had invented "The Twist." Cassius Clay had won the light-heavyweight Olympic Gold Medal in Rome. There had been race riots in Florida and UFO sightings in California. Richard Nixon and John F. Kennedy were going to debate live on national television. But the most historic thing was happening in our house. Pam was starting school!

My parents had conducted an ongoing and lively debate about keeping her out of public school and getting her a tutor, to reduce her exposure to infection. Pam put the question to rest by insisting on the life my father had so vigorously touted.

"I want to be normal, Daddy. I don't want to be different from the other kids."

That decision out of the way, my mother invited Pam alone into the living room for a talk, advising her not to push too hard to keep up with the other kids.

"I don't want you to make yourself sick," I heard my mother say as I eavesdropped in the hall, holding my breath. "Just go at your own pace."

"You never said that to me," I blurted, poking my head around the door and starting a hissy-fit.

My mother went down to Greenbrier School to explain about Pam. She gave both the teacher and principal a pamphlet titled "A CF Child Is in Your Class." Pam and I rode our bikes in circles around the school, peering at the windows into the empty classrooms while we waited for Mom.

"You'll have to stop sucking your thumb now," I instructed.

"I know that."

"Big girls don't suck their thumbs, you know."

Pam stuck her tongue out at me. We pulled up to the front door of the school.

"See that?" I asked, pointing through the glass wall of the foyer. "We have assembly every morning, and we all have to repeat what's inscribed on that wall. It says 'Incline thine ear, and hear the words of the wise, and apply thine heart unto knowledge.'"

"You think you're so smart," she mewed.

On the first day of school my mother dressed us in matching outfits, and since it was a special day, allowed us to leave through the front door, usually reserved for company. Getting ready I'd had trouble tying my shoe laces, as usual. No one in those days knew the word "dyslexia." Pam had patiently shown me that morning for the umpteenth time, repeating softly as her clubbed fingers worked their magic, "See, left over right…make a loop here…" and so on. *So much for being the smart one,* I thought, but I was grateful. Once I was securely tied into my Oxfords, we stood together on the front porch in the crisp September air, all fidget and sighs, buttoning and unbuttoning our sweaters, double-checking our pockets for apples and wax-paper-wrapped oatmeal cookies.

"My heart's pounding," Pam confided.

"Don't worry," I whispered, "I'll be right there with you."

My mother straightened our white cotton collars and

brushed our shoulders with her elegantly shaped, work-worn hands. Gregg toddled to the doorway, begging to be held.

"Let's go," demanded Pam.

"You've got plenty of time," smiled my mother. She grunted softly as she hefted Gregg up into her arms.

I took Pam's hand but she yanked it away and started off down the front lawn without me.

"Wave bye-bye," my mother coaxed Gregg. I could hear in her voice that she would cry as soon as we were gone. She held Gregg's chubby little hand and waved it.

Pam waved back at Gregg and then turned on her spindly white legs and took off.

"Hey wait up," I shouted. "I'm supposed to be taking you to school."

"There's Molly McGregor!" she called out, running to catch up with her friend.

"But I'm supposed to watch out for you! *Mom said*," I hollered. Tears welled in my throat. Confused and bereft, I turned back toward my mother, who smiled and shrugged her shoulders.

"You'd better get going or you'll be late."

Each day on our way to school, during recess and lunch, and again on our way home, I did watch out for Pam, keeping my antennae alert for kids who might tease her. If I hovered too closely, she shot me warning glances. It was a consternation that my independent sister refused to let me act as her Protector. Nevertheless, I remained vigilant.

One day, while on our way home from running an errand to Stan's corner store, Peter and Paul Florence tore up on their bicycles. The Florence boys, as they were known, were identical twins who were in Pam's Grade One class. She had confided to me that she had a crush on both of them. Her face lit up as they approached.

"Skinny Minnie. Is she ugly or what?"

"Yeah, she ain't normal."

My sister's smile evaporated and her eyes filled with tears.

"Shut up!" I yelled. "Leave her alone."

"Oooh, big sister's going to get tough, eh?"

They parked their bikes at the side of the road and stooped to pick up a handful of pebbles from the gravel.

"Don't you dare," I shouted.

They drew their hands back to throw.

"Run Pam, RUN," I yelled, squatting to grab my own ammunition.

I was not fast enough. A tiny gray stone left one of the boys' hands and arced through the air in slow motion, hitting Pam square in the forehead. Her knees buckled; blood spurted from her skin. Her eyes rolled back in her head, and she sank to the ground.

"You've killed her," I cried, "Pammy, *wake up*."

She lay in the gravel, limp as a rag doll. My heart exploded. The boys took off. I scooped Pam into my arms and began to run. Our house was only a block away but I felt like it might as well have been on the moon. I ran as fast as I could, clutching her body to mine, her limbs dangling crazily, my legs straining as if under water, my lungs burning. Finally, I reached our side yard. My lips opened and closed but no voice came out as I called for my mother. She saw us from the kitchen window, raced to the side door, lifted Pam out of my arms, and headed for the bathroom. I followed, blubbering, "Is she dead? Is she dead?"

My mother laid Pam on the counter and bathed her face with cool water. Pam came to and sat up, wobbling. Her forehead swelled with a nasty red lump, but the bleeding had stopped. My mother wiped my tear-stained face with a cold washcloth and asked what happened. I hiccupped hysterically as the story lurched out of me.

"Okay, okay, it's going to be all right," she murmured. "Blow your nose."

I blew.

"I'm going to get Pammy a baby aspirin and call Mrs. Florence. You get her to lie down and stay with her 'til I come back."

Pam scooched down off the counter. I trundled her down the hall to our room and pulled back her pink chenille bedspread. She climbed in at my command, her saucer eyes gazing up at me intently.

"I hate being skinny," she swore. "It's the thing I hate most about my CF."

My sister turned over and curled up, her thumb in her mouth. She closed her eyes. My mother returned to sit with her. She stroked Pam's hair and turned to me.

"Are you okay?"

I nodded yes.

"Then go on now, and set the table for dinner."

My mother had no idea how much I needed to be held, wrapped up in her arms, on her lap in the wicker rocking chair. I needed to be held against her warm breast forever and ever, I needed her to make it all okay. But it would never be okay. She could not make it better. She could not keep the boat that held the child from hurtling over the Falls. She could not bandage the scrape on my heart with gauze and white adhesive tape from the medicine chest. I knew that, and the knowing only made the needing worse. I knew my mother didn't have time to hold me even when she wanted to, because she had to hold the dying child, my sister. Yet I was dying too. Dying to the innocence of childhood, and the right to my own needs as I came to understand that Pam's needs were greater. Dying with Pam, as I promised I would. Dying to feel safe, and to be held by my mother in the wicker rocking chair, falling into heaven as she sang softly, "Row, row, row your boat, gently down the stream…"

CHAPTER SEVEN

"...none of us, who ever came back
From that long lonely fall and frenzied rising,
Ever learned anything at all
About swimming, but only
How to put off, one by one,
Dreams and pity, love and grace –
How to survive in any place."
— MARY OLIVER, The Swimming Lesson

I have always been afraid of the water. My mother sent me for swimming lessons at the Y that same year I turned eight, and celebrated the news that I had what the instructor called "an Olympic stroke." Sadly, I had no heart for the deep end of the pool. With eyes squeezed tight I always swam kitty-corner, making a beeline for the side edge at the halfway mark, just where I knew the bottom gave way and the water went over my head.

When I was nine, I nearly drowned in my cousin's pool. After a brave leap from the diving board on a dare, my so-called Olympic stroke disintegrated into panic and I went under. A dark-haired girl named Brenda Martin dove in to save me. Many years later, as a young woman whitewater rafting in the Oregon wilderness, I nearly drowned again. I wanted to, in fact, newly separated from my first husband and bereft in a world without my sister. Instead, the Rogue River found a way to give my life back to me when I thought it had all but ended.

The Hudson River is deep, and the current swift. On crisp, sunny days, the 79th Street Boat Basin across the way from where I now live appears to be no more than a stone's throw from my balcony, but you wouldn't want to try to swim it.

I stare at the Hudson, remembering my fear.

"No one tests the depths of a river with both feet." So goes an old Ashanti proverb.

Sometimes you're forced to. My mind wanders, gazing down towards the Verazzano Narrows where fresh water is exchanged for ocean salt. The same exchange takes place in human cells, but in Cystics that is what kills them. They have excess salt in the water carried by the cells. It turns into thick, brackish sludge, drowning the victims.

I think of those who've drowned at sea, of lungs filling with salt water. Where did I hear that drowning is a pleasant way to die? I don't believe it.

My brother Jeffrey is an expert with a whitewater kayak. From the day my mother's water broke onto our kitchen floor and he was born the youngest child, and according to every good fairy tale, the last hope, Jeff has paddled the small boat of his life along the River Styx. After getting lost among a few dark shoals, he has settled on an ascetic life of solitude, contemplation, and challenge: his dog Cougar, his kayak, and the river.

He understands how a river can reclaim a life. I cherish my photo of him plunging over a waterfall on the Ottawa River. On the back of the picture he has written, "Elevator Shaft, 21 Feet, 6 on the Gauge." He holds his paddle high, blocking his eyes to the camera. His mouth is open wide. I can hear the sound streaming from him, a carnival-ride cry of terror and glee.

"Control in chaos...," he tells me, smiling wickedly. Each time Jeff takes his kayak over a waterfall or negotiates a tough rapid, he enters the threshold between life and death, thrilling to that dangerous proximity and to his fleeting, golden mastery over it. He treasures the high he gets from it, but it is more than a metaphor for him. Whitewater kayaking has become as much a means of fending off death as it is his preparation for it.

He quotes Barry Lopez to me, telling me that rivers bind the earth, that when you put your hands into a river, you can actually feel the binding.

Memory is the same. But I am still afraid of the water.

The Canadian Cystic Fibrosis Foundation grew rapidly, opening fifteen chapters nationwide. The attending publicity that surrounded us continued, causing me to question my place in the scheme of things. Who was I besides "a Summerhayes," or "Pam's sister"? How could I make myself seen or heard? What must I strive to be or do to be valued, by my family, my friends, or the world at large?

Articles about the foundation and my family, or more to the point, my parents and Pam, appeared under headlines like "Saddened Father Tells Cystic Fibrosis Story."

I was both embarrassed and disturbed to see my father characterized this way, though I knew it was true—my father was indeed sad, profoundly sad. He tried not to let anyone know how sad he was. He tried not to let himself know. He distanced himself from sorrow with activity. He was always on the telephone or on the fly. Out the door, in the car, off to the lumberyard. Late for a meeting, gone to make a speech, rushing to the airport. Even when he was home, he was distracted.

Night after night, my mother waited dinner until long after he told her to expect him, buying our patience with raw carrots and celery. Gregg pressed his nose to the window, watching the daylight hours fade, waiting for his dad to come home and play with him. Finally, my mother simply had to feed us and, of course, that's just when Dad would walk in the door. After dinner, he filled up the nebulizers in Pam's tent while Mom cleaned the kitchen, and then he disappeared behind the newspaper, or watched *Gunsmoke* and yelled at us to be quiet. Before long he was asleep in front of the TV.

His mind was always somewhere else. He constantly forgot things. He forgot to pick up milk on the way home after my mother phoned and asked. He forgot to mail the electric bill. He forgot where he put his keys, or his wallet, or the speech he'd written for the meeting he had to attend in ten minutes.

"Oh damn," he swore, scratching his head and looking about like a frantic bird. "I just had it in my hand!"

He took me with him to the lumberyard in Tillsonburg and told me to wait in the car.

"I'll just be a few minutes," he promised. Two hours later, when I wandered into the showroom complaining that I had to pee, he looked at me stunned and asked me where the hell I'd come from.

A few months later, on a cold January afternoon, he forgot to pick me up from my ballet lessons at the YWCA. I waited and waited, watching the shadows lengthen outside the lobby window. I phoned home. No one answered. I phoned Dad's office, and was told he had left for the day. I had no dimes left to take the bus.

He did not come for me. It got dark. Finally, I made up my mind to walk home.

I slipped and stumbled down the glistening sidewalk in the freezing twilight, hatless, bootless, without mittens, wearing only my coat, ballet slippers, and leotard.

I had walked over a mile and was inching my way precariously up icy Terrace Hill when I glimpsed my father racing past me in the car in the opposite direction, toward the Y. Frantic, I yelled and waved. He made a U-turn in the middle of the hill and sped back to where I stood. I clambered into his car, all snotty and frosted red. We did not know whether to laugh or cry. He handed me his big linen hankie so I could blow my nose.

"You forgot me," I exploded in tears.

"Aw, come here," he said chuckling, folding me up in his long arms and pulling me to his chest.

"Why, Daddy?" I wept into his overcoat. "What made you forget?"

"I don't know." His arms fell away from me. He removed his glasses and pinched his nose between his eyes. He sighed deeply. "I guess I've just got a lot of things on my mind lately."

We sat quietly together in the car, staring out through the cold windows into the dark. The streetlights blinked on. My father sighed again. He yanked a fresh hankie from another pocket and nervously wiped his nose from side to side.

"I love you," he said.

"I know. I love you too."

As an adult, I've read studies that claim fathers of chronic or seriously ill children sometimes cope by absenting or detaching themselves from their families. Not that it would have made a difference to me to have had this information as a child—studies mean nothing to lonely kids. How much of my own father's absence was truly necessary, and how much he used his work as an escape, I'll never know. I do know he felt torn. I know that he now thinks he did justice to neither his business nor his family. I know he looks back with regret; my mother and I often have to ask him not to castigate himself.

During those years when I felt his absence, however, I thought perhaps the answer to getting his attention, anyone's attention, was to become famous.

I fantasized that someday people would come to The House

at 16 Brier Crescent and visit it as a historic place, not as the location where the CF Foundation was started, but as the childhood home of that celebrated ballerina, Heather Summerhayes. I imagined little velvet ropes draped across the doorway to the living room, where folks would stand to peek in and see where I practiced my first dances. I could see the glass cases set up in our bedroom, containing pink satin toe shoes stained with blood and champagne, old programs from the theatres where I danced my greatest triumphs, and perhaps even a tutu, its sequins faded and dull, its feathers limp, from the time I performed "The Firebird" to such acclaim.

"I want to be the next Anna Pavlova," I confided to Margaret McGuiness, the secretary for the CF Foundation. She sent me a newspaper clipping from the *Toronto Star*, showing a photograph of students from the National Ballet School of Canada. The girls were only a year or two older than me, and touted as future stars. Here was my chance, I realized.

"Please, please, let me try out," I begged, waving the clipping in my mother's face until both were wilted with my desperation.

In the wake of a Valentine's Day blizzard, my parents drove me to Toronto to audition for the National Ballet School of Canada. They had warned me my chances were slim—I was four months short of turning nine, and the school rarely admitted students under the age of ten. Sitting in a dark corner of the rehearsal hall, my parents watched from the shadows while Betty Oliphant, the school's director, put me through my paces.

"Push the clouds away. Push them away, gently. No, gently, softly. That's it. Slow down, don't run so fast. Push the clouds away…no dear, you're trying too hard now. The clouds are very soft, very light. Just push them away gently, gently…"

In April, a letter arrived to inform us that I was the youngest person ever accepted into the summer program. I was entirely too pleased when my mother phoned everyone we knew to tell them about it, then took me shopping for pink tights and a patent leather dance bag. Thrilled, I pranced around in my new belongings until Pam started to pout and my mother told me to stop because I was making my sister jealous. Good, I thought. I'd been jealous of her enough times.

On Mother's Day, a telegram and a prize bouquet arrived at our door. My mother shrieked so loudly and laughed so hard that both Pam and I came running. Our neighbor, Ivy Johnson, had secretly nominated my mother for a "Mother of the Year" contest sponsored by the Florist Telegraph Delivery Service. The *Brantford Expositor* ran the story the next day:

MOTHER OF THE YEAR RUNNER UP HERE

A Brantford mother last night was named runner-up in a Mother of the Year contest and didn't believe it. Mrs. Douglas (Donna) Summerhayes of 16 Brier Crescent was not even aware she had been nominated. "I thought somebody was pulling a joke on me," she said today. But now she sees it as a chance to publicize the work of the Canadian Cystic Fibrosis Foundation which she and her husband have worked so hard to form...

The article went on to say that *"she was chosen because of her devotion to her six-year-old daughter, Pamela, a Cystic Fibrosis victim."* I scrutinized the page carefully, searching for my name, or Gregg's. We were not to be found, even upon a second reading. It was bad enough that Pam was mentioned exclusively in the newspaper columns covering my father's local or national speech giving and fundraising on the foundation's behalf, but to be left out in this instance was unbearable. I threw down the paper and ran out of the house bawling.

"I thought you won because you're our mother too."

The failure of the newspapers to acknowledge my existence

convinced me that I amounted to nothing. Ballet school would change all that. It had to.

Counting the weeks from my ninth birthday in May until my sojourn in July, I kept myself busy planning an entertainment for the June CF Board meeting. Hunting through my mother's closet in search of new costumes, I came across some funny-looking baggy dresses.

I trundled out to the kitchen, where my mother stood at the sink peeling potatoes for dinner.

"Mommy, are those pregnant dresses in your closet?"

"In the first place," my mother continued, "the dresses aren't pregnant, I am. And in the second place not a word to your father about this. I haven't had a chance to tell him yet."

"Oh Mom. What do you want—a boy or a girl?"

"Gee, I didn't know. Another boy would be nice I guess. Then we'd have two of each, eh? It really doesn't matter though, just so long as the baby's healthy."

As my mother spoke, her hands deftly slipped a paring knife in circles beneath the wet skin of a potato. The skin curled into a heap on the soggy newspaper she had laid down to protect the countertop. Though it was a chilly spring day, sunlight the color of buttercups poured through the kitchen window. The radio crooned the theme from *A Summer Place."*

"Here, I know you like this." She slipped me a piece of raw potato. I chewed thoughtfully, sorting through my feelings. It would be great to have a baby to play with, a real live doll. Then again, a baby would be just one more thing to take my parents' attention.

"Mom..."

"What is it, sweetheart?"

"Will the new baby have CF?"

My mother laid down her knife and knelt beside me. The warm air from the floor vent ruffled her apron.

"I don't know, sweetheart," she said softly. "I hope not. We'll just have to wait and see and cross that bridge when we come to it. Run along now. Dinner's almost ready. You can set the table any time."

I ran along as I was told, but stopped to ask another question. When I turned around, I saw my mother standing with her hands over her mouth, staring out the kitchen window.

I knew by then what one-in-four meant. The odds were good the new baby would be healthy. Was that why they were having it, I wondered? Was it to replace Pam in case she died? How dare I even think that?

By the time July arrived with its promise of ballet school, my mother was wearing her pregnant dresses, and I was torn about leaving. I would miss everyone, but would I be missed? Pam grinned and waved at me with excitement as the car pulled out of the driveway. I choked up.

By the next day, however, my doubts disappeared into the dust motes that glittered in the molten light pouring through the tall, arched windows of the National Ballet Studio. The air rang with the tumbling notes of Tchaikovsky played with gusto on upright pianos. The rehearsal hall smelled of stale sunshine, rosin, and sweat.

"Chassé, glissé, pas de chat, changement!" the ballet mistress called out the combinations sharply. *"Plié, ronde de jambe, battement!"*

I whirled and leapt, out of breath, struggling with my *porte de bras*, trying to keep my elbows soft, remembering, then forgetting, to keep my thumbs tucked into my palms. I learned to "present" myself, head erect, knees turned out over the feet, imagining all the time that I was onstage, wearing a flowing yellow tutu made of tulle. Demanding as it was, I became smitten with the place, and myself in it.

My mother and father came to visit almost every weekend.

My mother was "showing" more each time I saw her. The three of us shopped and went out for dinner, or to the theatre.

Pam sent her love, they told me. She missed me terribly. She had another staph infection in her chest, but Dr. Cleary was trying to get that under control.

"Will she have to go in the hospital?"

"Well, we're hoping we can avoid putting her in, at least until you get home. It would be too much for us to have her in Cleveland and you up here. Don't worry though; Emmett is taking good care of her. We don't want you to worry. Just concentrate on what you're doing here and make us proud."

My days were full with the joy and discipline of dancing, but my nights were disturbed by a new recurring dream.

I am in a dark place. Sounds of moaning and crying fill the air around me. Suddenly I come upon a casket, floating on a velvet-draped catafalque. My heart beats wildly as I approach. My blood runs cold, but I am drawn to the casket. I cannot turn away. I look in. Pam is lying there, so white her skin shines with rays of light all around. Her eyes are closed and her arms are crossed over her chest. "Pammy," I call out. "Wake up, wake up, WAKE UP...!"

I returned home at the end of the summer, swearing to God I would never leave my sister again. In my absence she had wasted down to purplish-white skin and bones. Some days her lips were the color of violets. Her fingernails blushed the same hue, and the clubbing of her fingertips had grown worse for lack of oxygen. Her cough, thick and explosive, sounded as if it would blow her wide open. Her breathing was fast and shallow. After a few minutes at play, she looked like a fish on dry land, her lips pursing as she fought for short gulps of air, her chest heaving up and down. She called this state "puffy."

"I'm all puffy today," she said, laughing breezily as though it was a joke, smiling so we shouldn't worry. She wheezed like an old radiator. My parents decided it was time to take Pam to Cleveland to see Dr. Lee Matthews.

While they were gone, I prayed for Pam. I prayed in the morning when I rose. I prayed walking to school. I prayed at recess. I prayed when I was supposed to be doing my arithmetic. I prayed sitting in her empty mist tent when I came home for lunch, and again after school. In the night I woke up and got down beside my bed to pray on my knees, keening the absence on the other side of the room. *Please God, don't let my Pammy die.*

My father came home after a few days so he could return to work. He explained to me that Pam was on intravenous antibiotics. He described the needles, tubes, and bags, and told us that the drugs were supposed to kill the staphylococcus infection raging in her lungs. He told me because I wanted to know, demanded to know.

My mother stayed in Cleveland with Pam. One night the phone rang. My father listened carefully, hung up the receiver, then slumped at the kitchen table, holding his glasses in his hand and pinching his nose between his eyes.

"What's the matter, Daddy?"

He sighed deeply. "Mommy had a talk with Dr. Matthews today about Pammy." He looked as if he wasn't sure he should continue, but he couldn't help himself. He tried to tell me, in words he hoped I would understand but not be frightened by, that my sister's heart had enlarged to twice its normal size, because she had to work so hard to breathe. Her tiny lungs were a mass of scar tissue, due to the repeated pneumonias. The damage to both organs was irreversible. Her pancreas was almost completely failing to produce digestive enzymes so she was virtually starving, and the rest of her body, her kidneys, her liver, even her bones, were not growing the way they needed in order to sustain life. What my father didn't tell me was how amazed Dr. Matthews was that Pam was still alive at all.

My father's voice choked and his eyes turned pink.

"But she takes the granules," I protested. "Does this mean

she's not going to get better? Does this mean she's not coming home?"

"No, honey, she's going to be better, just not as much as we hoped. She'll be home soon. And Mommy will be home tomorrow. She almost had the baby today, and it's way too early."

Years later, my mother herself would tell me about that day, the stifling heat of the hospital, the sharp stench of blood, vomit, and disinfectant, the groans of gravely ill children and the agonized weeping of other parents. On the way back to her hotel, she had stared bitterly at the other passengers on the bus, wanting to shout, "My child is dying! How can you all go on with your lives as if nothing matters? My child is dying!" Her emotions had induced several hours of premature labor.

My mother arrived the next evening, her face lighting up as she saw me waiting in the door. I ran from her embrace, immediately accusing.

"You left her there alone."

"You need me here, too," she tried to explained.

"Then it's all my fault!" I wailed, running to my room and slamming the door.

Within a few days Pam was ready to be released, and my father flew down to retrieve her. The $3,000 hospital bill astounded him. He told them he'd have to pay it over time. They told him he must pay up immediately, in cash, or they'd hang on to his daughter. Devastated, my father was forced to leave Pam alone for three additional days while he returned home to raise the cash, while those extra days were added to the bill.

Hat in hand, he went to Grandma Bill and Uncle Frank, executor of the estate, asking for a loan. They were sorry, but the answer was no. If they gave him money now, they reasoned, he'd expect it again later, and this wouldn't be the last time Pam got sick. It could drain the estate.

Swallowing his tears and pride, my father went next to the

bank manager, who made him "jump through hoops" to get a second mortgage on the house.

After Dr. Matthews saved my sister's life, my parents drove or flew Pam back and forth to Rainbow Children's Hospital in Cleveland every four to six weeks for a checkup. Occasionally, I was invited along to keep her company. Despite the underlying tension of wondering what Pam's new prognosis might be, the trips down were fun and had a vacationlike quality, especially when we flew. The stewardesses found the two of us "darling" and solicited our help in passing out menus or mints to the other passengers. Pam was especially admired for her pale skin and elfin physique, but it annoyed her when passengers oohed and aahed, speaking to her in goo-goo language.

"I'm not a baby," she announced to them, indignant. "I am seven years old."

It annoyed me that having come that far I was never allowed to go with Pam right into the clinic. I found myself relegated to the stuffy, vaguely furnished waiting room. Being almost nine, and a precocious reader, I passed the time scanning *Reader's Digest* accounts of people rescued from blizzards or burning buildings, saved miraculously from the brink of death. Shifting on the hard, wooden chairs, waiting for my sister to finish her tests, I thought long and hard about miracles.

Once, I read about the sole survivor of a plane crash who wandered for several days through the mountains with a broken leg. I fantasized about my own survival in such circumstances, watching myself in my mind's eye, heroic as I survived on wild berries, while limping through the brush, scaling cliffs and making my tortured way to safety.

My father chatted amicably, and vocally, with the nurses and other parents.

"How was the little (so and so) girl doing? I didn't see her and her family here today."

The reply came *sotto voce*. My father's cheeks flushed. He pulled out his hankie and wiped his nose.

"Oh no! Oh, I'm so sorry to hear that."

He came to sit beside me, sighing deeply.

"What's the matter?" I asked him.

"Oh, a little girl we used to see here once in a while with Pammy has passed away since we were here last. Don't say anything to your sister. Your mother and I will tell her when we get home."

Almost every visit brought news of another death.

Pam trotted out from her exam—tired, cranky, ready to roll. The trip home was subdued. A day or so later my parents would take my sister aside and say softly, "We have something sad to tell you."

"You don't have to tell me anything," she'd retort, setting her jaw, and casting her glance sideways into the frozen distance. "I already figured it out for myself." Her back stiff, she turned, slipped into our room without a sound, and shut the door.

"How did she know?" my father asked, incredulous each time.

"She has a sixth sense," shrugged my mother.

Dr. Matthews replaced Pam's granules with dark green capsules, called Cotazyme, which contained the same enzymes in a powdered form and were easier to swallow. Still, she took thirty or more with each meal, and a handful with anything else she ate, even a piece of toast or an ice cream cone. I gagged just watching her.

Dr. Matthews introduced two kinds of therapy for Pam. One was a type of physical therapy called postural drainage, the other was a type of inhalation therapy we named The Mask. Pam had both therapies three times a day, four if we were afraid she was coming down with an infection. The mask and physio were done back to back, and took forty-five minutes to an hour. We referred to the entire process as Pam's Treatment.

Pam's morning treatment, her lunch treatment, her after-school treatment, and the occasional before-bed treatment divided our daily routine.

The ritual of making tea always accompanied the treatment. Mom made Pam's mask while Dad put the kettle on to boil. Mom pulled a vial of medicine called Ventolin, a "bronchodilator," from the fridge, where we kept a box of them next to the milk. Carefully, she mixed the Ventolin with .09 percent of saline solution, and poured the sticky mixture into a plastic receptacle which screwed onto the mask. The mask was a filmy green plastic affair reminding me of the oxygen masks I'd seen on Second World War pilots in the movies. It was connected by tubing to an air compressor, a miniature of the one that ran the tent and vibrated with the same grating, high-pitched rumble. Pam strapped the mask over her nose and mouth with a wide green elastic band. The compressed air filtered the Ventolin into a mist that Pam breathed for twenty minutes.

In an effort to encourage and support my sister, I took the mask a couple of times. The odor, a rotten egg, yesterday's garbage smell, was already familiar, since it saturated the entire family room. Breathing it directly into my nose and mouth made me want to retch. It had a bitter, metallic taste, and left a sticky residue on my face.

With Dr. Matthews' encouragement, Pam had already developed a tacit acceptance of this therapy in the hospital in Cleveland. She knew she had no choice. She had to do treatments three or four times a day, every day. This would define her daily routine for the rest of her life.

Although the treatments were quickly accepted as custom in our house, the feelings I had watching Pam go through them never went away. In the pit of my stomach lay a faint, dull ache that I learned to ignore, an ache made up of equal parts compassion for Pam, and sickening guilt for my unspeakable gratitude having been spared her fate.

While she took her mask, she read or did homework or watched television. Gregg and I lolled nearby, trying to ignore the pungent odor of the mist as it floated across the den to the kitchen, where the steam from the bubbling teakettle drifted up to meet it. We turned the TV set up louder so we could hear *Rawhide* or *Kraft Theatre* over the grating drone of the compressor.

When Pam was finished with her mask, she coughed a bit while Mom made the tea. Once the woolly tea cozy hugged its pot, it was time for Pam's physio.

Dad had built a giant slant board out of pine, which stood on tall legs so the working surface was slightly higher than a grownup's waist. The board itself slid up from a flat position to a forty-five-degree angle, and back down again. Pam climbed up there onto a thin mattress.

"How do we start, Pam—front or back?" my mother always asked. It was good for Pam to have a choice, because it made her feel like she had control over the proceedings.

Usually they started in on her back. Pam lay face down as Mom and Dad tucked a pillow under her tummy and tilted the slant board up until Pam was virtually hanging upside down. She lay with her arms at her sides, dispassionate.

My mother or father, whoever was doing the physio, raised their arms above Pam's rib cage, hands cupped, and pounded or clapped her with great force in a steady rhythm.

The lungs are divided into five lobes. Vigorously, my parents clapped and pounded each of Pam's lobes, front and back, to dislodge the thick, suffocating mucus, which had hopefully been loosened by the mist from the mask.

When it was time for her to turn around and do the other side, she stopped for a brief rest and coughed, spitting mucus into a Kleenex that she dropped into a paper bag at the foot of the physio table.

I learned how to do Pam's treatment too, so I could relieve my parents when their arms tired, or the phone rang, or they were out giving a speech and we were left with a babysitter. It was harder to get babysitters now that we had to do treatments on Pam. When Auntie Ruth came, she would do Pam's physio. When Auntie Elsie or anyone else came, I did it. Pam made her own mask.

The up and down thumping of Pam's fragile torso lasted thirty minutes to an hour. Every rib was sharp beneath the flesh of our palms, each vertebrae was a granite knot. We struck her fluttering barrel chest and her bony back repetitively, until her skin glowed pink beneath her flannel pajamas, until our arms ached and our palms were stinging and red.

My mother sang to her, we all sang together, we told jokes or had spelling bees. This distracted Pam, and ourselves from the pain of it all – her body, our hands, our hearts.

"How do you spell quiet?" I asked.

"Qu..u..u..i..e..e..e..t..ee..ee..." she spelled back to me, the sound of her voice vibrating and coming out all jiggly on the vowel sounds as she was pounded. Sometimes it made us laugh so hard the treatment had to stop completely while we composed ourselves.

At other times, though, Pam would wince or cry out a little, and the pat-a-pat rhythm of the clapping broke for just an instant.

"Are you all right?"

Pam gritted her teeth, nodded yes, and though her eyes may have brimmed with tears, she motioned to begin again.

On occasion, her face creased with such pain that she pressed her lips together and closed her eyes while fighting for composure. When she could take no more, she waved at us to stop, sat up, crumpled forward, and wept silently. Then within minutes, she was laughing through the tears that streaked her face, joking, "You guys always manage to beat the truth out of me." She blew her nose and lay down again, smiling gamely. Then her eyes grew passive, almost steely, and she gestured at us to resume pounding.

When the physio was done, my mother gathered the cups and the pot of strong, steeping tea, and brought them to the kitchen table. Pam sat in Dad's easy chair in the family room and coughed. Often, I sat with her.

She grabbed a handful of Kleenex, girded herself on the arms of the chair, and took a deep breath. Her cough started deep inside the cave of her chest with a dark, wet rumble that rolled up and out of her like the sound of thunder with heavy rain. The sound poured into my ears, making me shiver. I stared at the soft floral pattern of the needlepoint rug, steadying my insides. I caught myself clenching my fists.

My sister's body heaved and groaned like an erupting volcano, racked by one cough, then another, and another, a crescendo of coughs, each growing in intensity until a huge glob of mucus bubbled up into her mouth. If a plug became stuck in her chest or her throat, I was there to pound her back hard with my fist, and bang it out. She spit it into the Kleenex or a kidney basin, her eyes quickly appraising. She knew if it was pink, or had a green tinge, it meant either hemorrhage or infection. When she was done, she sat quiet and trembling, her eyes watering and her lips blue. She caught her breath, and allowed a mantle of dignity to settle on her spare shoulders.

Now it was time for tea.

My mother's water broke as she fried eggs for breakfast on a Saturday morning seven days before Gregg's fifth birthday, two weeks before Christmas of 1961. Pam and I sat fidgeting in the basement all morning, watching *Lassie* and *The Lone Ranger* on

TV. Halfway through *Sky King* the phone rang. Auntie Elsie called down from the top of the stairs.

"Girls," Elsie giggled, "you have a new baby brother."

"Yay!" Pam and I danced around the room while Gregg stood by looking betrayed.

From the moment my mother brought Jeffrey home, I looked for signs. He had a herniated belly button that wouldn't go away on its own and had to be fixed surgically.

Pam was vigilant as well. "He's so pale and skinny, Mom, and he isn't getting fatter. Everything he eats goes in one end and right out the other, just like me if I don't take my pills. And, his poo STINKS!"

"Lots of babies grow at different rates. As for his digestion, well, maybe he's just allergic to cow's milk. Lots of babies are. And, by the way, poo stinks!"

"I think he tastes salty when I kiss him," Pam whispered to me. We closed the door to the nursery and kissed the baby several times.

Pammy licked his tiny arm for good measure.

"I can't tell," she sighed.

"Of course you can't tell. You taste too salty yourself."

I licked the baby.

"I can't tell either."

Walking in on our examination, my mother cautioned, "You girls worry too much."

"The baby's fine, the baby's fine, there's nothing wrong with the baby," went the new litany in our house, but we were all suspicious.

It took three sweat tests before we knew for sure. Our new baby brother, our sweet, last hope, had Cystic Fibrosis.

"Subclinical," Dr. Matthews said. "We can start treating him right away. Chances are he'll have a fairly good prognosis."

The house fell silent.

Dr. Matthews prescribed a mist tent for Jeff, just like Pam's, and told my parents to give him gentle physio. A pound of prevention really was worth an ounce of cure.

My parents' new grief was awful to witness. My mother's quiet tears as she folded the laundry. My father's stricken face, staring out the window. Their determined cheer and flinty optimism encountering acquaintances at the supermarket. I wanted to fix it, to make it better. A soft April rain bleated against the windows of the lumberyard office as I awkwardly punched the stiff keys of an old black Smith Corona, painstakingly typing a secret letter for the 1962 *Chatelaine* magazine Mother of the Year contest:

Dear Sir:
I should like to nominate my mother, Mrs. D.K. Summerhayes as "Mother of the Year." She has four children to look after, of which two have a rare disease called "Cystic Fibrosis." She is very patient and cooperative with them and gives both of them three treatments of physiotherapy a day. She puts them in the oxygen tents every night and never loses hope that someday they may be cured. She manages to prepare delicious meals and keeps the house sparkling clean. Once a month she takes Pam (8) to Cleveland to have a check-up. At any special occasion, such as a birthday or Christmas, she always turns up with lovely things for us. She is, at most times, very happy and she has brought Pam (8), who is afflicted with CF, up to her age with much difficulty. However, she just goes along the best she can. We all try to help her out, but there isn't much we can do. Everything is so hard on her she hardly gets a chance to rest. She is awake all night with Jeff, about five month's old, who is also afflicted with CF (Cistic Fibrosis). She is giving me the advantage of going to National Ballet Summer School

in Toronto. I would appreciate it if you would choose her as
"Mother of the Year" for she would certainly enjoy it and it
would help her very much in a way that words cannot
explain.

Yours sincerely,
Heather Summerhayes (age 10)

I did not win the prize for my mother, and decided that made
me a failure as both a daughter and as a writer. I didn't know
which was worse.

Ever since Mrs. Hetherington, my fifth grade teacher, first
assigned us to write a poem, I was sure I had found my calling. I
had, in fact, come to fancy myself as the reincarnation of our late
local heroine, poetess, and literary vaudevillian, E. Pauline
Johnson. The urge to write, once let loose, broke the surface of my
being like a trout flinging itself up out of the water into the sun.

Words carried my feelings outside of me, emptying the ache
in my chest in a way that sighs and weeping did not. Putting
words on paper became a compulsion. I filched pads of creamy
Vellum along with the fine pen from my mother's desk, and fer-
reted them into the Big Woods. In the shade of a pine tree, on
the damp, cool earth, I sat until twilight, filling yards of paper
with crude plays and poetry.

"That's very nice, Heather," my mother said when I brought
my scribbling home to her, "but I've warned you time and again
about sitting on the ground like that. Little girls shouldn't do
that. It's bad for your bladder. And I hope you put my good pen
back where you found it."

Books became my friends, and I filled the empty spaces of my
life with them. I read anything I could lay my hands on: Nancy
Drew, Cherry Ames R.N., ghost stories, biographies of Njinski
and Pavlova. I stole books off my parents' shelves: *Exodus, The*

Silver Chalice. I made pilgrimages to the library every Saturday after ballet class, and spent the entire afternoon reading. I brought home armfuls of books and hung onto them for months, until my mother discovered that I owed several dollars in overdue payments.

In bed at night, I whispered to Pam how I wanted to be a famous writer, and chattered on about the fantasy life I would lead as a great ballerina by night and an illustrious poet by day. Nobly justifying my ambitions, I told her, "The more famous I am, the more money I can raise for CF."

My sister listened quietly in the dark.

Most nights I tried to stay awake until I was sure Pam was sleeping well and soundly. The nebulizers in the tent hissed softly. White mist filled the space inside the plastic until I could barely make out my sister's form. Soon she curled up and disappeared like Brigadoon.

I slept with one ear cocked for a change in her breathing, or for coughing spells, dreaming the same dream night after night:

I am swimming in the ocean. Three huge brains foam up out of the water on the heads of giant pins. They converge on me. I try to swim away, but I run out of breath. The brains surround me, pushing me under. My mouth fills with their gray puffiness. I am drowning. I am suffocating. I am walking through a jungle. The path opens to a clearing. The earth is smooth and tan, inviting. I step into the clearing. Quicksand. I am sucked down to my waist, to my shoulders, to my neck, to my chin. I push again and again with my right leg, trying to escape. "Save me, save me," I cry out, but no one comes.

BOOM! The compressor in the basement started up and I was suddenly awake, gulping for air, shivering, hugging my knees to my chest, my covers kicked into a tangle at the end of the bed. My eyes adjusted slowly to the darkness. Weird shapes and patterns moved across the wall, shadows from the trees outside our window.

The compressor shut itself off. The tent hissed. The wind moaned. The house was still as a tomb. I strained my ears to hear if Pam was breathing. I was scared she would die in the night, without warning. No one had told me how a person dies, what the signs were. I only knew what death looked like from seeing a drowned lady at the beach when we were little, and from watching Bela Lugosi and vampires on *The Late Show*."

I sat up and peered through the black filter of night across the room to my sister's bed, looking for signs of life. In the mist of her tent, in the dark, in her deep sleep, she seemed as dead as I imagined someone could be. I called to her softly.

"Pam...Pammy?"

No response. My heart began to pound and my palms broke out in a cold, clammy sweat. *Go touch her*, I told myself. *I can't.* Sharp pains, jagged threads of electric current, shot through my chest each time I took a breath.

You have to tell Mom and Dad. Mom and Dad...Oh my God! I have to tell Mom and Dad that Pam is dead!

Long minutes passed. I lay paralyzed, tears running silently down my cheeks and behind my ears, soaking the pillow.

Go! Go! Finally, I forced my legs out of bed. My joints screamed with panic. I could not run. I could not even stand up. Crawling on my hands and knees I inched my way toward the door, keeping a wide berth from my dead sister in her bed, recalling those vampire movies. I knew dead people could suddenly sit right up and grab the living ones.

Keep going. You have to tell Mom and Dad.

I did not take my eyes off Pam for a second. I fought for breath.

Suddenly, Pam flopped an arm down outside the bottom of the tent, and coughed lightly. A shock of terror, then relief twisted my heart, wildly pounding inside the small cave of my chest. I crumpled gratefully to the cold linoleum floor, catching my breath. After a few moments, I pulled myself to my feet and wobbled back to bed, feeling shaky and stupid.

Thank you God for keeping Pam alive.

I pulled my covers tight around me and cried myself to sleep.

Before long Pam woke up gasping for breath, fighting the rising tide of mucus, hacking into her pillow so as not to wake the baby. Her cough rose and fell like storm waves crashing on rocks. She shot up from her pillow and ripped back the tent flap with an angry swipe. White mist poured out from behind her, fogging the room. She coughed and coughed, desperately grabbing the tent and the sheets and the sides of the bed. Mucus caught in her throat, gagging her.

I leapt from bed, turned on the light, and called for my parents.

They flew into the room and swooped down on her.

"Spit it up! Spit it up!" my mother shouted. Pam bent forward, cleaving to my father, clenching his arms to steady her while my mother doubled her fist and pounded the back of my sister's rib cage. Pam's chest heaved and cracked and growled. The dam burst with a great dark explosion of air. A sticky yellow glob spewed from Pam's mouth into the handful of Kleenex my father held like an offering below her chin.

"Good girl, that's a good girl...," my mother murmured gently as Dad wiped around Pam's dry, cracked lips and dabbed at her wet eyes with a fresh tissue.

My mother patted Pam's back tenderly, moving her hands up and down to smooth away the blows she had just rendered.

"There, there. Are you all finished? Was that all of it? Are you all right?"

Pam huffed and puffed, trying to catch her breath as she nodded yes.

"Good. Now, take some of this cough syrup. It might help you sleep better."

Pam strained her neck up and opened her mouth wide like a baby bird as my mother slipped two teaspoons of sticky red Benylin syrup down her shivering gullet. I sat up in bed, riveted, arms wrapped tightly around myself, holding my breath.

Pam lay down under her covers. My mother closed up the tent and tidied the night table. Dad turned off the lamp. They came over and kissed me lightly on the forehead.

"Go on back to sleep now. Everything's all right."

My parents made their way back down the hall and shut off the light. In minutes the house was quiet, as if I had dreamt it all. I stared into the blackness, wide awake, telling my heart to slow down, telling myself I must sleep because I had school in the morning.

I was afraid to sleep. I was afraid to dream. I was afraid of drowning.

At the other end of the house, Jeffrey began his long siren baby-wail. My mother groaned and my father sighed, "Oh no." The compressor boomed on again in the basement. I pulled my pillow over my ears and forced my eyes shut.

CHAPTER EIGHT

"Faith is not belief. Belief is passive. Faith is active."
— Edith Hamilton

*"My faith demands that I do whatever I can, wherever
I am, whenever I can, for as long as I can with whatever
I have to try to make a difference."* — Jimmy Carter

When I was ten I believed in God, because I was taught by my parents and by the Reverend Cyril Squires that I should, although I think I always had my own innate sense of a greater power. I believed that God made everything and God saw everything. He punished us when we were bad, and rewarded us when we were good. Sometimes, though very rarely and only under extreme circumstances, He granted miracles in exchange for prayer.

It was God's Will that accounted for most of what broke our hearts. God's Will seldom seemed to be that we have joy. Thinking about it now, I don't recall anyone whispering and nudging on a happy occasion, "It was God's Will."

Having faith meant believing that God intended the best for us, even by employing His Will in giving my sister and baby brother Cystic Fibrosis.

Prayer meant saying "Please, please can I have...?"

This was all part and parcel of religion which, I was told, would give me that faith I so needed.

If only it had been, if only it were, that simple.

Tragedy can cause people to lose their faith, or conversely to discover it perhaps for the first time. Seeing children suffer and die can cause a loss of faith, and yet it is a powerful testimony to witness the faith of a child, especially one facing death.

The spring of 1962 brought with it the sweet, metallic fragrance of melting snow on damp earth, the purple hues of budding crocuses, and my beloved poplars sprouting their new green leaves. Our faith in spring had sustained us through the winter, and God had not let us down.

I heard a lot about faith in those days.

John Glenn had enough faith to orbit Earth in February. John F. Kennedy inspired our faith that he could save the Free World from Krushchev and the Russians. Pam and I had been to the Capital Theatre to see *The Miracle Worker* with Patty Duke, and learned that Helen Keller's family had no faith, but Annie Sullivan had lots.

My parents kept telling us we needed to have faith. We got it by attending church every Sunday, just like we went to the service station to gas up the car. We went to church to gas up our souls.

On Sunday mornings, Pam and I loved to let Mom and Dad sleep in a bit while we got up early to surprise them. We set the table specially, folding pink Kleenex paper napkins into little fans, dissolving into giggles trying to get them to sit upright on the breakfast plates. We squeezed oranges on an electric juicer that sounded like a jet engine at takeoff, and our laughter grew more hysterical. We clamped our hands over each other's mouths in useless attempts at composure. Pam's left the taste of salt on my lips.

"What's going on out there?" Mom and Dad called from their bedroom. "You'll wake the whole neighborhood!" My parents' shuffling footsteps sounded in the hall as they got up to wake the boys.

"Don't come out yet, not 'til we say!" We laughed so hard we couldn't hold each other up, tumbling to the linoleum on top of each other in a heap of wriggling flannel pajamas.

"Donna," teased my father, "I think we'd better go see what those girls are up to!"

"Wait, wait," we sputtered, our laughter reduced to wild smirks as we scrambled to mop up the orange juice we had just spilled on mother's clean floor.

"Okay, we're ready. SURPRISE!"

"Aah," cooed my mother. "Look what my two girls have done!"

Pam and I exchanged grins.

"Well," Mom chirped, "let's get this day started off on the right foot!"

Still wearing her nightgown, she strode into the kitchen with the same determination that characterized all of her movements. She commanded the space between the fridge, stove, and sink with the dexterity of the basketball player she had once been, slam dunking eggs into a bowl, hurling strips of bacon into a pan, eyeing the game clock, pouring milk into a pitcher, turning to check the table setting we'd created and making the necessary adjustments.

I ran to strip Pam's mistogen-soaked bed, and make mine. Pam took her mask while holding Jeff in her arms and feeding him his bottle. Gregg disappeared back into his room with orders to get dressed.

Dad polished our shoes, a Sunday morning ritual that I loved. He spread newspaper out over the kitchen floor and folded his tall, wiry frame into a corner between the sink and the stove, sitting cross-legged at my mother's feet, six pairs of shoes lined up in a neat row in front of him.

"For heaven's sake Doug, don't sit there, I'll trip all over you!"

"Where else should I sit?"

"Anywhere but there."

"What's wrong with me wanting to be close to my beautiful wife?" he said, so sweetly you could gag.

My mother sighed and rolled her eyes. "Oh, it just makes me crazy when you do this!"

My father stayed put, chuckling. Parked next to him on the floor was the shoe basket, a four-quart wooden apple basket, the kind we collected candy in on Halloween, this one stuffed with polish and brushes.

Dad began with Jeff's tiny white baby shoes and moved up the line carefully applying polish with a flannel rag. Gregg's small brown Oxfords, Pam's and my matching black Mary Janes, Mom's high heels, his own large brown spectators. This done, he began once again at the head of the line, shining every shoe with a big soft brush that "thmacked" against the leather as he whipped it back and forth. The waxy smell of polish mingling with the aroma of sugar-cured bacon was almost enough to sweeten the stench of Pam's mask. After Pam's physio was done, we ate breakfast, slipped into our glossy shoes and the dresses or suits that we'd "saved for good," and piled into the big maroon Dodge to head for church.

Pam and I loved First Baptist Church. We loved to climb the wide staircase and pause with appropriate solemnity on the landing where the names of the dead from the Great Wars were engraved on the wall. Here the staircase split in two, ascending gracefully to the left and right, leading up to the doors of the sanctuary.

We always went up to the right. I assumed this was because my father, who was a deacon of the church and on the board of management, was superstitious in the knowledge that Jesus sat at the right hand of God.

We loved to sit upstairs in the first row of the balcony at the back of the church, commanding a superb view of the congregation. Pam and I secretly agreed it made us feel that much more important than everyone else because we were higher up and therefore closer to God in Heaven. The rest of the Summerhayes clan sat close by. Grandma Bill, formidable in the midst of her many grandchildren, dispatched tiny red cough drops that went so sticky in our mouths it was hard to open them. This had the intended effect of keeping us all quiet.

Reverend Squires stood tall and angular at the front of the church, behind the maroon-robed choir, beneath a huge stained-glass frieze of Christ standing in a doorway holding a lantern. The lantern had a bulb in it that shone like a candle flame. The frieze was the only decorative piece in the church, and was inscribed with the words "Behold I stand at the door and knock. In loving memory of John William Widdup from his Beloved Wife." It served to remind us of the biblical passage, "Seek and ye shall find. Ask and it shall be given. Knock, and the door shall be opened unto you."

Below the frieze, behind Reverend Squires, hidden by burgundy velvet drapes, was a baptismal tank the size of a grave. On Baptismal Sundays the tank was filled with water, the pulpit was pushed into the floor, the curtains were parted, and Reverend Squires donned wading boots to baptize sinners below a hand-painted mural of the River Jordan. Afterward, glass thimbles of grape juice and tiny squares of bread were passed among the congregation for those who wished to participate in Communion.

Reverend Squires delivered long, lusty sermons in the cadence of his native Scottish brogue. He quoted Shakespeare and the great classic authors, gesticulating earnestly, his black robes flapping like giant wings. Pam and I clung to each other, stifling our giggles, imagining what would happen if he fell backward through the curtains into the empty tank.

Every Sunday, Reverend Squires said that we could look forward to the Resurrection of the Dead, and the life of the world to come. This gave me hope that if Pam died, someday we'd be together again. All the same, every Sunday I asked God to cure Pammy and not make her die, or if she did die, would He please raise her up again like Lazarus so I wouldn't have to wait for the Resurrection of the Dead? So far as I knew, while I prayed to God asking Him to save Pam's life, Pam was asking Him if He would make her fatter.

When the service ended, the congregation poured out onto the front steps of the church to chat. Then, like leaves falling one by one from a great tree, they drifted slowly off home. Sometimes my mother hitched a ride for herself and the boys with Auntie Ruth or Uncle Lloyd, going on ahead to get the roast in. Pam and I stayed behind to wait for Dad while he took forever to count the collection.

We played alone together on the church steps, casting furtive glances at Thorpes Brothers Funeral Home, a large white manicured Victorian house that stood twenty feet away across an immaculate lawn.

"I dare you to go over and peek in the window," I challenged my sister.

"I'm not going over there. They have dead people."

"Scaredy-cat, scaredy-cat."

"So? I dare you to go," she said. "I double dare you."

I dared. Sort of. "I'll go if you go with me."

Pam's face broke into a devilish grin as she offered me her hand. Together, we snuck across the velvety grass and craned our necks up over the concrete windowsills. Heavy drapes concealed the view on the other side of the glass, except where the drapes parted slightly in the center of the window. There we stood, two breathless conspirators on tiptoe, noses pressed against the pane, straining to see inside.

Suddenly, the drapes quivered.

"Aaaaagh! I see one, I see one!"

We shrieked in unison, racing all the way back to the church, falling down on the steps clinging to each other, laughing until we were out of breath and Pam launched into a coughing spell.

"What are you girls up to?"

Our father's voice behind us made us jump, sending us into more squealing spasms of laughter.

In the afternoon, while the roast was in the oven, we all went out for a Sunday drive, or stopped in at one of the grandmas for tea.

After dinner in the evening, my parents sat smiling and exhausted on the big Duncan sofa in the living room listening to the strains of Ray Coniff or Mitch Miller on the stereo. Pam and I pranced and somersaulted while Gregg played with Jeff on the carpet.

"You see," smiled my mother. "God has seen us through another week."

I had questions about God that church didn't answer. When I was in the woods, in the company of trees, the wind, the water, the sky, and the earth, I felt a connection to God, and I was flush with my own divinity. God heard me in the woods, I just knew He did. When I prayed at church, I wasn't so sure. Maybe that was because there were so many people praying all at once in church, and it was hard for Him to pay attention.

In church, gazing up at that stained-glass snapshot of Christ knocking at the door, I imagined myself at the same door, rapping my knuckles politely at first, then pounding, trying to get God's attention.

It was never like that in the woods, where I had all His attention. The woods felt like what I imagined was on the other side of that door, a place already full of thanks and praise, already singing, already praying, all the time, as if this was where God actually resided from Monday to Saturday, really being Himself, before He had to put on His Sunday Best and climb up onto His great chair in the clouds and be what everyone wanted Him to be. I waited in the woods for God to speak to me from a burning bush, or for an angel to appear, telling me what offerings and sacrifice I should make to Him so my sister could live.

On a hot July Sunday morning, at the age of ten, I accepted Christ as my Savior and was saved by the rubber-wadered Reverend Squires in a tank full of water beneath a painted mural of the River Jordan, in full view of the First Baptist congregation.

I left for the National Ballet Summer School straight from church, clutching my baptismal certificate in one hand and my dance bag in the other, a young girl on a holy mission. The woods and the dark nights I shared with Pam dissolved into the horizon through the back window of my father's Dodge. Ray Charles blared from the dashboard. "I Can't Stop Loving You."

I knew I was going back on my promise never to leave my sister again, but in the Communion classes I'd taken to prepare for my Baptism, I had learned about the Parable of the Talents. I understood that my talents came from God, and that He expected me to make something out of them. Becoming a famous ballerina was no longer a flight of fancy, but a religious calling.

"It's not fair," Pam complained, "Heather gets to do everything."

July 1st/62
Dearest Heather,
...I am so proud of you going to ballet school. We are telling everyone about you and hope you like it and are doing well. I hope you like the food and are getting enough rest.

*Jeffy's teeth are through now and he is not so
cranky…Gregg is still trying to learn to ride Pam's bike. I
don't know which is going to fall apart first—Gregg or the
bike!!…I bet you are glad not to have the noise of the tent
bothering you, eh?…Well I must go and do the dishes now so
will close with all my love and you are in my thoughts always.*

July 10/62
*…Gregg was sleeping with Pam in your bed as she is very lone-
some at night…Pam is going to Cleveland with Karna and
Mr. Ivey in Mr. Ivey's plane. I hope they will be safe. In any
case I suppose I shall worry about them (Dad and Pam) until
they are home again safe and sound…Today there was a terrible accident behind our house on the highway and a 14 yr. old
boy was fatally injured. He was Patty Brazil's brother…Right
now we are without hydro and I am writing by candlelight.
We are having a terrific thunderstorm and the neighbourhood
is in complete darkness…I may be bringing Vicki Young back
with me on Sun. so that Pam will have someone to play
with…Please don't make any more phone calls unless absolutely
necessary as they are costing far too much…*

God Bless you,
Love, Mother

Reading my mother's letters, I could picture her writing in the flickering candlelight, surrounded by her melancholy and the dark. I
could feel her anxious heartbeat as Pam flew to the clinic in
Cleveland, and hear in her ears the sound of ambulance sirens
screaming up the King George Road, too late to save Patty Brazil's
brother. I was reminded of Pam's dejection since her best friend,
Vicki, moved away.

Thoughts and questions plagued me. Was it my fault that my sister was lonely? What if Pam died while I was gone? Maybe I'd be to blame for leaving her alone. Maybe she'd choke to death in the night when I was not there to wake up with her. Maybe Pam's death would be God's judgment on me because I was self-ish and wanted to be famous. How could God offer me a calling and punish me for accepting it at the same time?

I closeted myself in the hot, airless phone booth down the hall from my room and sat for a long while, working up my courage. I stared at the silver dial of the big black pay phone, fingering the graffiti carved into the wooden shelf below, hearts and arrows, strange names, rainbows and peace signs. My stash of dimes grew sweaty in my palm. I would pay for this call myself, and not reverse the charges. My heart beat until I could hardly breathe. My fingers trembled as I dialed.

"I want to come home," I whimpered into the receiver, "come and get me."

My parents were dumbfounded.

"I don't like my roommate," I barreled on, "and she doesn't like me. Anyway, I have a sway back and my legs aren't long enough. Barbara Malinowski got her picture in the *Toronto Star* because her legs are longer than mine. And my hair is too short, so I can't wear it in a real ballerina bun. I look stupid."

"We'll let your hair grow out then, if it's that important to you," said my mother, bewildered. "I don't see what your hair has to do with leaving ballet school."

"We had a hard time finding the money to send you there," my father's voice penetrated the receiver sharply. "We're not letting you give up that easy."

The following weekend they drove up and took me out to Scott's Steak and Seafood Restaurant. My father let me have two Shirley Temples.

"You've worked so hard," my mother said, "and I know how

badly you want this. If you leave now, I don't think they'll let you return for the winter school."

I sipped my second Shirley Temple and deliberated. I was about to try my Chechetti exams for acceptance into the full-time curriculum. If I passed—and there was a good chance I would—I would be on my way to becoming a professional ballerina. The next seven years of my life would be predetermined, with only the occasional weekend, one week off at Christmas, and two weeks in the summer to go home. Pam was likely to die in the interim. Then I would have to live on with the knowledge that I abandoned her, and gave up knowing her to pursue my own selfish ambition. In the meantime, who would be there for her when she woke coughing in the night, or when the Florence boys threw stones? My instincts were strong not only to protect Pam, but to safeguard my relationship with my parents. If I stayed at ballet school, it would be easy for them to forget me, and then Pam would really get all their attention.

I stared at the fish in the aquarium next to our table and poked at my steak. I thought about Abraham and Isaac. Reverend Squires told the Communion class how God told Abraham to sacrifice his son as proof of his love for God, and when God saw that Abraham was willing to sacrifice what was dearest to him, He spared Isaac and rendered His blessing.

Maybe that was the whole point. Maybe God gave me my talent so He could test me with it. If I loved God enough to give up ballet, maybe God would let Pam live.

"I don't want to come back for winter school. I don't want to stay here now. I just need to come home." I sounded whiny and childish instead of like the grownup I wanted to be. There was no way to explain it. If I told the truth, they'd make me stick it out.

My mother looked at me skeptically and sighed. Her disappointment passed like a chill breeze between us. My father removed his glasses and pinched the bridge of his nose between his eyes.

"We want you to stay another week before you make up your mind about coming home," my mother said briskly as we walked back to the ballet residence. "Because once you leave, there'll be no coming back."

I waited out the week and phoned.

"Are you sure?" asked my mother. "Are you absolutely sure?"

"Yes. I'm sure."

They came to get me and watched while I took my last class. I danced badly, as if to prove I'd made the right decision. In the car on the way home, pains in my chest were so sharp I could barely breathe.

Entering the house, I was sorrowful and relieved all at once. My heart leapt when I first saw Pam, but she greeted me without a hug, hands on her hips, defiant.

"Why did you come home before you were supposed to?" she demanded. She followed me into our room, her eyes snapping as I unpacked my bags.

"Leave me alone."

My sister studied me as if I were a glass-bottomed boat and she was trying to peer through me all the way down to the murky depths.

"I said leave me alone." I wanted to hug her and shove her to the floor all at the same time.

We ate dinner in silence, save for the sound of my sister's legs paddling her chair as she continued to eyeball me.

Afterward, my mother sat me down in the living room to talk once more about quitting.

"This is so like you," she started in. "Whenever something doesn't go the way you want it to, you just give up. I don't want this to become a pattern. Heather, you'll have to learn sooner or later that you can't simply throw in the towel every time the going gets rough."

"I didn't give up!" I shouted, "I just…oh, you wouldn't understand."

"Don't you raise your voice to me, young lady. You're not living up to your potential and I'm just trying to find out why. Even your teacher last year said you are one of the brightest kids in your class, yet you're just getting through by the skin of your teeth. You've got too much going for you to be an underachiever. So what is it? Do you simply not care to apply yourself?"

"You sent me away so you can pay more attention to Pam, that's why I quit, and I'm not letting you get away with it. I'm your daughter too, and you have to pay attention to me. I'm never going to let you send me away again." I threw myself to the floor sobbing loudly. My mother, too, began to cry.

"What's going on in here?" my father bellowed. "I won't have you behaving like this and upsetting your mother after she's tried everything she could to make you happy. Go to your room."

I stomped down the hall. Pam sat on her bed in our room, stony and sad.

"It's all your fault for having CF," I wanted to shout. Instead I smacked her in the face. She did not make a sound, but absorbed the blow in her stoic way, staring at me, rubbing her cheek where I had struck; her jaw clamped forward and her eyes became suddenly ancient, glittering with tears. The look on her wan face told me that she understood all too well what I had given up, and what it cost. She had already done the job of blaming herself. My stomach pitched and I wanted to throw up.

All that stuff about God and Abraham and Isaac seemed like a poor excuse now, something I invented to suit my needs. I was afraid and ashamed that I simply did not have the courage to fight for my own life the way my sister fought for hers.

I couldn't know then how my decision to quit ballet school would come to haunt me and burden Pam. I only knew I had suddenly lost faith in myself, and in God. I had a sick feeling in my bones, and the faint, nagging instinct that I'd let us all down.

Time rusted the last days of summer, and the trees turned brown before we knew it. On Saturdays we helped to rake the leaves. All the families in Greenbrier brought their kids out to do this. Up and down the streets you could hear loose chatter, laughter, the scraping of rakes across dry grass.

The sun was strong but the air was crisp, as the wind blew in from the north. Wearing gloves and heavy pink sweaters that Grandma Bill hand-knit for us, we bent over our rakes while sticky yellow poplar leaves swirled about our ankles. With infinite patience, working in a steady rhythm, we drew the leaves into huge piles, but the skittering leaves taunted us, urging us to play.

"I dare you to go jump in the leaves," I teased my sister.

"No," she smiled, "you do it."

"Uh-uh. Mom and Dad will yell at me. You're the only one who can get away with it. C'mon, I dare ya ... I double dare ya."

A mischievous grin blossomed on Pam's face.

"C'mon, Pammy. I'll do it if you'll do it."

Pam let go a peal of laughter and ran screaming down the lawn in wild delight. She was so small that when she leapt into the air, she floated for a brief moment before plowing into the great pile of leaves with a soft whoosh. She turned her head and grinned at me. I tore down the lawn after her. In an instant, Gregg jumped in with the two of us. We rolled around, frolicking and pushing each other into the leaves, squealing and shouting. The leaves crumbled beneath us, crispy brown bits stuck to our sweaters and caught in our hair.

My mother shouted from the kitchen window. "You kids quit making a mess and come in and get washed up!"

After dinner, we went out again to help my father burn the leaves. We huddled together in the cool, descending twilight roasting marshmallows, our hands and faces warmed by the fire.

The night air grew rich with dew and smoky perfume. We speared the marshmallows on the ends of twigs, holding them in the flames until they formed charcoal shells that peeled off to ooze molten white sweetness. When our fingers were sticky with the last ones and the leaves had turned to ash, Pam and I skipped across the driveway to sit on the Wishing Rock. Since I left ballet school, wishing on stars made just as much sense to me as praying to God.

"Time you girls were in bed," said my father.

"Please can't we stay out a little longer, please?"

"All right. I'll get the boys to bed, and then it's your turn."

My father hoisted a sleepy Jeff onto his shoulder, took Gregg by the hand, and disappeared into the house.

We scrambled up onto the pink granite Wishing Rock, sitting with our arms around one another. The sky stretched above us like a great veil of mourning. My heart ached inexplicably.

"You go first," said Pam, and I began.

"Star light, star bright, first star I've seen tonight, wish I may, wish I might, have the wish I ask tonight…"

For thirteen days in October of 1962 we stood at the edge of the world holding our breath with everyone else, watching events unfold in Cuba, and wondering if this would be the end. My family barely had time to sigh with relief before November arrived, and Pam was admitted to Brantford General Hospital. No one had to tell me her prognosis was poor. I stole my mother's Bank of Commerce calendar and hid it in my room so I could mark the passage of time—our own thirteen days—'til Pam came home, wondering again if this would be the end.

Mom and Dad went up to the hospital several times a day, preferring to do Pam's treatment themselves. They ferried her school assignments and stayed late to help her study, returning home with toys and gifts sent to Pam by well wishers from church, or from Summerhayes Lumber, or who knew where else. Too much stuff for her hospital room. It overflowed. The tributes were piled on her dresser and bed at her end of our room.

"Now don't you touch those," my mother warned, "they're for Pam when she gets home from the hospital." I clenched my jaw. I wanted to cry. I wanted to hit someone. I wanted Pam.

I had to get away. I had to fly on my bike Tornado, to McClures' woods. It was larger, and farther afield than the Big Woods of my early childhood. I'd be alone there. I'd be safe. I could cry freely there, and not face the question my mother was starting to ask repeatedly.

"What's wrong with you?"

I pumped the pedals of my bike as hard as I could. The wind filled my mouth in gusts. My ears pounded. Greenbrier rushed by in a blur of poplars and red brick. At last I reached the woods. Leaping down, I pushed my bike along the soft, rutted earth until the path disappeared, and I was finally in the deepest, leaf-carpeted heart of the forest. Panting, I shoved Tornado up against a maple tree, threw myself on the ground, and let go the fierce tears that had been pushing at me from inside. The incessant knot of pain that sat in the well of my chest burned red up through my esophagus and screamed out along the path of my tongue. I sobbed and heaved against the pungent earth. My nostrils pressed to the dank soil, I inhaled the sweet, piercing scent that soothed my hot head. The fallen leaves were damp and cool against my cheek.

I sat up and wiped my face with the back of my sleeve. Mom had just washed my jacket. She'd be mad when she saw the mud.

I staggered to my feet and wandered in aimless circles beneath the towering elm and maple trees. They flailed and danced as the wind rose and fell like ocean tides through their branches.

Bronze leaves fluttered and drifted. Far off, at the edge of the woods, the sun glazed the stubble in the late autumn fields. Here, beneath the umbrella of my misery, the sun seemed gray.

I fancied myself a soothsayer, a prophet, a child who had the gift of reckoning. I was a child of whom listening was demanded, but to whom no one would listen. Like Alice, I saw life on the other side of the mirror and had fallen down the hole.

I wept softly, muttering, "I can't compete with Pam. I can't keep up with Mom and Dad."

They were preoccupied with hope and optimism, with structure and routine, and exemplary behavior on the face of things. They rallied, they organized, they took the blows and turned the other cheek. I followed my parents into battle, eyes fixed firmly on the enemy in our midst, watchful, waiting for the ugly disease to make its next move, never turning my back or sleeping too soundly.

"I try, I try!" I shouted, beating my fists on my forehead and jumping up and down on the ground until my bones stung. My despair echoed through the trees.

CF wasn't the only thing. I got an F in self-control on my report card. Carol King's back got broken when I suddenly jumped off the seesaw and sent her flying. She'd kept me up there, high in the air, laughing at me all through recess, but that was no excuse for what I did. Then I told my classmates that Mrs. Hetherington had cancer, and was probably going to die. That was true, but I got into trouble anyway. My marks weren't as good as Pammy's, with all the days she'd missed.

I heard voices in my head.

"You're not trying hard enough."

"I am so trying."

"All we ask is that you do your best."

"I *am* doing my best."

"No, you're not. Do better."

When I returned home, I found my mother down on her knees in the kitchen, a pair of old woolly socks drawn over her hands up to her elbows. She rubbed Johnson's Wax into the linoleum with hard, keening strokes, thinking I did not see the tears that ran off the end of her nose and fell softly into her aproned lap.

"Why are you crying?" I asked her, my own eyes still pink from my trip to McClures' woods.

"Take your shoes off before you come in here, I'm waxing the floor."

"I'm sorry, Mom. I'm sorry if I did anything to upset you." I was on the verge of tears again as I hung on to the wall and slipped my shoes off without untying them.

"Don't take your shoes off that way. You'll ruin the backs."

"Sorry," I repeated, bending down to untie the Oxfords that lay askew at my stocking feet.

"How did you get that mud on your jacket?"

"I fell off my bike."

"I just washed that jacket."

"I know. I'm sorry." I hung my head and picked at the dried mud on my sleeve.

"Throw it back in the wash now. As soon as I've finished here we'll sit down together and have some tea. I baked some cookies while you were gone."

When my mother tucked me in that night, I begged. "Don't leave me, Mommy. Sing like you do when Pammy's here."

But it was not a time for singing.

"It's lucky you didn't ruin those new shoes." We hugged each other, both hurt and helpless, "I love you," our minds on the other side of town.

Pam came home, wispy and white, and Christmas arrived, and my mother baked more cookies and put up more decorations than any Christmas previous, attempting to ward off the melancholy stirred by Pam's deteriorating condition and the usual family politics.

We rang in the New Year of 1963 with false bravado. Watching my sister's decline through the weeks that followed, we felt bitter and cold, no matter how high my father turned up the furnace.

Sure enough, Pam went in again for sixteen days in March. I learned the news by coming home from school and finding her bed stripped empty. I thought how often I'd complained about the sound from Pam's tent and compressor bothering me at night. Now the sight of her bare mattress turned my stomach, and I was sleepless. I lay in the dark, wrestling with my need to do something.

How was an eleven-year-old girl to mitigate the dire circumstances of her life? What power did she have to bring comfort, ease the tension, lessen the pain? By the time Pam came home from the BGH, I had come up with a plan. I would help raise money for a cure and become famous. I would be Judy Garland and Mickey Rooney rolled into one. I would put on a show!

My invalid sister watched me rehearse, hiding behind corners, trees, or chairs, observing slyly as I shaped my material. I couldn't tell if she admired me or thought me ridiculous. Finally I invited her to stop hiding. She sat in the corner of the living room, curled up against the fluted back of our rose-colored upholstered wing chair, knees pulled up beneath her nightie, her bare toes, clubbed like her fingers, peeking out from beneath a flannel ruffle.

I pranced around singing to *Porgy and Bess* on the stereo, "Bess, you is my woman now, you is, you is…" I leaped and twirled to Chopin's *Polonaise in A flat* and the overture from Strauss's *Die Fledermaus*, pretending to be Lois Smith, prima ballerina of the National Ballet Company of Canada.

"Maybe I'll dance between acts in my play," I panted, taking a deep bow as my sister applauded wildly.

"Tell me what your show's about."

"I'm writing a play about Queen Victoria and Prince Albert.

They loved each other very much and then he died young and she grieved for him the rest of her whole life."

"Oh."

"I'm giving the money to Cystic Fibrosis. Maybe the *Brantford Expositor* will even come and take pictures. Mom said she might call them."

My sister carried the Scotch tape and tore it off in neat strips with her clubbed fingers, as I stuck our magic-marked, bristle board posters to the streetlights around the neighborhood. My father delivered benches from the lumberyard and set them up in the carport for my audience: my mother, Pam and Gregg, Ivy Johnson from across the road and her mother, "Granny East Who Survived the Blitz," Mr. and Mrs. Jarvis from next door, and Nick, who worked for my dad and showed up earlier than expected to pick up the benches and return them to the lumberyard.

It poured rain. I sold orange Kool-Aid and brown paper lunch bags full of soggy popcorn, a nickel a bag, prior to rushing through my performance. I took my bows to polite applause. When everyone had left, Pam helped me set pots out in the driveway and under the eavestroughs to catch the soft rainwater. Later we would wash each other's hair with it at the kitchen sink. We stood with our mother in the carport doorway, watching the basins fill while Nick, completely soaked, loaded the benches onto the flatbed truck. I could feel my hair frizzing up around my ears in the dampness.

"I'm no good!" I pouted. "Nobody came."

"It wasn't your fault," said my mother, hugging my shoulder. "I think the weather kept folks away."

"But I wanted to be famous and raise a lot of money for CF!"

Pam squeezed my hand and patted my back. "We saw you," she said. "We loved it. You can have all the money from my piggy bank if you want."

"No," I stomped my foot, "that's silly. *I* am supposed to get money to help *you*. *You're* not supposed to give money to help *yourself.* I'm nothing but a big failure."

"Don't be so hard on yourself," said my mother.

How could I not be? I was flourishing, while Pam lived by inches. She could not gain weight no matter what, or how much, she ate. We fed her bowls and bowls of her favorite, pink Junket. She devoured Borden's Eagle Brand condensed milk right out of the can. We filled her with butter tarts, macaroni and cheese, and blueberry pie. Dad gave her the pieces of meat with the most fat on them, though fat was difficult for her to digest, and she got terrible cramps if she didn't take extra Cotazyme. She had cream on her cereal as a snack before bedtime. Nothing worked. My sister was starving to death right in front of us. How long could she go on?

"Just as I am, without one plea, but that Thy blood was shed for me..."

The collective voice of the congregation rose in song and my heart stirred. My tiny sister, four feet one inch of spit and vinegar and forty pounds soaking wet, stepped carefully down into the water of the baptismal tank, beneath the stained-glass vision of Christ holding the lantern and knocking at the door, front and center at First Baptist Church. She had stepped back from the brink of death.

During the cold spring of 1963, while she was in the hospital, I had filled the lonely hours pretending I was Little Peggy March or Lesley Gore, wandering McClures' woods, belting out the lyrics to "I Will Follow Him" and "It's My Party." Pam, meanwhile, sat in a hospital bed coming to terms with her life, and her unreliable prognosis, as well as a nine year old could. She returned home sober and pensive, asking to be baptized.

I objected to this on the grounds that she was a year too young.

"I had to wait until I was ten. Why doesn't she?"

I also protested the fact that she was going to receive a white Bible, to mark the occasion. This gesture stood in direct violation of a long-term understanding that a white Bible was to be our special gift for turning twelve. I was still going to have to wait for mine, so I'd been told, and I was spitting mad.

I knew full well that Pam was getting hers now because my parents had good reason to believe she wouldn't live to see twelve. The underlying threat of my sister's mortality meant, generally speaking, that she always got what she wanted, when she wanted it. This latest crisis in the hospital had only upped the ante. Understanding this did little to help me accept the injustice. On the other hand, I didn't have the heart to argue with my mother that I might not see twelve either. *Remember Patty Brazil's brother?* I wanted to say. *I could get hit by a truck just as easily.*

So there I stood, itching and jealous, anxious and proud, as Reverend Squires reached out toward Pam, trailing the black-winged sleeves of his gown in the water. She leaned into his long, outstretched arms, and he lifted her gently down beside him. The water lapped around her chin. The Reverend offered to hold her up so she wouldn't get a mouthful, but she shook her head no and tried to stand on tiptoe. She glanced up at the mural of the River Jordan and I had to giggle, knowing that she was pretending to be there.

The church was packed, yet so hushed I could hear the spring breeze rustle the yellow forsythia outside the stained-glass windows. Silent prayers for my sister flew up all around me. My skin prickled with the sensation.

"Pamela Gaye Summerhayes," intoned the Reverend, "I have known you since the day of your birth. I know you to be a good

Christian, that you have studied hard, and completed the learning required of you to be baptized. I know that you wait upon the Lord. Are you now ready to accept Christ as your Savior, before God and this assembly?"

"I am," she replied, coughing. The raw, jagged sound that poured from her echoed through the rafters above our heads. Her hands flew instantly from the water to cover her mouth.

"Then in the name of the Father, and the Son, and the Holy Ghost, I baptize thee."

Pam held one hand to her nose as Reverend Squires dunked her beneath the water. The congregation exploded again in song. Pam bobbed up spluttering, shaking her wet head like a terrier, her Junior Choir robe melting thickly along her twiglike arms. Reverend Squires picked her up and handed her off to my mother, who stood out of sight with a towel, ready to dry Pam off. Mrs. King, our Sunday School teacher, wept openly, front and center in the choir where the whole church could see. All over the church, people were dabbing their eyes.

My father let go of my hand. He removed his glasses and pinched his nose between his eyes. His cheeks went pink.

A sharp pain rose in my throat, and I knew suddenly that leaving ballet school was not a right choice or a wrong one, simply the only one. Whatever my ultimate destiny, I knew that my calling right now was to be here with Pam, for as long as she had need. Time and circumstance, my own needs and inner longings, would come to test my faith in that belief. Moments of struggle lay ahead when I would question my fidelity to that calling, but for this moment the organ bellowed magnificently through the tall brass pipes behind the choir. The singing voices thundered heavenward, filling my ears and swelling my heart. I raised my thin soprano voice to join the others, the words of the old familiar hymn suddenly rich with new meaning.

"Oh Lamb of God...I come, I come."

CHAPTER NINE

"My mind tells me to give up, but my heart won't let me."
— JENNIFER TYLER

The great mountain range that is Manhattan floats upside down on the water's surface, shimmering and dissolving before my gaze. The Hudson River glistens in the sun, and glimmers beneath the moon. Great oil tankers and cruise ships maneuver the shipping lanes, dwarfing small pleasure boats and single-man kayaks. Mesmerized as I am by its breathtaking beauty, it is easy for a moment to forget what lies submerged, the cold and treacherous pull of the currents, the whirlpools, obscure shoals, and the rocky ledges below. Rogue logs, called deadheads, float perilously shrouded by waves and whitecaps.

Beneath the great city that I so love, beneath the tall condominiums lining the Jersey side of the river, beneath the forests and farms of the Upper Hudson, ground water seeps through the porous rock and fractured aquifers. With steadiness and stealth, it permeates the interconnected cracks and crevices, slowly saturating the seemingly impermeable clay and shale, creating underground rivers that flow unseen into the vast tidal estuary.

As I think back to my family in the year leading up to my twelfth birthday, I wonder that we must have mesmerized those who gazed at us from the outside into thinking that we were negotiating the currents of our life quite well. Perhaps we also mesmerized ourselves. There were sunny mornings and glimmering evenings, a house filled with music and laughter as we tapped our toes to Mitch Miller and The Beatles. There were warm hugs, hot milk and oatmeal cookies, buttery popcorn and the Wizard of Oz on our new TV. We had peach cobbler, goodnight kisses, and Sunday drives in the country. Pam learned to sew and my mother put up strawberry preserves. Yet, while my parents worked to create harmony and joy in our lives, we were still pulled by the hazardous undertow of a hidden dread for the future. Fear seeped like groundwater through the rock we thought of as our family.

Death was hiding in plain sight, so we tried to hide from Death, from the full and complete realization of it, from the unbearable anticipation of it. We took shelter in the warm and lovely parts of our life, the same way we burrowed safely beneath the covers with our parents during thunderstorms.

I know now that the harder you work to conceal a truth, the more that truth becomes self-evident. I know that when you concentrate on the rocks or whirlpools in a river that is precisely where you'll end up. Focusing on fear can lead you straight into the danger you are trying to avoid. Renouncing your fear can be even worse, as you negotiate the river blindly, denying your survival instincts, and finally wondering where that rock came from when you wreck your life upon it.

We hide our fear in our need for perfection. We bury it by keeping busy, working overtime at the office, cleaning out the garage, buying stuff we can't afford. We drown it by overeating, drinking too much, or turning to drugs. We stave it off by starving ourselves. We overreact and strike out in anger at those we love, trying to hide our fear.

Pam was in her twenties when she counseled me, "You can't control life by being afraid of it."

"Face your fears," she told me. "Then move beyond them." She first learned this the year she was ten. It has taken me much longer.

⁓

The child who is dying says, in that case, I'd better have some fun before I go. The child who sits next to the child who is dying asks, how dare I have fun when my sister is dying?

Fun didn't seem so hard for Pam, as far as I could tell. She was ten years old, in and out of the house with Molly McGregor and June Tranmer, up and down the street on their bikes, down in the basement giggling, in the backyard running around. Her friends waited for Pam to cough, for her to catch up and get her breath. Then on they all went, having fun.

I played alone with my Barbie doll, working on a project to build a house for her out of a big cardboard box I had dragged home from Woolco. I decorated it with scrap wallpaper and carpet, Formica samples and pieces of wood molding from the showroom at the Summerhayes Lumberyard. Once in a while I spent the night at my friend Jane Wilson's house, where I got to read contraband like *Millie the Model* comic books, and watch *The Saint* on TV after nine o'clock. After school and on Saturdays, I rode Tornado, with no hands, exulting in the wind on my face. I was twelve, and had secret crushes on Brent Cook and John Van Stalduinen. But I wasn't really having fun. I was just working at it. I sat on the Wishing Rock and sang when I thought no one, not even Pammy, was around to listen. *Someday I'll wish upon a star and wake up where the clouds are far behind me...*

I wondered if Pam sang these words too, when no one, not even me, was around to hear. *Somewhere over the rainbow, skies are blue...any dreams that you dare to dream really do come true...*

The difference between Pam and me was that she really believed somewhere over the rainbow existed, and I just wanted to.

On top of that, the world was "going to hell in a hand basket" as my mother was fond of saying. For months, ever since the Cuban Missile Crisis, we had been diving under our desks at school whenever the air raid siren went off, practicing drills in case the Russians dropped The Big One. Mrs. Hagey, my seventh grade teacher, said that in the event of a nuclear attack we were to squeeze our eyes shut so we weren't blinded by the flash. What was the point, I wondered, of saving our sight if we were all going to die anyway? I wanted to see the light if it were the last thing I'd witness on this earth.

I'd heard we'd have twenty minutes from when the siren went off until the bomb hit. I figured that might be just enough time to grab Pam out of her fourth grade classroom, and Gregg out of Grade One, and hightail it down the street home so we could die with Mom in the basement. Or make it to the bomb shelter that Dad kept talking about building. Of course, Pam couldn't run that fast, so I might have to carry her, which would slow me down a bit. Something to consider.

If we had a bomb shelter, of course, we'd have to live in it for years because of the radiation. I wondered, though I was afraid to ask my parents, if Pam was to die of CF while we were down there, what would we do with her body? Wrap her in a blanket, and then what?

Of course, whatever happened in the end was all up to President John F. Kennedy because the decisions he made would affect all of us in the Western Hemisphere. That's what my mother said. Lester B. Pearson may have been our prime minister, but JFK was our hero.

On November 22nd, 1963, I was down in the basement sick with a cold, wrapped in flannel and slathered up to my eyeballs in Vicks VapoRub watching a Western on TV, when Chet

Huntley and David Brinkley appeared abruptly on the black-and-white screen, in the middle of the movie, in the middle of the day.

"The president has been shot."

I stared at them in disbelief. I got out of my chair and flipped the channel. There was Walter Cronkite, fighting for composure. The president had been shot.

"Mom," I shouted from the bottom of the stairs, trying to take the steps two at a time on weak knees, my cheeks already wet with tears.

"MOM!"

The blood drained from my mother's face when I told her, and she quickly turned on the family room TV, moaning a long, low "Oh no..."

She kept us home the rest of the week, "to watch history unfold." We stayed glued to the television screen. We wept at the sight of Jackie in her blood-stained pink suit. We gasped as Jack Ruby shot Lee Harvey Oswald right in front of our eyes. We sat speechless as the cortège moved down Pennsylvania Avenue, followed by the riderless horse, and we bit back tears when John-John saluted.

Jackie's face was staggering and bereft. I saw, for the first time, what grief looked like. I read my own future in her face.

I didn't know what to be more afraid of then, the end of the world or my sister dying. They both seemed like the same thing to me. Some nights I lay in bed turning it all over in my mind, wishing they'd drop the bomb so we could all die together, rather than have to watch my sister slip away. We could melt like the Wicked Witch of the West in a tangerine-pink mushroom cloud. Gone straight to heaven before we knew it—Pam and I bravely holding hands, instead of me frantic by her bed as she suffocated slowly or coughed to death violently, while I was powerless to do anything, powerless to feel anything but pain as God took her from me.

God controlled people getting assassinated or dying. My mother controlled everything else. She washed, mopped, and spray-polished the chaos out of our lives. Pine-Sol, vinegar, and Lemon Pledge were not merely household cleansers, they were weapons in the battle against helplessness and unarticulated fear. From the expression on my mother's face, the way she held her tongue, and the ferocity with which she wielded scrub-brush and flannel cloth, I learned that scouring and hand-waxing the floors on bended knee were potent ways to deal with unspoken anxiety or unexpressed rage. Our floors shone, yet she lamented, "There's still dirt there I can't get at. It gets trapped in the linoleum and hides in the corners I can't reach." Like fear. Like grief.

She cleaned the house the day before Mrs. Kathom, the cleaning lady, was due, and rearranged the furniture every other week. She rearranged me too, controlled me, dumped my dresser drawers upside down, turned my whole insides out and made me put them back, all my feelings, my entire wild spectrum of emotions, organized into straight lines and folded into neat piles.

"I want you to put your things away so that your drawers look like Pam's drawers."

Not only did I have to aspire to please God and my mother, I also had to live up to my sister's ideal behavior. I was never as neat, never as smart, and never as composed.

If my mother asked me to do a chore and I complained, she said, "Pammy never behaves like that when I ask her to do something," to which I argued that she hardly ever asked Pam. When I became frustrated with a homework assignment, my tears were answered with "Pammy takes her time with things. You lose patience with yourself. You give up too easily." I didn't "apply myself," but Pam managed to "keep up and get good marks in spite of being sick and missing so many days of school." When Pam cried, they asked her what was wrong. When I cried they told me to stop, because I was "getting upset over nothing." It was a small house and Pam was usually within earshot, which made these comparisons more humiliating. In my worst moments I asked myself: if Pam is so good and I am so bad, then why didn't God give me CF instead? What sense does it make to kill the good person and let the bad one live?

My clearly superior sister had no sympathy for me as I tearfully rearranged my belongings. She perched smugly at the end of her bed as if she were the Deputy Drawer Police, watching me to make sure I followed my mother's orders.

"That's not how you're supposed to fold your undershirts."

"There's nothing wrong with the way I'm folding them."

"You're supposed to fold them in half down the middle and match the armholes, then fold them in half again the other way."

I did as I was told.

"You know," she said, "if you would learn to be neat in the first place instead of just stuffing everything in there, Mom wouldn't have to dump it all out."

"Why does Mom care how my drawers look as long as I find everything?"

"The way a person keeps their drawers is a reflection of the way they are inside," my mother called through the door.

I took that to mean I was a mess. Pam pursed her lips and shot me a snotty look to underscore my mother's remark.

I stuck out my tongue at her.

"Don't," she snapped, pushing me.

"Don't touch me," I spit, and grabbed her wrist.

"Leave me alone," she cried, jabbing at me with her free fist.

I slapped her face. I couldn't help myself.

For a fleeting second she registered shock, and her eyes filled with tears. I gasped.

She exploded in a white heat, socking me right back, putting the entire force of her iron will and her wiry body behind the blow. In an instant we were all over each other, scuffling and throwing blind punches. I rained blows on her shoulders as she twisted round and sank to the floor, her arms raised over her head. She rolled into a tight ball, shrieking, "Mom, Mom, Heather's hitting me again!"

"You're spoiled rotten," I shouted. "You get away with murder just because you're sick and people feel sorry for you."

"That's not true," she squeaked. Pam's face crumpled and turned scarlet. "I can't help it if I'm sick," she cried hoarsely, "or if people feel sorry for me. I didn't ask them to. It's not my fault."

"Then whose fault is it?"

She didn't have the breath to answer. Her lungs crackled as she gasped for air. Her body trembled and she began to cough.

My mother's feet pounded down the hallway and around the corner. She blew into the room like a gust of arctic wind.

"Break it up, you two."

My mother took my sister by the hand and led her out the door.

"Heather, you stay here in your room until I tell you to come out."

"Why doesn't she have to stay? It's not fair."

I flung myself on my bed and sobbed loudly into my pillow.

My mother's gentle, muffled voice echoed down the hall, followed by my sister's cough.

"Are you all right? Did she hurt you?"

I lay in a mangled heap of tear-dampened, half-folded clothes, imagining my mother with her arms around Pam, telling her to never mind me, patting her back, stroking her hair, loving her more than me. "I hate my sister," I thought. "I hate her stinky mask, and the time her treatments steal from me and Mom. I hate her stupid tent. I hate having to wake myself up at night to make sure she isn't dead. I hate that she gets away with everything. I hate her, I hate her, I hate her."

Later, my mother opened the bedroom door and poked her head in.

"Did Pam come back in here?"

"No, I thought she was out there with you."

My sister had a habit of hiding when she was upset.

"I'm sorry I upset everything," I sniffed. "Can I help you find her?"

"No thanks. I think you've done enough for one day."

"I'm sorry. I'm sorry."

"Sorry isn't good enough. You've got to learn to control that temper of yours or one of these days you'll do some real damage."

My mother shut the door. I held my hot head in my hands, feeling my blood pulse with shame. Last week I had told Pam I wished she had never come home from the hospital. It wasn't true, I didn't mean it, but I was so mad. She cried for days after. I was sorry then. I was sorry all the time. I was sick of being sorry, but sorry was all I had. I knew it wasn't good enough, that I wasn't good enough. How could I be good enough if I hated my sister? Except I didn't hate her, I just hated that, next to her, I didn't feel good enough. Self-pity welled up and spilled through my fingers, salty and wet, while my mother hunted through the house from room to room, opening and shutting doors, calling out Pam's name.

⌒

My sister was a virtual skeleton. She had a staph infection raging in her lungs. She was up at the Brantford General Hospital for the second time that spring, and it looked like she might not come home. Dad said they were giving her high doses of antibiotics, but the drugs had caused Pam to lose her appetite and with it, more precious ounces. The nurses shot her up every six hours. My mother told me there was hardly an inch of her arms or legs or her tiny little bottom that wasn't bruised from the needles. One morning, she said, Pam got up to go to the bathroom and collapsed. My sister had not been able to walk since, and had lost all sense of feeling in her limbs. She slept more and more. Awake, she snapped angrily at the nurses.

"You know that's not like her," said my mother.

Lately she had refused food altogether, but that was not the worst thing, my mother sobbed. "She keeps insisting that the room be kept dark. Oh, that frightens me. Every time I go in there to open the curtains, she yells at me to close them."

I had read the statistics in the green CF Foundation pamphlets, which bluntly stated that 75 percent of children with CF died before the age of six, while the other 25 percent faced almost certain death between the ages of six and twelve. Pam's original prognosis when she was diagnosed in May 1958 at age four was six years at the outside. It was now May 1964. Pam was ten years old. It had been six years.

She had just gotten out of the hospital after spending sixteen days there in April, when they turned around and put her back in. In the few intervening days, crocuses and hyacinths sprouted in my mother's flower beds, and buds burst green on the trees. Just as Pam came home again, one last blizzard struck, taking us all by surprise. Gregg and I bundled Jeffie up and had one last snowball fight in the backyard, while Pam watched from the bedroom window.

Now a winter melancholy clung to her shoulders. She had grown quiet, distant, and contemplative.

I told stupid jokes, trying to make her laugh.

"What's black and white and read all over?"

When that didn't work, I messed up her underwear drawer, hoping to get a rise out of her.

"Leave me alone," she murmured, closing the drawer, looking at me as if I were the village idiot, and walking away. Frequently, she hid from us. Roaming the house in idle moments, I would stumble upon her squirreled away in a corner or behind a piece of furniture, sucking her thumb and staring into space.

One Saturday morning she disappeared altogether. No one could find her, and when she didn't show up for lunch we really began to worry.

"Where on earth is that child?" fumed my mother. "Have you been fighting with her again? You know she's not up to that."

"No, Mom."

"Have you looked all around the house?"

"Yes."

"Then she must have gone to Molly's, or June Tranmer's. I'll drive over and see." Meanwhile, Gregg and I gathered our friends and combed the neighborhood on our bikes. My mother took to the streets in her little beige Hillman. I tossed my bike in the tall grass by the roadside and ran through the Big Woods, calling my sister's name. Meanwhile, my father came home from the lumberyard and made another sweep of the house.

"I still can't find her!" I cried an hour later, plowing through the side door on the verge of tears.

"It's all right," said my father. "She's here."

My parents sat together at the kitchen table with the tea things spread out in front of them. My mother's eyes were hope-worn, puffy, and red-rimmed behind her glasses.

"She's asleep in your room. Leave her alone for a bit."

I slid into a chair at the table. "Where was she?"

"Hiding under the Duncan chesterfield," my father replied.

"What was she doing there?"

My father looked as if he had been taken completely apart and basted back together.

"What's the matter?" I asked.

He hesitated, put down his cup of tea, and looked for help from my mother.

She looked back at him and shrugged. "I think she's old enough."

My father sighed deeply and poured himself another cup of strong tea, adding two heaping teaspoons of sugar and a dollop of milk. I was suddenly aware of his long fingers, callused and rough from his labors at the lumberyard, quivering as they spilled milk onto the tablecloth.

"Pam was hiding so we wouldn't see her crying."

"What was she crying about?"

My father let go yet another sigh and swallowed hard. He pulled a large white hankie from his back pocket and wiped his nose side to side with it, as he always did when he was uncertain.

"While the rest of you were out searching, I decided to take another look around here." He had heard some strange choking sounds coming from the living room, so he tiptoed in and tracked them to the big Duncan Fife sofa, calling my sister's name. The sound had stopped abruptly.

"I got down on my hands and knees and peered beneath the couch. And there she was."

"Then what happened?"

"I asked her what the matter was."

"What did she say?"

"Not a damn word."

Slowly, carefully, my father inched the heavy, overstuffed chesterfield away from the wall, got back down on his knees, and crawled in behind. Pammy sat up and stared at him with eyes so red and hollow they looked as if she had been staring into her own grave. These were not the eyes of a ten year old. Neither was the candor in her voice when she asked him, "Am I going to die, Daddy?"

My father's eyes glistened and turned pink as he told this. He fluffed his hankie and blew his nose.

"Is she?" I asked, my throat closing against my will.

"Is she what?"

"Going to die? I mean, for sure this time?"

My father flinched. His eyes shifted. He wanted to hide the truth from me, hide it from himself, but he couldn't.

"She might."

My heart felt suddenly like it had stopped pumping blood, and instead was pushing cold air through my body.

My father shrugged his shoulders, trying to collect himself. "I guess this last time in the hospital sort of scared her. I guess maybe she just finally realized..."

I fell off the cliff of my father's unfinished sentence. Reading something in a pamphlet, even hearing it said out loud, was not the same as knowing it in your own heart, or as Pam knew now, for the first time, in her soul.

"What did you tell her?"

"I told her that all of us have our time to die, and when it's our time, it's our time. I said it was God's decision. I told her she wouldn't necessarily die from having CF."

"What did she say?"

"She seemed to accept it."

My mother stared silently at the damp wad of Kleenex in her troubled hands.

I asked to be excused, and rushed from the table before anyone could answer. I threw on my ski jacket and ran into the street, my mother's voice echoing after me that it was still cold out and I should wear a hat. "You might get an ear infection..."

"I'll be okay," I yelled over my shoulder, running as fast as I could to the sanctuary of the Big Woods. I climbed to the top of my Lookout Tree.

"Please, God..." I cried, but my voice died in my throat.

The sun began to set. Salt from my tears stung my cheeks in the damp cold. Pink and violet bled across the shivering sky, becoming a deep, velvety blue.

In bed after lights out, Pam and I made believe that nothing had happened. She left her tent open for a while before we went to sleep. The bitter-smelling mist poured out, a silvery fog filling the dark room.

"'Night 'night. Don't let the bugs bite."

"Or the lions lick!"

"Or the turtles tickle!"

We giggled and then lay in weighty silence, each waiting for the other to speak of what had happened.

Finally, I called out to her, "I love you."

"I love you too."

"Let's say our prayers together."

We repeated our nightly prayer in unison.

"Now I lay me down to sleep, I pray Thee Lord my soul to keep. If I should die before I wake, I pray Thee Lord my soul to take. God Bless Mommy and Daddy..." Pam stopped to inhale deeply from moist, heavy lungs, and coughed sharply. Her voice penetrated the dark.

"It's getting worse."

A Prayer for My Sister, Pamela
Oh, Lord why is thine hand upon her?
And why this ill disease?
That not a man can conquer
Oh, tell me if you please!
She cries because she knows now
Her life is soon at end,
But she cannot understand
Why heaven's round the bend.
It is not what I wilt
But what thou has in store,
But must I live with heartbreak
For now and evermore?

Oh please Lord, do not take her
Unless thou take me first
Or else my heart shall fail me
And belief in thee shall burst!

Amen

Heather Anne Summerhayes
Age 11, April 1964

Within days she was back in the hospital. I could tell everyone thought this was IT. No one discussed it flat out, but the
house was starched with tension, worse than I'd ever known. My
parents tried to hide their fear, not realizing how they gave themselves away, alternately speaking to us too sharply or hugging us
too long and too hard. I asked over and over why Pam was in
again so soon. My father patiently explained that Pam never really got over the infection she had in April, and that the antibiotics
she was taking at home weren't doing their job. This left me to
wonder what would happen if the hospital antibiotics didn't do
their job either. Why didn't they send her to Dr. Matthews in
Cleveland, I wondered? The answer I came up with made terrifying sense. They didn't want her to die so far away from home.
    As usual, my parents made the effort to be up at the hospital
to do Pammy's treatments at least two and sometimes three times
a day. Mrs. Sloane, Pam's fourth grade teacher, took schoolwork
up to her, along with get well cards from the class.
    We were all like paper cut-outs at home. My father worked;
my mother cleaned the house, bought groceries, tended to the
boys. It was ritual, it was doing what had to be done, but my
parents' hearts and minds were somewhere else. They applied
their energies where they saw the greatest need, but my sense of
abandonment was keen. I behaved petulantly with my play-
mates, and then stormed off to weep in the high branches of the

Lookout Tree in the Big Woods. Returning home, I threw tantrums at my mother's feet when she asked me to set the table.

Fears took root. I refused to go to sleep without my doll Susie, and I kept my poetry, which I had bound into a small manuscript, right next to me, in case our house burned down in the middle of the night. I was certain the sharp chest pains I felt were small heart attacks. My mother rubbed me with Vicks VapoRub and said maybe I had a touch of pleurisy, but it was nothing to worry about. I suffered frequent, severe abdominal pains. When I complained of this to my mother, she told me that if I would just stop sitting on the cold ground in the woods, the pains would go away.

"I can take you to see Dr. Cleary if you want," she offered, but the look on her face told me she did not need another sick child.

I knew that my small discomforts did not compare to Pam's and soon realized it was better to spare my parents much whining about them. I should speak up only if it really, really hurt, or if there was blood. This was not because my parents were unwilling to suffer with me, but because Pam's suffering was life and death, which was clearly of greater value. As painful as it was to accept this, I did understand. Soon I learned not to voice my pain at all, if I could help it. In any case, I wanted to be stoic, like my sister. As time went on, I learned to relinquish the right to own my own physical pain, and suffered the death of my ability to voice it. At times I scorned such pain, treating it with a kind of contempt, challenging myself to hide it as much as possible.

Many nights throughout Pam's absence I awoke in the middle of the night, stood up on my bed, and stared out the window, watching the wind sway the dark trees while my mind followed a path down King George Road, around the bend past the cemetery, and up to the doors of the red-brick hospital, where my sister slept and where I was not allowed to go. After a while, I crawled back under the covers to contemplate her empty bed and think what I would miss most about her.

I would miss her laugh. I loved how we made each other laugh. We didn't laugh with anyone else the way we laughed with each other. Her laughter was contagious, a jumper cable wired straight to my heart. We laughed at everything, at nothing; our laughter swooped and turned like a roller coaster. We laughed until we were weak in the knees, until we had to hold on to each other, until we fell to the floor and ran out of breath and she coughed so hard we had to stop laughing, but still we couldn't.

I would miss her snooty airs, yes, even those, and the way her lips puckered and her eyes frosted over when she was disgusted. I would really miss our bedtime chats, and the way she listened when I read my poems. Our games, her mischievous spirit, her serenity, and her tough-mindedness.

Tears slid down my cheeks when I thought of how I would miss the way she forgave me after we fought, putting her tiny hand on my cheek and looking into my eyes as if offering salvation.

I was sorry for the times I'd said I hated her, told her to her face even, because I loved her, I loved her so much it made me wonder, if Pammy died, who would I be without her?

Memories grew more precious as I realized that memories might soon be all I was to have of her, of us together. Through the lonely nights I came to understand the importance of memory, and vowed that from then on, if God let her live, I would make it a point to memorize every single thing I could about Pam, and our life together. Before sleep returned to claim me, I stood up on my bed once more, gazed through the window, and searched the sky to see if God was up there. It was hard to have faith in Him, yet I was learning sometimes faith was all there was. So every night I offered the same prayer.

"Please God, let my Pammy live. Let me have more of her to remember, and let me remember it all."

Gregg, now a sturdy seven year old with a charming, crooked smile, was missing her too. Even more, he missed our father's mindfulness and our mother's cheer. Though he was otherwise quiet, obedient, and unobtrusive, earning him the moniker of "a good boy," he teased Jeff mercilessly, and was punished for acting out at school, where he struggled to keep up his grades.

While Pam languished in the hospital, my twelfth birthday came and went. I celebrated with forced excitement, feeling as if I'd betrayed her. I breathed in guilt, and breathed out longing.

I longed for Pam to come home, and to be well. I longed for a life free from fear and sorrow. I longed to understand the meaning in all of it, why God made us suffer.

Pam had been gone a month, and already there were moments when I could not remember her face.

GONE VISITING
We used to sit six places
At the table, but now
Their is only five,
You see, Pam got an invitation,
To a home that's up above.
She's just gone visiting
We'll see her soon
And give her all our love again
When we get an invitation from above.

Like humidity on a hot summer's day, the longer Pam remained hospitalized, the more fear and tension built up in our house. I longed for the storm to break, although I sensed that when it did, there'd be no place to hide.

One night my father came through the side door like thunder, full of deep sighs and ominous rumblings. He never simply entered a room at the best of times, hurling himself through doorways and down corridors. On this night it was as if his limbs shot lightning as he took off his coat and hung it in the closet. He had just come from the hospital.

"How's Pam tonight?" asked my mother.

"I don't know," he replied tersely.

"What do you mean you don't know? Didn't you stop in and see her on your way home from work?"

"Yes, I saw her."

"Well? And?"

My father tried to explain, and as his story poured out, I pictured the whole thing. On his way home from work he had whisked into Pam's room, behind schedule as usual. He looked at his watch and apologized to her, all half-finished sentences and scattered nervous energy. He swept over and tried to kiss her hello, but my sister jerked her head away from him and waved him off, wordlessly, and rather viciously, with a bony arm.

The thought of it made me smile.

Nonplussed, my father pulled up a chair and sat down. "How has your day been?" he asked.

Silence.

He asked a few more questions.

More silence.

Pam sat on the bed so still, so small and white, that she almost disappeared into the tumble of sheets, her face carved in stone. She stared into the corner farthest away from my father, not so much as batting an eyelash.

"To heck with it then," my father said finally, his voice thick with hurt. "If that's the way you're going to be, I'm going home."

He walked to the door and lingered a moment, waiting for a response. Pam could have been catatonic for all she did or said. He left then, and brought home thunder.

His story told, he removed his big linen hankie from his

pocket, wiped nervously at his nose, and waited for my mother's reaction.

"Well," she said, fiercely mashing potatoes, "you must have said something to upset her."

I stood riveted, by the table, clenching the silverware. They were going to fight again. They had started fighting with each other more since Pam went in. My father protested, as usual, that he had done nothing wrong.

"Listen," he said, "Pam just takes after your mother that way. They can both really give you the silent treatment when they want to."

"You leave my mother out of this. My mother isn't the problem here."

"Oh. I guess that means I'm the problem."

All the while my mother ground the masher furiously into the potatoes while the peas boiled over on the back burner and tears ran off the end of her nose. She had also been up to the hospital at lunchtime, and Pam had refused to speak to her as well.

"Maybe she'll speak to me," I piped up, my mouth dry and afraid.

"You stay out of this. Go get into your pajamas and leave us alone."

"But I haven't finished setting the table..."

"Just go and do as I say," Mom barked, waving the masher at me. The phone rang. "I'll get that."

I went to my room, closed my door loudly, and then opened it a crack, standing with one ear glued to the conversation that was taking place across the hall.

"She what? When did this happen?...I'll be right up."

"What is it?" asked my father.

My sister had crawled to the bathroom and locked herself in. She refused to come out. All the nurses, including Miss Greenfield, Pam's favorite, had been trying to talk her out, to no avail. They had sent for a master key but thought it best if Mom came up and tried talking to Pam again in lieu of dragging her out by force.

My mother took her coat from the closet and raced out the side door. The engine of her little Hillman revved up, the tires squealed, and the gravel crunched beneath them as she drove off.

"Jeez Murphy!" my father swore loudly, his voice cracking. I changed into my pajamas and crept out to finish setting the table. My father hunkered down in the den, hiding behind his newspaper.

I fed my brothers and got them both into their pajamas. My father tucked the boys in while I tidied the kitchen, wiping the counter three or four times like my mother always did when she was waiting for bad news.

The phone rang.

"Hello," answered my father. "Jeez Murphy...all right." He hung up sharply and went to the closet.

"What are you doing?" I asked in a small voice as he fastened his coat.

"I'm getting ready to go back up to the hospital. Your mother's not getting anywhere with Pam, so she wants me to try again."

"Take me with you," I begged, "please. Pam will talk to me, I know she will."

"I'm afraid I can't do that, honey. They won't allow you up there."

"But I'm her sister. You already said she wouldn't talk to you. Maybe I'm the only one who can help!"

"Heather, I said no and I meant it. Stop trying to make things worse."

"But why?" I cried, close to tears and stamping my foot.

"There's your mother's car. I've got to go." He kissed me swiftly on the cheek and stepped out into the darkness. I stood shivering and lost in the open doorway, waiting for my mother to come inside.

We sat together on the couch, wringing our hands, waiting for the phone to ring. My father had promised to call if everything was all right.

"Tell me what happened," I demanded.

"Well, after they called and I raced up there, my God, I just flew out of that elevator and down the hall to her room. And when I looked and saw that empty bed..." My mother choked back tears. "Miss Greenfield was standing at the bathroom door waving me over, so I went and knocked on the door and whispered, 'Pammy, are you in there?' I could just feel my heart pounding and I was trying to catch my breath. She didn't answer me, so I knocked again and called 'Pammy, please, open up...it's Mommy, honey...' and she didn't make a sound, she didn't even cough."

I saw it all as if I had been there myself, feeling my mother's terror as my own. Pam's silence was as powerful as the grave, the locked door a closed casket on which my mother pounded in vain.

"So then I said to her, 'I'm going to call your daddy,' so I called him, and then I went back to the door and pleaded with her, and I said 'Pammy, please don't do this to me, you're scaring me half to death. Please, just say something. Tell me you're all right.'"

The door stared back, mute. My mother pulled at it, shook it.

"Oh God, oh God!" she moaned. "What if she can't answer? What if there's something wrong with her? What if she's..."

My mother rocked herself back and forth, got up and stood at the window, walked over and stared at the phone, came back to the couch and rocked herself again. I slid over and put my arms around her. We waited for my father to call.

"I wish Daddy had let me go with him."

"Oh sweetheart, there's nothing you could have done."

I did not cry or speak another word, frightened of upsetting my mother more than she already was.

My mother went to the window again, and the phone.

"Honestly, if she's just pulling some stunt to punish your father and me..."

The phone rang. My mother grabbed it as if it were a life preserver being tossed to her from a passing ship. She listened intently, weeping, collapsing into a kitchen chair, saying "Uh-huh, uh-huh...," and blowing her nose. I crept to the edge of light that separated the kitchen from the den, and waited in the shadows.

"Okay," she said into the phone, "we'll put the teakettle on and see you in a while." She hung up. "Your father's coming home."

He soon arrived, bristling as he searched through the closet for an empty hanger, jerking our coats and jackets sharply back and forth. "I sat on the floor talking to her through that damn door for over an hour," he growled. "All she would say was that she wants it to be over. That's all she said...she just wants it to be over."

"She just wants what to be over?"

My father threw his coat on a wire hanger he had bent yanking it from the closet, and glanced around the room, as if the words he needed were hiding from him in the bookcase or behind the toss pillows on the couch.

"Listen," he said, "I think she's just got fed up with everything. She's been cooped up there for weeks and she's not getting any better, and everyone's prodding and poking at her and telling her what to eat and when to sleep...she can't see any of her friends or Heather or the boys...she doesn't have any control, and it's making her angry."

Frantic, my mother's eyes flickered about my father's face as he stood there, frustrated as all get out.

"For heaven's sake, Doug, stop beating around the bush and just spit it out!"

My father looked at my mother like he was trying to figure out what she meant, when I knew he knew exactly what she meant. He hung up his coat and sighed from the bottom of his shoes.

"I'm just trying to protect you, Donna."

"I don't need protection!" my mother shouted. "Just tell me what she said."

He whispered something that made my mother look as if she had been split down the middle with an axe. Her voice came out soft and full of tears.

"What did you say to her after that?"

"I said it was up to her. I told her we would all help her live but we won't stand by and watch her give up and die without a fight. I said she could think that over and call us when she makes up her mind."

"And then you left her there? Oh Doug, oh Doug...how could you?!"

"What else was I supposed to say? What did you want me to do—break down the door and drag her out of there kicking and screaming? Miss Greenfield is right. Pam has to make this choice for herself, Donna. It's the one thing we can't do for her."

My father swallowed his tears.

I stole quietly to the kitchen and put the teakettle on, got the milk out of the fridge, gathered cups and saucers from the cupboard. I made the tea and brought it to the table. We sat down, speechless and spent. When the phone rang, we all jumped.

"Hello," said my father.

"Daddy?" It was Pam. She was crying. I could hear her through the receiver. "I'm sorry, Daddy."

"It's all right, honey, it's all right."

"Miss Greenfield had a talk with me after you left," Pam

sobbed, "and I'm calling to apologize for the way I acted. Will you and Mommy come and visit me tomorrow?"

"Of course we will."

"Let me speak to her," said my mother, taking the phone. "Pammy?"

There was no need for me to hide now, for I had become invisible. I slipped off through the dark hallway and climbed up onto my sister's bed, giving myself over to a night of tears and bad dreams.

Pam had survived the measles and chickenpox. She had survived several bouts of staph and pneumonia. Each time, we had counted it as a miracle. How many miracles, I asked myself, was one family allowed?

In the days that followed, I called to God from the Wishing Rock, but heard no answer. I looked for Him vainly in the woods. First Baptist was bereft of Him. The choir sounded hollow, and the church was full of coughing, whispering, and dead air. Even Reverend Squires seemed a caricature of himself.

My parents didn't know how to help me any more than they knew how to help themselves. They seemed old to me, but in fact they were quite young. My mother was barely thirty. They were still learning how to cope with their own feelings and with facts about the disease that remained vague and uncertain. They were good at sharing those basic facts with me, but there was still much that frightened me about Pam's condition and prognosis, especially when my imagination got going. It was always worse when Pam was in the hospital, and my callow instincts were alarmed by my parents' deep sighs, their anxious eyes, and tight-lipped smiles.

Children react to the worst thing they can imagine. The worst thing I could imagine in my twelve-year-old mind was Pam's death, in a violent, painful, bloody coughing spell, with me not there to help save her life, or at least to hold her hand.

There was no place to put my imaginings. I carried them around in the dark inside of me, where they waited for a time and a place to leap out and unleash their holy terror. With pubescent hormones beginning to rage, I was already in a perpetual bad mood. Added to this was the constant pressure of my parents' compelling need for me to get things "right," to control my thoughts and actions and refrain from causing further upset. Caught each day between crisis, fear, and obligation, I was set up to react to anything as if it was the worst thing, to overreact, and I often did.

One day, I went over the edge.

"Where do you think you're going, young lady?" My mother's tone of voice was sharp. I ignored her.

"Heather Anne!" She used my middle name only when she was angry.

"Jane Wilson invited me over to watch cartoons."

"You're not going anywhere until you get that room of yours cleaned up. It's a pigsty. I can't walk in there anymore."

"Then don't."

"Now you listen here, we're not having another fight over this. You've got to learn to settle down and do as you're told."

All the time, it seemed, I was being told. To be quiet, to shut up and to listen to what I was being told, instructions on how to be quiet, how do a task and do it right the first time. "I do listen!" I wanted to protest, to the birds and the wind, to the song of the poplar trees, and to my own heart beating in the dark of night.

"Did you hear me? Get downstairs and clean your room!"

"I don't feel like it."

"Well, that's too bad because you're doing it anyway!" She grabbed my arm and hauled me down the basement stairs. "You begged us for your own room and now I expect you to keep it clean!"

Dad had answered my anxious pleas, and built a room for me

in our half-finished basement. My mother had bought me new furniture, and hung the old curtains from the den. It was not the cozy refuge I had anticipated, however. In daylight hours, as I had discovered, my room failed to offer the privacy it warranted. My mother entered uninvited, scouting my room from time to time like an army sergeant seeking contraband. At night it felt like a bomb shelter, lonely, dark, and damp. Hidden away from the rest of the family, helplessly submerged in nightmares, I woke and no one heard me cry out. I stared wide-eyed into the shadows, heart pounding, physical pangs of guilt like knives in my chest, knowing that when, or if, Pam returned from the hospital, I would no longer be able to keep watch over her and listen to her breathe.

On the other side of my wall lurked the compressor that ran both Pam and Jeff's mist tents. It shattered sleep, vibrating my bed, reverberating through the cavernous black furnace room, echoing off the cement walls and floor, droning like an airplane ready for takeoff. Woken again and again through the night, I lay alone in the dark, wondering if my independence was worth it.

"Just look at this mess!" my mother barked, shoving me through the door and into the room. "This room has to sparkle before you go anywhere."

"Cartoons will be over before I'm done. Jane is expecting me. Why can't I clean up when I get back?"

"Because by the time you get back it will be time to help me unload the groceries and do Jeff's treatment. Now do as I say and get busy."

My stomach churned with sudden rage. A piercing, violent disembodied shriek found its way out of my mouth. I threw myself onto the bed as if possessed, pounding and screaming. My mother strode toward me on her basketball legs and yanked me to my feet. I shoved her to the floor and hurled myself around the room, screeching, crying, bouncing off the beige pressed-wood paneled walls. With one mad swipe I sent everything crashing off my dresser. My mother lunged forward and grabbed me by the shoulders.

"Let go of me!" I shouted, "I hate you!"

I kicked and punched blindly while my mother lurched backward. I clenched my fists and ran at her. She jumped out of my way. I careened toward the wall. My right fist smashed hard against the pressed-wood paneling. I sank to the floor, my body shuddering with deep sobs.

"Oh my God," gasped my mother, "are you all right?" She stretched her arms out toward me.

"LEAVE ME ALONE!" I screamed. "I HATE YOU! I hate you. I hate you..."

The blood drained from my mother's face. She turned slowly and left the room.

"I hate you, I hate you," I incanted, until I was out of breath. Weeping, I sat up and surveyed the damage. I had thrown tantrums before, but never this bad. I was scared and shaken, yet for a moment, the sense of my own power had been exhilarating.

I picked up the lamp, straightened the shade, and placed it back on the dresser. The curtains drooped where I had yanked them and bent the curtain rod. My arms trembled as I pushed them aside.

I crept upstairs, slipped quietly to the closet where my mother kept the cleaning supplies, pulled a dust rag from the paper bag full of old cloths, and tucked a can of spray polish under my arm. Gregg appeared in the hallway door, staring at me as if I was a complete stranger. I turned and ran back to my desecrated sanctuary, away from the anguish and awe in my little brother's eyes, away from the sound of my mother sobbing in the kitchen.

Downstairs, I dumped out my drawers and reorganized them so they looked like Pam's drawers, underwear and T-shirts neatly folded. I made my bed with crisp hospital corners the way my mother had taught me for my Girl Guide Housekeeping Badge.

I hunted down an old cardboard shoebox from the other side of the basement, and filled it with my hair curlers.

As I tried to write "Curlers" on the side with a magic marker, my right hand would not work. I shook it. It flopped awkwardly, sending shards of pain up my arm. Once more I tried to write, putting the magic marker between my thumb and index finger. Painstakingly, I scrawled the label. Using only my left hand, it took me two hours to dust, vacuum, and put my room in order.

"I'm finished," I informed my mother tersely.

"I'm just giving Jeff his physio. You wait for me downstairs until I'm done."

Though he was not sick the way Pam was, the doctors still wanted Jeff to have the standard three treatments a day. It was all my mother did anymore—give Pam and Jeff their treatments, strip their beds, wash their sheets, and set up their tents. I took these ministrations so for granted, I never considered how burdened she might have felt.

I slunk back to my room. My hand was a throbbing, swollen purple mass. I sighed deeply and stared out the window at the careless poplar trees. Jeff coughed upstairs. The treatment was over.

My mother's footsteps were sharp and sure as she descended to the basement, to my room, my neat hell. I stood almost at attention, determined not to cry. Her gaze fell on the dresser, the bed, the night table. She lifted the bedskirt and checked underneath for dustballs. She looked me in the eye and said she didn't want to see anything like this happen again. She was controlled, remote.

"I'm sorry," I mumbled, close to tears.

"I know," she replied curtly, "I'm sorry too." She walked to the door, then stopped and turned back toward me. "Heather, I don't know what to do to make you happy." The ache in her voice broke the dam in my heart. My eyes flooded, and spilled as she left the room.

Denying the pain in my hand, or stealing aspirin to ease it, I managed to hide the injury from my mother for almost three days. When she discovered it, she ran me up to B.G.H. I had x-rays in Emergency while my sister lay in her bed up on the ninth floor.

"How did this happen?" asked the doctor.

"I fell out of a tree."

The doctor looked at my mother doubtfully. My mother stared at the floor.

They put me in a cast up to my elbow.

"Pammy will want to know how I broke my hand," I mumbled in the car on the way home.

"Why don't you just tell her what you told the doctor?"

I turned my face to the window, and wept with shame.

Within the next few days, we got our miracle. Dr. Matthews discovered a new antibiotic in England and arranged to have it sent to Dr. Cleary. Pam's subsequent retreat from death's door was swift.

Though I was not allowed to visit her, I knew this was true when I saw her picture in the newspaper. It was a relief to see her, smiling wanly, skinny arms and legs hanging out from her baby dolls and her hair flat from weeks in bed. The photo had been taken at the Brantford CF chapter's general meeting up at the hospital. "Brantford's Lisa" the caption read. Pam had been chosen as the poster child for the CF Foundation.

More publicity. They were going to put Pam in ads and on posters like Timmy for Crippled Children's and the March of Dimes. I didn't know what to make of this. One minute my sister was at death's door and the next she was the centerpiece of a major ad campaign, sporting a fake name while plans were being made to buy her a new dress and have her hair permed. Confusion gave way to jealousy, all mixed up with plain old heartache and longing to see her.

"All right," my father relented, "hop in the car and I'll take you up with me."

"See that window up there?" he said as we parked the car across the street from the hospital. "That's where Pammy is."

I scrambled out and hopped up and down with excitement, ready to race across the road and through the hospital doors.

"Now just hold your horses there," said my father. "You can't go inside and see her, the hospital won't let you. I just brought you here so you can wave up at her. She's expecting you, so she's waiting up there in the window. Go on, wave."

I could not believe that my father would make such a fool of me, or that I could have been so stupid. I squeezed my mouth hard to fight back tears and waved dutifully up at the dark window, not willing to admit that I couldn't see anyone waving back.

"See her?" smiled my father, waving and pointing. "There she is."

"I see her." I lied to please him.

"You wait here in the car now, and I'll just run up for a minute and say hi. I won't be long."

We acted out this charade a couple of times. No matter how many tears I shed, my father could not be convinced to take me any farther than the parking lot. Hospital rules, he incanted sternly.

He may have been able to say no to me, but he couldn't say no to Pam. She demanded to see me too, so my father, caught between the two of us, devised a plan.

On the appointed day, when we arrived at the hospital, my father took me for a snack in the coffee shop. After a few minutes, I excused myself and went down the hall to the ladies room, which was right next to the stairwell. Dad casually paid the bill and rode the elevator to Pam's ward on the ninth floor while I counted slowly, "one Mississippi, two Mississippi," all the way to a hundred. When I was done, I poked my head out of the ladies' room door to make sure no one was watching, then raced nine flights up the stairwell and flattened myself into a corner of the landing, where I waited panting and breathless for my father to come and get me. The door swept open and my heart jumped.

"Quick, quick," he whispered, "run straight across the hall!"

I dashed blindly into my sister's room. The cloying disinfectant smell burned my nostrils and choked me. Pam was perched high on her hospital bed, giggling, her hands bunched excitedly over her mouth.

I reached up and threw my arms around her neck, dizzy with joy, breathing hard against the tears that wanted to come.

"Don't cry," she said, "I'm all right."

"I know," I replied. "Anyway, I'm no crybaby." I wiped my nose with the back of my hand and stared up at her.

"If anyone comes," she said, "you can hide in that cupboard," indicating a pair of doors below the sink behind me.

"How have you been?"

Pam laughed and rolled her eyes. "I had kind of a rough time there for a while, but I'm okay now. Dr. Cleary said I should be home in a few days."

"I saw your picture in the paper."

"Oh," she groaned, "I'm so embarrassed about that. Don't I look awful? Nobody warned me. Mom tried to comb my hair but it kept sticking up." She giggled again.

I told her I was writing another play to raise money for CF."

"It's about Henry the Eighth and all his wives, but I'm waiting to do it until you get home."

We discussed the fact that Dad had built me a room in the basement, and how weird it would be not to sleep together anymore.

"I think it will be good for you not to have the tent bother you," Pam said. "What happened to your arm?"

I glanced sheepishly at Dad and told Pam I fell out of a tree, the lie sour on my tongue. She offered to sign my cast.

Pam showed me a giant scrapbook. She had been keeping busy gluing in get well cards from Summerhayes Lumber, First Baptist Church, the John Noble Home where Grandma Birdsell worked, from school, and even from people she didn't know who'd read about her in the paper. News of Pam's plight had also been broadcast on the radio since the "Lisa" picture appeared in the *Expositor*, and the radio station sent her a Kookie Doll.

I perused the five-inch-thick scrapbook and admired the beautiful doll, taking it all as evidence of how much more my sister was loved than me.

"Quick," my father blurted, "into the cupboard."

I shut the cupboard door on myself and held my breath.

"I see you've got visitors," the nurse said.

"Just one," Pam lied, "just my dad."

"Yes, I can see that. Let's take your temp."

I waited in the dark cupboard, tensing my muscles to keep still.

"Mmm-hmm, okay, that's normal. Have a good visit with your dad. Your sister can come out now, but then she has to go."

Dad opened the cupboard and the three of us convulsed in laughter.

"It's a good thing you're the actress in the family," Pam giggled, "'cause I'm terrible at it."

My father lifted me up on the bed. Pam was so fragile I was suddenly afraid to touch her. I reproached myself for the envy I had felt. The skin around her eyes was puffy and dark. Red and purple track marks ran in bright, neat lines up and down her arms and thighs. She covered her legs self-consciously.

"Looks like we'll have to stuff you with butter tarts when you get home."

"Ya," she smiled. "Hospital food is yucky."

"Okay girls," my father said. "Time to go."

"See you in about two weeks," I chirped, squeezing Pam's hand.

"Before that if I can help it," she replied. She reached out her arms and pulled me close, kissing me on the cheek. I held her, trying once more not to cry.

"Dad," I asked as we walked down the hall to the elevator, "has Pammy's room always been on that side of the building?"

"Yes. Why do you ask?"

"Because her room doesn't face the parking lot. Just who have I been waving at?"

By the time Pam came home she had been gone forty-eight days. I was hyped up, live as a snapped wire. It was the end of June and school had just let out for the summer. I had passed into Grade Eight, although I had to write my finals in the cast, and lost marks for poor penmanship.

Pam passed as well. Although she missed fifty-three and a half days of school, her marks were excellent. Mrs. Sloane, Pam's teacher, gave me her report card to bring home. It was full of comments like *"Pam is a lovely child"* and *"How I will miss that sunny smile next year! Pam is a credit and pride to any classroom."* My report card bore no such remarks. None of this would be lost on my father.

Jane Wilson waited with me for Pam on our front porch. I stared impatiently up the street while Jane played with her dog Tammy and talked on and on about how great it would be to be in Grade Eight next year and maybe get to wear nylons.

I didn't care just then about nylons, I only cared that Pammy was coming home. We would make tea and celebrate.

My mother's little beige Hillman came into view. Instantly my heart began to pound and my breath came short and sharp. I stood up as the car turned into the driveway. Pam smiled, waving at me from the front seat. The backseat was loaded with "get well" presents. The report cards went soft in my sweaty palm. My mother got out of the car, but I did not move to greet her. Instead I stared at my sister, who was not only sweet, brave, and smart, but alive, a wonder to all, no less than a miracle.

Jane's dog jumped up and barked as my mother made her way around to the passenger side of the car. Pam clambered at the window while I stood paralyzed. My mother put her hand on the car door, turned the handle, and stared at me with hard eyes.

"Well," she said, "did you pass?"

I thought she meant she'd expected me to fail.

Suddenly the whole year caught up with me. Unkempt dresser drawers dumped on the floor, Jackie Kennedy in her bloody pink suit and black veil, hiding places and Lookout trees, dark nights and lonely hours, air raid drills and locked bathrooms, nightmares and empty beds, publicity campaigns and living miracles. My sister's report card. *"That sunny smile."*

Tears flowed so sudden and swiftly I could hardly see. The report cards soared like yellow birds into the sky where I had flung them. I watched as if I was standing outside myself. Everyone was staring at me, moving in slow motion, as if we were all under water. An anguished, wailing sound brought me back into my body, and I was shocked to hear my own voice, so loud that the neighbors peeked from behind their curtains to see what the commotion was.

My mother sent Jane home and banished me downstairs to my room, "to reflect on my behavior." The sound of teacups clinking on saucers upstairs, the padding of footsteps back and forth across the floor, the soft click of the refrigerator door opening and closing, all hurt me. My sister's cough echoed eerie and ragged down through the heating duct from the kitchen, her voice sobbing.

"It's all my fault for being so sick."

"Nonsense," my mother said. "Heather's just mad because

you got all those presents. She knows better than to behave like that."

I didn't understand why behavior was more important than feelings. *We need to set a good example for the other CF parents,* my dad had said. What did that have to do with me, and the way I felt? Why should I have to worry about setting an example for people who didn't know or care about me?

I knew I was letting my parents down. I didn't like my feelings or behavior any more than they did, but it all felt beyond my control.

Later, my mother called down the stairs, telling me to come up and set the table for dinner.

"You've had enough lying around down there and feeling sorry for yourself."

I dragged myself upstairs, shrinking in disgrace as I folded paper napkins and counted out the stainless silver, while my mother muttered in the background, pushing pots around the stove.

"I wish I had the luxury to mope in my room. I can either fall apart or keep going, you know. I don't have time to sit around and chew over every little thing. I'm too busy just putting one foot in front of the other."

My mother had no time for nonsense, no time for playing games, no time for histrionics or for anything except cooking and cleaning, doing another load of laundry, going out to buy groceries, stripping Pam's bed, sterilizing the tent, making Pam's mask, doing Pam's treatment, doing Jeff's treatment. She was busy brushing our hair, ironing our clothes, baking us cookies, breaking up our fights, reading us stories, picking up our toys, putting us in our places, or putting us to bed. She had foundation business to be accomplished, phone calls to make, checks to be written, and bills to be paid. There were drugs to be stocked, clinic appointments to be kept, prayers to be uttered. A marriage to hold together.

The day in and day out of chronic illness is like removing stones from a field, so many stones over so many days, that one day you look down and the field, once small and green, has become a vast gray quarry. The stones have gotten larger, and heavier, and still they must be picked up and hauled away.

How sick of hauling stones my mother must have been. How she must have ached to go out and take a carefree walk in the sun, or sit in the backyard with a glass of lemonade and watch us play, laughing without having to worry about the sound of Pam's cough. She must have longed to just pick up and go to a movie with Dad, or make time for more potluck dinners with friends without having to fret about fitting in Pam's treatment, or being too tired to go out after doing it. There must have been countless nights when my parents fell into bed exhausted, each of them thinking *I can't do this anymore,* not wanting to do it anymore. Or mornings after, when they opened their eyes and looked around to realize that they had no choice, that they were essentially alone in this, and there was no one to take over and do it for them, or even with them. How afraid they must have been of failing the foundation, the CF families, their own families, Pam and Gregg and Jeff, me. *Mortally afraid,* my father would admit to me, once I was grown.

I was too young to know.

The summer stumbled past.

Lounging in the backyard, looking for four-leaf clovers in the grass, Pam told me about a girl who had been in the hospital in the room next to hers.

"She had the blinds drawn and the door closed and the sheets right up to her neck, sealed in darkness. Is it any wonder she died. I won't die like that. I want the shades up and light coming in."

I was too astonished to know what to say, but Pam's talk of dying made me more determined to produce my Henry the

Eighth play and Variety Night so I could raise a hundred dollars for CF. My mother baked squares for sale at intermission, and allowed me to wear her bridesmaid's dress from Aunt Barb's wedding. By the time I'd finished rehearsing my friends, selling the tickets, doing the costuming and arranging the lawn chairs in Marci Jacklin's backyard, my chosen venue, I'd had run-ins with nearly everyone except my mother, who said I was trying too hard.

Gregg played Henry the Eighth pretty well for a seven year old, except he sat up too often during his death scene (surrounded by all his wives), and I had to keep pushing him back down. Wendy Smith and I were a big hit with our choreographed version of "Who Put the Bop in the Bop-She-Bop-She-Bop," though it had little to do with Henry the Eighth.

Later in the month, Pam and I both helped out at the annual wine and cheese CF fundraiser, passing out plates of cheese on Grandma Bill's big side lawn. In July, the National Board met in our living room to pick out a Christmas card design.

Our attention turned to Gregg that summer, as he repeatedly got himself into trouble, giving Pam and me memories we would laugh about right up to the end of her life. First, he got lost playing hide and seek in McClures' cornfield. When Dad found him hours later, Gregg got a legendary spanking. Next, he tore his ear half off riding his bike up onto the front lawn at twilight, when he flipped headlong over a skipping rope that Pam and I left tied between two trees so we could practice high-jumping. It wasn't funny, but we couldn't help laughing 'til we fell on the floor, when he came home swathed in gauze like a swami wearing a turban.

Meanwhile, my father had taken over Summerhayes Lumber. For a few months he was over the moon, but one night after dinner he made a startling announcement. Summerhayes Lumber was going out of business.

Pam and I looked at each other nonplussed, then back to

Dad, who sat at the head of the table like a marionette with every string pulled taut. He jerked his hankie from his back pocket, blew his nose, and stuffed it back into his pants.

My mother rattled around on the other side of the kitchen, filling the sink with soapy water and scraping the dinner dishes into a brown paper grocery bag at her feet. She looked tense, but infallible. My mother was involved with living, in the deepest practical sense. She kept herself busy, especially in times of crisis.

"Donna," said my father, "come here and sit down while we talk about this."

"I don't know what I have to add to this conversation." She hefted the tray crowded with tea things and carefully made her way across the freshly waxed floor in her stocking feet.

I sat slack-jawed at the news. Pam stared at the pile of pills in front of her and took them slowly, one by one, instead of by the usual handful. Even Gregg fixed my father with an incredulous, penetrating stare.

Mom pulled Jeffie onto her lap. "You're getting too big for me," she huffed, and reached across him to pour tea.

"What do you mean it's going out of business?" I asked. "You just won the Building Dealer of the Year award. Why are you getting rid of the lumberyard? I thought it was doing really well."

"So did we," my mother snorted. An odd look passed between my parents. My father looked down into his tea, and then jerked the cup to his mouth and sipped loudly.

"Well," he said, "I've got a meeting to run off to and I'm going to be late if I don't hurry." He planted a kiss on my mother's cheek. She pretended not to notice. "Pam, I'll try to get home early enough to do your treatment before you go to bed." He whipped out the door, leaving us in shambles. I guessed that was the end of the talk.

As it turned out, it was the business that was in shambles and had been well before it was turned over to my father. He did not know this until the bank did an audit, and found, in my father words, "irregularities." Once again, fingers were pointed back and forth between him and his brothers. Accusations were made.

"I guess I'm the fall guy," he sighed to my mother.

I learned this by eavesdropping at my parents' bedroom door.

There were members of the family, and some in the business community, who thought less of my father because he declared bankruptcy, because he didn't hang on to the company and try to rebuild it. No one gave him credit for how hard he fought to save it. I wanted to tell them they didn't know what it was like to be the father of two sick kids, what it takes out of a man. I wanted to tell them how hard he tried, how much he gave, to us, to the CF Foundation, to everything he did, how much he bled for that stupid lumberyard. There were limits to how thin my father could spread himself. I wanted to walk up and down Colbourne Street with his Dealer of the Year plaque and a megaphone.

He wept behind closed doors, swore in front of us, and kept long hours starting Summerhayes Industries, a new business building crates and pallets for shipping. My mother ironed my father's hankies, pressed his shirts, steamed out his suits, and told him to go to Ludlow's for a new tie and a pair of shoes so he would feel good about himself.

We did not have time to catch our breath before Jeff was admitted for a week of retesting at Sick Children's Hospital in Toronto. He was almost four, and his health was much better than expected, so good in fact that Dr. Crozier, who had started a CF clinic there, wondered if my brother's initial diagnosis had been correct. My mother came home anguished, telling us how Jeffie had leaned out of the hospital crib, his arms outstretched, screaming over and over again, "Don't leave me, Mommy!" His tiny, desperate voice followed my mother down the hall, ringing in her ears all the way back to Brantford, a sound that broke her heart each time she recalled it, a sound that has haunted her for the rest of her life.

For the rest of the week we functioned like automatons, moving perfunctorily through the hours and days, careful, oh so careful not to hope too much, not to breathe too deeply. When the news finally came, bad as it ever was, and we knew once and for all that Jeff had CF, my mother fell to her knees and waxed every floor in the house, her tears dripping off the end of her nose into her aproned lap, her sobs echoing down the hall like tragic arias.

My father banged doors shut, shouted "Jeez Murphy" and "Goddammit" and slammed the countertop with his fist, sighed deeply and snapped his newspaper open curtly as if warning us to keep away. Pam and I went underground, weeping with our arms around each other in our rooms or tiptoeing quietly down the hall to visit the boys, staring at Jeff as he napped, consoling Gregg with kisses and hugs. We fled to my downstairs bedroom, closed the door, turned my transistor radio up to a blare, and sang along with Peter and Gordon that we couldn't live in a world without love.

The last days of summer wafted away on the sugary smoke of fallen poplar leaves that my father burned at the end of our driveway. Pam signed up for Brownies and piano lessons. Gregg became a Cub Scout. I kept on with Girl Guides and Saturday afternoon ballet. We all registered for skating lessons.

My mother bucked up and went shopping, bringing home new school clothes and flinging them like rainbows across our beds. She stood square in the kitchen, leafing through the red Purity Flour Cookbook, feeding us on homemade chili sauce, cabbage rolls, pot roast, and the remnants of her lost dreams. She planted fall marigolds and dug in tulip bulbs for the next spring. She tucked love notes in our school lunchboxes. Knowing that staphylococcus, infection's friend and a Cystic's #1 enemy, could grow anywhere, she scrubbed the house too clean for death to get a foothold. She brushed our hair and bathed us. She sang to us in the night.

"Away in a manger, no crib for a bed…"

"Brighten the corner where you are…"

The CF Foundation made plans for a new ad campaign. In the same vein as Timmy, the poster boy for the March of Dimes, we'd have Lisa. Guess who? The Brantford chapter would buy a half-page ad in the *Expositor*, featuring Pam as Lisa, to appear at Christmas. She had already posed for the photograph, along with the doll she received as a gift from the radio station when she'd been sick last spring.

"I should have had my hair permed," moaned Pam.

"I think it's a very sweet picture," said Mom.

"That bow you stuck in my hair was too big."

"I still don't understand why you have to call her Lisa," I complained, churning with envy. "She should be able to use her own name."

"Lisa, Lisa," Gregg giggled.

"Lisa," Pam said under her breath, smirking.

"Here's what's going below the photograph," my father grinned, giving us the copy to read.

This delightful child requires life-long intensive medical treatment. Until science finds answers, Lisa depends for survival on costly drugs, complex breathing equipment, a devoted family.

The ad would also list the accomplishments of the Brantford CF Chapter throughout 1964.

- *Summer medical student grant*
- *Search clinic and teaching centre*
- *Supported medical and lay information*

- *Provided inhalation mask for Brantford General and St. Joseph's Hospitals*
- *Paid $500 for patient inhalator equipment*

Even I was impressed.

My father entered two floats in the Labor Day Parade. One was a shiny new Kelly green flatbed truck loaded with crates and pallets, with "Summerhayes Industries" painted on the cab door to advertise his fledgling business. Nick, Dad's friend from the lumberyard, rumbled it along in a slow procession of Brantford Fire Department trucks, police cars, the mayor's Cadillac, and a few dozen children riding go-carts and bicycles festooned with multicolored streamers.

Dad followed, driving the second float, an exhibit for the Brantford chapter of the CF Foundation, a rented flatbed truck draped with streamers and handsome blue-and-white signs that read "Give a Child the Breath of Life." We had set up Pam's bed, tent, mask, compressor, and physio table behind the truck cab.

Pam and I begged to ride the float together. Ever the aspiring actress, I gave Pam "sample" treatments, doing her postural drainage on the physio table, clapping her back and chest up and down the parade route. She took her mask while I threw green CF pamphlets to the stunned crowd. We waved and laughed as the mist from the tent and the mask wafted behind us down Colbourne Street. After the parade, we gathered at Grandma and Grandpa Birdsell's for a picnic.

The living room at Grandma's was cool and dark. The blinds were pulled and the curtains drawn against the sun. A couple of electric fans chugged softly side to side, strategically placed to circulate the air. I sat cross-legged on the carpet watching a man perform miracles on television.

"HE-al, HE-al," he drawled, pressing his hands dramatically on the heads of sick and dying people. The lame walked, unseen cancers disappeared. "Praise the Lord," the man shouted, "Hallelujah!"

I squinted at my sister's silhouette as she opened the door and entered the room, the light from the kitchen a lemon halo around her.

"What are you watching?" she asked, plopping down beside me on the carpet.

"Oral Roberts. He heals sick people."

"Oh."

We watched agape as Oral Roberts pressed his hands to another head, incanting "HE-al, HE-al!"

"Maybe we can get Mom and Dad to take you there."

Pam looked at me as if I had three heads. She got up, turned off the TV, and sat down cross-legged in front of me, taking both of my hands in her own.

"Heather," she said. "Oral Roberts can't make me better. Nobody can."

My throat clotted as I fought back tears, and my lips drew tightly downward. I gazed at my little sister, her face pale as moonbeams, her hazel eyes charged with intent. She sounded grown up, more grown up than me. How was this possible?

"When I was in the hospital last spring, I figured that out. It scared me, and it made me mad. I hated being sick. I hated being told what to do. 'Pam, take your mask. Pam, take your pills. Pam, have your treatment.' I was sick of it. They couldn't fool me. I knew I was going to die no matter how many treatments I had, or pills I took, or needles they gave me. I thought it was all for nothing, and that I was too much trouble for everyone. If that was the way my life was going to be, I just wanted to die right then and get it over with. So I locked myself in the bathroom. I crawled under the bathroom sink, rolled up in a ball, and prayed to God to strike me dead right there and then. Then I squeezed my eyes shut and waited for it to happen!"

She giggled at the thought of it. I wondered how she could do that when I was ready to cry. This was the first time she had spoken to me of that night.

"I don't want to be a burden on the family. I hate being sick, but mostly I hate seeing what it does to everyone."

"It's all right," I squeaked.

"No," she said. "It's not all right."

We sat for a few moments, silent, staring down at our intertwined hands. My heart thudded loudly.

"What I finally realized," Pam softly continued, "was that God gave me a life, and it's up to me to live it the best I can, for as long as I can. All we can do now is to love each other, and keep hoping the doctors find something new." My sister hugged me, and looked away. Her eyes turned steely and she set her jaw.

"Don't worry," she promised. "I'm not giving up."

CHAPTER TEN

*"Anger storms between me and things, transfiguring,
transfiguring."* — MARGE PIERCY

It's an angry afternoon on the Hudson as I write. A forty-mile-an-
hour wind bellows and moans, rattling the windows. A driving
rain lashes across the landscape, blurring the dark silhouette of
Manhattan. The river is the color of cold steel. Whitecaps roil and
scud across its surface as the water hurtles past below me. Several
big seagoing tankers have hunkered down midstream for the
duration. The seas are wild out beyond the Verrazano Narrows
Bridge. Weather reports warn of coastal flooding. I shiver and
light a candle.

Storms once raged inside me, adolescent tempests that
unleashed vicious tornadoes and torrents of tears, gales that
howled and blew the doors off our house, shuddering the foun-
dations. I am still surveying the damage to this day.

Dr. Feldstein, my patient counselor, has guided me through
the whitewater of memory and emotion. I have told her how I
wish I could take back the destructive rage of my teenage years,
the harsh words, the bloody screams, the anguished wailing
and slammed doors. It is hard to forgive myself the pain I
caused, knowing how it must have marred my brothers' and my
sister's lives.

She assured me that my behavior was completely normal

under the circumstances; that I had to behave the way I did. She said that I was saving my sanity, that I was serving the family by acting out our collective rage. I was courageous to do so. She said.

Looking back, I can see that I was not so much angry as I was drowning in grief, shouting out how I too was afraid to die, afraid of the leaves falling, of the stars going out, of the river drying up. Afraid of being left behind. I was already bereft, alone in the cemetery at midnight. Anger grows from the hard kernel at the center of grief; the feeling of being utterly powerless.

Beneath our attempts to be normal, my family was hopelessly frightened, intolerably sad, shamed by our inability to ward off catastrophe no matter how courageous or capable we strove to be, and outraged at our circumstances. These underlying emotions were too raw and overwhelming to contain, and our defenses too tenuous.

Looking back with me, my mother now acknowledges the intensity, and the enormity of the feelings that she and my father both determined to keep under control.

"Giving in to them never seemed to do any good," she said. "And we were afraid to show our true feelings to the outside world in case people should think less of us."

Each member of a family has a role to play in the group dynamic, either chosen or assigned. It became my role to act as the lightning rod for the emotional electricity that crackled in the atmosphere of our "normal" family life. I gave voice to the unacceptable and the unexpressed. My parents and I struck an unconscious bargain where I became, in fact, responsible for opening Pandora's Box. And I paid the price. As I howled out our darkest fears, our most unacceptable emotions, there were many days when my family came to view me, and I came to view myself, as dark and unacceptable.

We weren't aware of this silent covenant we had made, and couldn't face the real source of my anger. All we could comprehend was that I got flat out mad and stayed that way for a long time, for "no good reason." Yet as much as our fighting exhausted my parents, it also liberated them. My explosions permitted release of their own dark, pent-up emotions. In the aftermath, once the dust had settled and we'd had a night or two of good sleep, we could all return to precious "normal" for a time, calm and patient, even light-hearted, ready to attend to the task at hand. Saving Pam.

In the late spring of 1965, we moved from the house at 16 Brier Crescent, a place we would remember often with laughter, bittersweet longing, and wistful silence—the only place we would ever think of as our true home.

Gregg begged harder than anyone to remain there. Years would pass before I realized how his eight-year-old heart broke to leave that house. Or rather, that a portion of his heart broke away from us as a family, and that rift was never to be fully mended.

Pam carried memories of that house within her as if they were precious jewels, bringing them out to dazzle and comfort her when life became too painful.

As for me, I would return there in dreams. In the dead of night, I would walk through its shadowy rooms, locking every door and window, vainly trying to make sure we were all safe.

I turned thirteen in a tiny rented house out on Highway 24, where we lived briefly while my father built my mother's "Dream House" with his own hands on a lot inherited from his father in Wyndham Hills, an exclusive subdivision created on acreage that had once been part of the family farm. The rental was only a short car ride from town, but for a young teenager, it might as well have been in the middle of nowhere. Under sodden skies, the spring fields lay waiting to be planted, surrounding the house as far as the eye could see. I waited like the fields, praying for the sun's return, unsure of the future, unsure of myself, unsure of everything.

None of us knew the exact details of the bargain my sister had made with God on that night only weeks before, when she picked herself up off the cold tile floor of the hospital bathroom vowing never to give up. She had changed, though. The new antibiotic had stabilized her health remarkably. She was bossier, that's for sure. More than ever, grownups treated her as if she were the Princess Royal. She knew she could get away with murder if she wished, and this gave her a certain confidence, a license, I thought, to try and do just that.

The remarkable obstinacy she had displayed during that scene at the hospital, and the epiphany she had subsequently experienced now served to underscore a new sobriety in her character, causing all of us to pay even more attention when she wanted her way. We were all just a little afraid of her now, this pale, saucy eleven year old with newly pierced ears and the prodigious will to live.

I had had no such epiphany, no electrifying moment through which to transform my fear, galvanize my resources, or otherwise cause my family to take me seriously. I had only the memory of the fear that filled the house while she was sick, and the certainty that no matter how well she now appeared, or how willful she became, she would come close to death again.

Aware of my sister's mortality, I began my passage through adolescence keenly attuned to the images of death that presented themselves on our TV set and in the newspapers through the late 1960s. The pock-marked face and shark eyes of Richard Speck and his slaughter of six nurses. A boy with a shotgun in a Texas bell tower, picking off students on a college campus as if they were wooden ducks at a carnival. Robert Kennedy and

Martin Luther King lying in pools of blood. Three young civil rights workers dug out of the stinking earth. American soldiers butchered in Vietnam. The naked running bodies of napalmed children. Four little girls blown up in a church basement in Georgia. *Four Dead in O-hi-o*, at Kent State, at the hands of the National Guard. These were the images that frightened and fascinated me, hanging like a backdrop to my life: images of death that struck close to home.

The fits I threw while Pam was in the hospital, such as the day I broke my hand, and my tantrum on the front lawn the moment of her triumphant return, were no longer isolated events.

In June we moved into the Dream House. My mother planted petunias, impatiens, and bright red geraniums around the perimeter. Dad rescued the Wishing Rock from 16 Brier Crescent, placing it at the foot of our new driveway.

In July we held a wine and cheese fundraiser for the Brantford chapter of the CF Foundation. Pam and I passed around platters of cheese, gave demonstrations of the tent, mask, and physio, and handed out pamphlets to tipsy, seer-suckered patrons.

"Do I look sick enough?" Pam coyly asked me, and we collapsed on the grass together, clutching our sides as we laughed.

In August Brian Mulder died, six years old, claimed by Cystic Fibrosis. We were close enough to the family to know his parents as "Auntie Mape" and "Uncle Joe." After the phone call, my mother sat right down with Jeff in her lap and began to brush his hair in soft, slow strokes.

Pam and I went to sit on the Wishing Rock. We wished that Brian wasn't dead. We wished that his brother Peter, who also had CF, wouldn't die now as well. Peter was Pam's age. Eleven.

We sat for a long while in the sun, Pam's jaw tight and her lips pursed, my chest burning with unshed tears.

"C'mon," she said firmly, "let's do Scout's Pace."

We ran count of ten, walked count of ten, ran count of ten, walked count of ten, up the wooded street and back, collapsing once more on the Wishing Rock, our grief barely spent.

Later that night, on my way to the bathroom, I heard the sound of my mother's voice floating down the hall on the soft gold light from the kitchen.

"I wonder if Peter will just give up now and follow his brother."

"I give him six months," my father replied, sighing.

I lay awake then, as I did many nights that summer, listening to the dark. I strained my ears to hear Pam breathing through the wall, as if I could, as if it would make a difference. I listened to the faraway drone of the compressor, the wind in the trees outside, the flush of the toilet down the hall, the running of water and snapping of lights as my parents went to bed. Later still, I woke to the sound of Pam choking, the swift padding of my parents' feet across the hall and into her room, the slapping of their hands on her back and their anxious voices murmuring, "That's a girl, spit it up, that's good, you're okay now…"

A few weeks before Christmas, Peter Mulder died.

My father took me to the funeral home but made Pammy stay behind, though she begged to come with us.

"It'll be too upsetting for her," my father quietly explained to me. "She's too young. She's not ready for this yet."

My sister stood stone-faced in the hall, watching me put on my coat, and then turned slowly and disappeared into her room, locking the door behind her.

"I don't want to go," I yelled back through the door. "Dad's making me."

My father guided me up the frozen steps of the funeral home.

"There's nothing to be afraid of," he murmured.

Grownups clustered, hushed and red-eyed, in the corner where Auntie Mape and Uncle Joe sat. My father walked me to the coffin, his hand gentle on my back. My breath stopped short as I gazed down at Peter's face, this boy I knew, so waxy and pale and stiff, his delicate eyelids rimmed with a purplish hue. My ears rang.

That night I dreamt of a drowned lady on a beach, and woke in the dark realizing that it was not a dream, but a real memory of something that had happened at our old cottage in Turkey Point. I was about eight then, and Pam was six.

We had just returned from a wild spin in the *Donna P.*, an outboard motorboat my father named after my mother. Pam and I climbed out of our wet, orange-canvas life preservers while my mother railed at Dad, "I'm not doing all that work to keep this child alive if you're going to go out and kill the lot of us in that boat!"

Meanwhile, a fire engine shrieked up the gravel road along the beach, and stopped where a crowd of people had gathered. Leaving Pam in the dust I ran to investigate, elbowing my way through the throng. Lying there like a fish on the sand was a young woman, her skin pearly white, her body limp. Her dark, wet hair, matted with sand, clung to her face. Her eyes stared wide open and empty. Water dribbled from her mouth, but she made no sound. Somehow I knew she was dead.

In the nights and weeks that followed Peter's death, I dreamt of the drowned lady over and over, but it was Pam on the beach that the firemen were trying to save, and I always arrived too late. I daydreamed too, dramatic fantasies about Pam's demise. Watching the rain smatter the windows of the school bus, listening to my friends jabber in the cafeteria at lunch, or staring right in Pam's face at the dinner table, I imagined how her death might take place, and where. Perhaps she'd cough herself to death in front of me while I was alone with her at home, and then Mom and Dad would arrive to find her dead in my arms, and they'd be mad at me and blame me for the rest of my life because I didn't save her. Or maybe we'd be on Colbourne Street eating French fries on a Saturday afternoon, and she'd collapse suddenly on the sidewalk, and I'd scream for help while passers-by ignored me.

Sometimes I envisioned Mom discovering Pam's corpse in bed when she went in to wake her up for school in the morning, and me waking to the sound of my mother's screams. Or I imagined that I was called out of class and told in the nurses' office that Pam had died suddenly, without me, and I screamed "No, no!" and went to pieces believing I could have saved her if only I'd been there.

"What's the matter with you?" my mother asked ten times a day.

"Nothing, leave me alone."

Every day after school I dumped my books and took off running to the snow-blown golf course across the street from our house. I stood on the peak of the highest hill, inviting the bracing wind to fly cold and straight into my eyes.

"Please God, please," I yelled out loud. "I'll do anything, anything, only please don't make Pammy die."

I stayed out as long as I could, until the gray afternoon slipped into twilight and the wind hushed. I knew I should go home. My mother would be waiting for me to come in and set the table.

Approaching the house, I could see my mother's silhouette in the golden light of the family room window, her arms crossed, looking up and down the street, looking for me. I rubbed my face with snow so she wouldn't see I'd been crying.

"How was your day at school?" she asked as I plowed through the door. My sister stared at me over the green proboscis of her inhalation therapy mask.

I tried to talk to my mother over the noise of Pam's compressor, then as she pounded Pam's back during her treatment, and once again as she busied herself in the kitchen peeling vegetables and browning meat. It was no use.

After dinner, I fought with Pam over doing the dishes.

"You wash and I'll dry," I instructed my sister.

"No, I always wash. You wash and I'll dry."

"I'm not putting my hands in that yucky water."

"It's not going to kill you."

"Heather," my mother called from the den. "Don't argue with your sister. She hasn't been feeling well today. Let her do whatever she feels up to."

One night, fed up with letting Pam do "whatever she felt up to," I banged the cookware around the counter, then slapped my sister in the face. She slapped me right back. I picked up the wet dishrag and threw it at her. She grabbed a one-quart copper-bottomed Revere Ware pot by the handle and threatened me with it.

"I know why you're angry," she shouted tearfully, "but don't take it out on me! There's nothing I can do about it!"

As I turned to stomp out of the kitchen, she heaved the pot at me, striking me behind the knees. I hit the floor like a fallen timber. Suddenly, we were both laughing.

"I didn't know you were that good of a shot."

"Me either!"

My mother rushed in from the den.

"I've had enough of this nonsense. Heather, you either straighten up and fly right or go to your room."

"You only care about me if I'm perfect!"

I scrambled to my room, slamming the door. Weeping, I lay on my bed in the dark, jealous of the bustling sounds I could hear down the hall as my family made tea, watched television, and laughed together.

Soon my mother came in to say good-night.

"I wish I knew why we fight so much. I wish I knew what's making you so unhappy."

I sighed deeply on the verge of tears, afraid to speak to her of Brian's death, and Peter's death, and my fears for Pam.

"You mustn't hide your light under a bushel basket," she said softly, kissing my forehead.

Some nights she sang me to sleep the way she used to in the house on Brier Crescent.

"This little light of mine, I'm gonna let it shine, oh this little light of mine, I'm gonna let it shine…"

The winter of 1966 felt long and sad.

Auntie Mape and Uncle Joe Mulder invited me to come up and stay with them during Easter break. They were kind, gentle, and bereft, still grieving for the loss of their sons. They cooked dinner for me, took me shopping, and listened patiently to my nervous chatter about school. I told them excitedly that I would be turning fourteen in six weeks, and then sat in dumb silence, appalled with myself.

Later, I lay stiffly awake in Peter's bed, alert to the starched lace Dutch clean emptiness of the night, listening to the big old mantel clock from Holland chime the hours, wondering if Peter's and Brian's ghosts would come to haunt me. The next morning, embarrassed and unable to explain, I asked to go home.

Overnight the trees in our yard had burst into bud. Tulips and daffodils had poked their way up through the soil.

"Was it too sad at the Mulders?" my mother asked.

I nodded yes.

"I thought so. Come on out on the porch with Pam while she has her mask. It's a beautiful day."

I followed my sister out to the big screened-in porch where tea things had been laid. My mother had baked Pam's favorite coconut squares.

"I'll join you two as soon as I'm finished in the den."

On the other side of the open, sliding-glass door, my mother polished the furniture. Dust motes flew in the beams of soft yellow light that poured through the windows. With blue flannel rags cut from my father's old pajamas, she rubbed the pine end tables, the fireplace mantel, and the cherry rocker, trying to kill the staphylococcus germs that could grow in my sister's lungs. With rhythmic strokes, she swiped away the oily film left behind by the Mucomist from Pam's mask. Later she would hang the curtains outside on the line, as she did every week, beating them viciously in the fresh air, hoping to rid them of the mask's rancid odor.

I nibbled coconut squares and sipped my tea, hurting, knowing that my friends' mothers were holding spring luncheons and choosing foursomes for golf while mine scrubbed our house too clean for death.

That summer came smelling like sun-warmed canvas on old deck chairs.

I got my first period. As I shared my news with Pam, her eyes grew large and wistful.

"You're a woman now," she said. "I wish I could be a woman."

"Don't worry, your time will come." I felt phony and glib.

Not wanting to grow too far ahead, or have her feel left behind, I stuck close to my sister. I curled up on the end of her bed in her cool, Wedgwood Blue bedroom to share girl talk. I swam with her in our cousin's pool. I sat next to her on the couch while she had her mask. I pitched in with her physio treatments. The two of us watched *American Bandstand* on TV, trying to figure out how to dance the Jerk, the Twist, the Swim, the Frug, and the Mashed Potato. We threw "Beauty Evenings" when my parents were out speaking for CF, and we babysat the boys. I loved to make up her face like Twiggy, the new model in *Seventeen* magazine. I gave her manicures, knowing how much she hated her hands.

"They're too big," she moaned, "and my fingers are ugly."

When I pressed my palm to hers, her hand indeed outsized my own. In, spite of their size and appearance, her hands were feminine and alert. I envied how deftly she could thread a needle, and adored the way her hands flew to her face when she was excited, bunching together beneath her pug nose, hiding her grin while her eyes shone merrily. Her fingers were long and slender, delicately boned yet strong, but her fingertips had grown bulbous because of her body's fight for oxygen. Her nails were splayed, and often glowed a pale lavender. I filed them into soft ovals and slathered them with frosted shell pink polish, which she quietly removed the next day. I forgot that she had to check her nails through the day to see if they were pink or blue, so she knew how much oxygen she was getting. If they were blue, she had an extra mask and treatment. Nail polish was not an option.

Summer rolled out its lazy, crazy, hazy days for us. We brought lemonade, baked ham, and potato salad up to the Bell Homestead for picnics. We took long, lazy drives in the country, stopping for ice cream at the Dairy Queen. Mom let us stay up past bedtime to watch Merv Griffin on TV while we ate cherry Jell-O and whipped cream. I began to think she was right about us getting a fresh start in the new house. A trickle of hope laid a silvery trail across my heart.

Then one day, the phone rang.

"Oh my god," my father whispered into the receiver, and staggered slightly as if a tremor had rocked the earth.

Pam looked up, her face turned white as plaster, as if she knew what was coming. Little Esther Anderson was dead. A cold she caught a week earlier had turned into pneumonia. She went quickly, we were told, as if that should comfort us.

Esther was Pam's best CF friend. Both twelve years old, they had known each other since the beginning of the CF Foundation, when our respective parents became friends. Through the years they often met up with each other at Dr. Cleary's office, at Sick Kids, and the B.G.H., and played together not only in each other's homes, but also at a special program for Cystics organized by my mother at the YWCA.

Pam rose stoically from the table and headed back to her room, where she hid like a wounded animal. I started after her, but my mother warned me off. We sat together glumly at the kitchen table while my father telephoned the other CF families to break the news.

"Esther Anderson just died," he said repeating the awful words, sighing deeply, removing his glasses, rubbing his eyes, putting his glasses back on, sighing again, promising to call later when he knew more details about the funeral, hanging up, muttering "Oh boy, oh boy" as he dialed another number.

When it came time for the funeral a couple of days later, Pam emerged from her room rigid with determination. She was still furious at not having been allowed to go to Peter Mulder's funeral.

"I am going to bury my friend," she insisted to my father. "Don't try to talk me out of it."

The service was held at Thorpes Brothers, where Pam and I had peeked in the windows and shrieked with laughter so often after church. Now we locked hands, took a deep breath, and went inside for the first time.

The place was airless and stiff as we had imagined. We stood next to each other, staring down into Esther's blank, porcelain white face. Her blonde hair curled softly against an ivory and lace satin pillow. She looked like a life-sized doll, dressed up and boxed for sale.

I wanted her to open her eyes and say it was all a mistake. I wanted her to sit up and just scare the living daylights out of us. Pam gazed implacably at her friend. My throat swelled. The room began to close in with the sickly sweet odor of cut flowers already dying, and the weight of heavy curtains obliterating the sunny world outside. Grownups milled about, moving as if under water, speaking in the hushed tones I remembered from Peter's funeral.

I wanted to flee. I wanted to grab Pam and race out into the glittering yellow day, to roll down a grassy hill with her and laugh, to breathe in the blue sky, the high clouds and the summer sun. I wanted to be a child in a world where children did not die.

Back at home I asked Pam if she wanted to talk about it.

"I think I saw her breathe once," she said. "I guess my eyes were playing tricks on me."

I was useless, stricken with dumbness.

"I'd like to be alone now," she said, gently closing her door in my face. "I need to think."

My mother changed out of her funeral clothes and went right to work. She cleaned out cupboards and closets, exclaiming that it was time we got rid of all our "junk." She waxed the floors and wiped the windows, rearranged the furniture, and moved the pictures on the walls.

My father left immediately for the lumberyard and continued to work himself ruthlessly, practically living there. He doubled his speaking engagements for the CF Foundation. When he was home he raised his voice, banged his fist on the kitchen table, and said no a lot, as if that word, spoken forcefully, made him feel he was protecting us from harm, real or imagined. In his spare time, he disappeared into the side lot with a chainsaw and axe, clearing trees and shouting at us to stay back as he set fire to piles of underbrush, as if they were pyres for his grief.

Gregg and Jeff, aged ten and five, squabbled constantly, appearing as a single four-fisted, four-legged whirling dervish, spinning from room to room around the house, punching each other, shrieking and wailing with my mother in hot pursuit.

"Get downstairs to your room and stay there, do you hear?"

More shrieks from the bottom of the stairs.

"Now you two stop it down there, just stop it!"

Pam's door remained closed, for days, for weeks. While my parents respected her need for solitude, often as not I came home to find my mother huddled in close conversation with Pam at the foot of my sister's bed.

"Shut the door, please," my mother said when I appeared, "your sister and I are having a talk. We'll be through in a few minutes."

It hurt to feel shut out.

"You know I need to help Pam sort through her feelings," my mother explained to me later.

"Your sister requires a lot of extra love and support right now so she won't give up," said my father. And then, as if sharing a confidence, "It could make all the difference..."

I sat alone in my room waiting for comfort that didn't come, getting mad, while my twelve-year-old sister sat in hers, confronting a grief and a terror far deeper than mine, determining how to come out of it in one piece. Who was I, I asked myself, to be upset and scared? She was the one under real threat, and no matter how many people rallied around her, she still had to face the night alone.

With my parents' encouragement, Pam meditated and prayed, coming back full circle to the notion that God had a plan for her. She would draw power and strength by putting her faith in Him. Ultimately, she simply dug in her heels and vowed, as before, not to give up. One day she came out of her room and we all knew that was that. Her jaw was set and her eyes were bright. Her mourning was over.

We sat together on the Wishing Rock. She announced that she had decided not to waste her precious time and energy being scared or angry, but rather to conserve it. Big words for a little girl, but hard times demanded big words, even from one so young.

"I'm just going to be grateful for each new day, and take it as it comes." She sounded suspiciously like my mother.

Pam had a clear enemy to fight and tactics at her disposal. Determined to meet this enemy on its own ground, she became scrupulous about taking her pills and her mask, getting enough sleep, eating enough food, not missing any treatments and sometimes adding extras. Her spiritual and physical practices demanded the kind of cloistered discipline usually reserved for Olympic athletes.

I admired the new Pam, but I didn't like her very much. I wanted my old sister back, the one full of mischief and laughter, my ally and my charge. She was growing away from me, taking her life into her own hands, and even that growing away felt like a death.

My enemy, meanwhile, was less clearly defined than Pam's. Esther's death had forced me to realize, for the first time, that my parents couldn't save Pam, not with their love or determination, not with their money or their blood, and I couldn't save her with my prayers. I knew of no specific task I could undertake, short of cleaning my room, to combat the constant, churning dread, or the waves of guilt that knocked me down each time I contemplated the future. How dare I think of growing up, of having fun?

My mother said I was my own worst enemy. My friends told me to lighten up, saying I was too intense. Pam said I was too hard on myself.

My father told me to have faith. I thought he meant that he wanted me to have his faith. First Baptist Faith.

We were all dressed up and ready to leave for church one Sunday morning in late August when I decided I just couldn't go. I faced off with Dad in the laundry room by the back door while the rest of the family waited in the car.

"How can I worship a God who lets little children suffer and die?"

"What do you mean?" he asked.

"Oh don't do that. It makes me so mad when you do that."

"Do what?"

"Pretend you don't know what I'm talking about. I mean Peter and Brian and Esther."

"Is that what this is all about? How many times have I told you kids? When life lands you a blow, you pick up and move on. That's what your sister's done, and as long as she keeps up her treatments the way she has lately, she's in no immediate danger. There's nothing to be afraid of, so there's no need for you to carry on like this. Now go on out there and get in the car."

"I'm not going."

"Oh yes you are, young lady. You won't get your faith back by staying home. Now c'mon, I know you'll feel better if you go to church."

"No I won't."

"Now look here, it's my responsibility as your father to make sure you go to church and I'm going to see to it. You're coming with us and you're coming right now."

"Your faith's been shaken too," I shouted. "Don't tell me it hasn't."

He cocked one eyebrow and stared at me. His cheeks flushed.

"Yes, I'll admit it. But God tests our faith by shaking it. Pammy still believes. She's still going to church."

"Pammy, Pammy, Pammy. I don't care what Pammy believes!"

I grabbed the nearby clothes iron and heaved it at my father. He ducked. The iron sailed through the air, narrowly missing his head, exploding through the back door window, showering the floor with shattered glass.

A terrible silence saturated the stillness that followed. My father stood red-faced and stock-still. My heart pounded through my chest.

My mother's voice echoed off the cement walls of the garage. "Jesus Christ Doug, are you all right?"

"I'm fine," he managed to call out to her. "I'll be right there."

I was flooded with tears. "I'm sorry," I sobbed.

My father looked frightened, bewildered, fed up. He was tired of putting up with this kind of nonsense and tired of hearing "I'm sorry." I was breaking his heart.

I didn't care. No, I did care, but I couldn't help it. My heart was breaking too.

Shards of glass crackled underfoot as he stepped gingerly toward the door. He didn't yell, but rather spoke to me in a dark whisper.

"All right. You want to be left alone? I'll leave you alone. But I want to see this mess cleaned up by the time we're back from church."

"For God's sake Doug!" My mother's tearful voice called out.

My father gave me a long, shattered look. He turned away from me and stepped through the door into the garage.

"What on earth went on in there?"

"I don't want to discuss it now."

The slamming car door went through my heart like a gunshot. The engine revved, and the car jerked abruptly into reverse. The wheels spun in the gravel as my father backed up and turned the Studebaker around.

Through the jagged windowpane, I watched my family disappear down the road. The sunlight dappled the verdant maples, a mourning dove cooed in the distance, my mother's petunias bobbed cheerfully in the breeze. God's picture-perfect day.

As I bore witness to Pam's illness, she bore witness to mine, for I became sick with rage. I stomped my feet, screamed, tossed chairs, kicked the walls, pounded the furniture, threw things to the floor, slapped my parents, slapped myself, pummeled my own head with my fists, slammed doors, wailed, writhed, sobbed, and moaned in despair. Little provocation was needed for me to turn a minor disagreement into a full-scale battle.

One afternoon a small confrontation over a missing button on my skirt turned into a screaming match, quickly escalating into pushing, grabbing, and wrestling.

Gregg ran downstairs and hid with his hands over his ears. Jeff ran outside and rode his tricycle up the block as fast as his little legs could carry him. I ran bawling to my room and slammed the door, leaving my mother slumped at the kitchen table. Her sobbing echoed down the hall.

"This can't go on," she repeated to herself.

She's right, I thought, *this can't go on.* I stood sniffling at my bedroom window, the sting of drying tears on my cheeks. Staring out at the summer day, the trees and peaceful gardens in our neighbors' backyards, I was jealous of the carefree lives I thought that other people lived. I wished I had someone to talk to, like the nice red-haired, pony-tailed guidance counselor at school who had been so good to me last year. Then I remembered some of my Catholic friends telling me about the Children's Aid Society. I took the name at face value. Children's Aid.

I snuck out to look up the address in the phonebook, emptied my piggy bank, and slipped quietly out the back door, catching the next bus downtown. I paced back and forth in the sun outside the grimy glass door of the CAS, took a deep breath, and walked in, my whole body shaking.

As soon as I tried to open my mouth, the tears came. "I need help," I squeaked to the first person I saw.

The woman showed me into a small, dingy office piled high with brown file boxes. I was so keyed-up, so terrified, my gaze ping-ponged about the room, and every detail, including the woman's face, became a blur of corrugated cardboard and acrylic wood veneer. The only surroundings I was aware of were my own turbulent emotions, and I heard the woman's questions as if from the bottom of a river.

"How old are you?"

"Fourteen."

"And what's the problem?"

I fixed my gaze on the fake wood grain of her desk and spewed out my sad tale of woe.

"...and I'm sure it's all my fault. My parents have a lot to deal with, and I guess I don't make things any easier for them. They keep telling me everything would be all right if I would just quit being so mad all the time."

When I was done, the woman explained to me how hard having two sick children must be for my parents, and I wondered if she'd heard a thing I said, but then she told me she'd call to have a word with Mom, and not to worry, as I had done the right thing and it would all work out. I sighed with deep relief, and felt proud enough to reward myself with a box of French fries from the market square. The sharp fragrance of vinegar stung my nostrils and watered my tear swollen eyes, but the warm, salty flavor comforted me on the bus ride home.

The late afternoon sun bled through the trees as I walked along Lakeside Drive toward my house. The birds chirped gaily. My spirits lifted. When I approached the house, my mother burst through the door of the second floor screened porch and ran full bore down the long outside staircase to the driveway, screeching.

"How dare you air our dirty laundry in public? What goes on between these walls is to stay here, do you understand? I won't have the Children's Aid coming here and taking away my children. I'm a good mother, and don't you tell anybody I'm not!"

She sobbed desperately, as if I had murdered someone.

"I was only trying to help," I choked, barely able to speak for shame.

I ran ahead of her up the stairs and into my room, weeping bitterly for what I had done, afraid that nothing between us would ever be the same.

⌒

Pam had gone to Girl Guide Day Camp, and earned her badge for Scout's Pace. When she wanted to go to "away" camp, however, there was no place that would take her with her mask and pills and treatments. Ultimately, though neither she nor any of us considered her disabled, the only place open to her was Lakewood Camp for Crippled Children.

After a two-week stay, she came home grinning, still unbearably thin but with a healthy pink glow on her pasty white cheeks. With the exception of herself and two other CF girls, Linda Henries and Wendy Stibbards, most of her other fellow campers had been in wheelchairs, suffering from thalidomide defects, Cerebral Palsy, Muscular Dystrophy, or Spina Bifida.

Pam showed me a snapshot of herself with a cabin mate. My sister had propped the girl up against a flagpole, and stood next to her in a pose of studied nonchalance, so at first glance you did not see that Pam was actually holding her friend upright.

"She's been in a wheelchair her whole life," Pam told me. "I wanted her to be able to see what she looked like standing on her own two feet." She laughed. "You know, I feel so lucky. I can walk and go anywhere, dress myself, comb my own hair, feed myself, put my arms around the people I love, and do all kinds of things most of those kids will never be able to do. Maybe they think I'm worse off than them, but I don't know. I might not live for very long, but I can do more than they can with the time I've got."

The following summer, at Woodeden, another "crippled children's" camp, Pam became the closest of friends with Darlene Bunyan and Patty Murphy, two other CF girls with whom she made a solemn pact to help keep one another alive with mutual support and encouragement. With such friendships to bolster her, she blossomed as she moved into adolescence, fashioning a vital, viable life around her illness.

In June 1968, in an evening of fanfare and strawberry punch, Pam graduated from grade school. She stood on the front stoop of another new house, a stick figure drawn with a pale yellow pouf-sleeved lace dress, white gloves, a bouffant hairdo and a wan smile, captured forever by my father's Polaroid.

In the aftermath of a fight with his brothers (we had sold our side lot to a Jewish family, and citing the rules of the Wyndham Hill Association, my uncles had objected), my father had moved us back to Greenbrier, to a smaller, mottled brick house on a cul de sac where the Big Woods had once stood. My Lookout Tree was gone, chopped down and paved over, a street lamp erected in its place. My father kept promising to go back to Lakeside Drive to get the Wishing Rock, but he never did. The magic pink granite that had anchored our wishes, and our childhood, became a meaningless lump at the end of someone else's driveway.

Despite her pale and sickly appearance, my sister was as well as she had ever been. Now fourteen and about to start high school, she was a spitfire beneath a peace-loving veneer. By now she had left Dr. Matthews' clinic in Cleveland, and had begun seeing Dr. Douglas Crozier at the Hospital for Sick Children in Toronto. Much like Dr. Matthews, Dr. Crozier was regarded by many as a savior, and as my parents often said, he certainly kept the fear of God alive in them. His bedside manner, as described to me, was brusque and unyielding. I met him a couple of times. He was tall, slim, and raw-boned, with thinning hair and side burns. His eyes were drawn and heavy-lidded with the death of children. A cigarette dangled inevitably from lips tired of delivering bad news.

Dinner table discussions of Clinic Day painted a vivid picture for me.

"What's happening with you?" Dr. Crozier barked at Pam when she entered his office at my parents' side for her monthly checkup. He snapped her x-rays up on the screen behind his desk and pointed out the damage from her most recent lung infection. He shuffled the results from an afternoon of tests on his desk, offering his summation bluntly, stubbing out one cigarette and immediately lighting another, looking dead straight at my mother and saying things like, "Donna, I know you and Doug have been doing your best with her, but unfortunately your best will have to get better. Her pulmonary function is down a good 20 percent. If it continues in that direction, well, I don't have to tell you where we're headed."

After dinner, when my sister had gone upstairs to her room, my mother shared more details of Dr. Crozier's report with me, while my father whispered the names of the children who had died since Pam's last visit to clinic. Usually, within days or hours of hearing such news, or if Pam's clinic report was worrisome, I plunged into a bout of histrionics. My outbursts, and Pam's clinic appointments, were by now woven so deeply into the fabric of our life that we never saw the connection.

The whole world was having histrionics in 1968, so I fitted right in. Political assassinations and rock-star drug overdoses. Even Art Linkletter's daughter dropped acid and threw herself out a window. Every Monday the *Brantford Expositor* ran front-page obituaries with pictures of schoolmates who had died stoned in car wrecks over the weekend. Every night we saw young American men and Vietnamese children machine-gunned and napalmed on our television set. Students staged sit-ins and protests. Women were on the march.

"I'm going to be a feminist," Pam smirked.

"You don't have a bra you can burn," I snorted.

Remarkably, Pam had not had a hospital admission in four years. She swallowed her pills, upwards of sixty a day—digestive enzymes, antibiotics, and vitamins—with a wink and several glasses of milk. The antibiotics were beginning to yellow her teeth. There were no sleepovers with friends, for she still slept in the tent every night.

My sister stood about five feet tall and weighed all of sixty-five pounds. Although fashion-conscious, she was not a slave to it like me. She got her ears pierced, however, which annoyed me only because I was too lily-livered to follow suit.

The only purchased clothing that would fit Pam came from the children's department.

Out of frustration and necessity, she sewed much of her own wardrobe—nifty bell bottoms, cute shift dresses, and ruffled blouses. She was so gifted that she could look at a fashion spread in a magazine and copy an article of clothing exactly. She could even cut her own patterns. This bothered me no end, for it meant she could have a smart new outfit whenever she pleased for the price of a little saved-up allowance and a few dedicated hours at the sewing machine.

In a fit of envy I tried to out-sew her, going at the unfamiliar old black Singer sewing machine as if it owed me a couture wardrobe. Pam watched, amused and concerned, shaking her head and attempting to warn me about the machine's eccentricities.

"Leave me alone," I crowed. "I know what I'm doing!" As the words left my mouth, I ran my finger straight beneath the rapidly pulsing needle. My sister rushed to my side. With deft patience, she pulled the heavy cotton thread from my finger, stanching the flow of blood while I blubbered in pain and humiliation. She tried not to laugh when we discovered that I had sewn my dress together backwards, but she couldn't help it, and finally I had to laugh too.

In many ways, we were ordinary teenagers with an ordinary, healthy sibling rivalry. One minute we were laughing together at a secret joke and the next we were at each other's throats.

The voice of Neil Diamond drove me nuts, floating on sugary notes from behind the closed door of my sister's bedroom, underscored by the hum of her sewing machine.

I turned up the dial on my radio to blast out Janis Joplin, and cracked open my door. Within moments Pam yanked her door wide open to emit the Monkees at top volume. Seconds later we were face-to-face on the landing like two alley cats hissing and scratching.

"What on earth is happening to you two girls?" my mother cried out from the bottom of the stairs. "You used to be so close!"

Pam kept her distance because my anger exhausted her, and she couldn't afford to be exhausted. I kept mine because there were times when I felt I couldn't trust Little-Miss-Goody-Two-Shoes with certain secrets.

I was positive she had given it up to my parents that I'd been going steady with Les Mannen when I wasn't allowed to. How else did my mother know where to find his ring where I'd hidden it under my mattress? Why had Pam stood beady-eyed in her bedroom door, watching the fight that ensued as I punched my mother in the nose and made a run for it with Les in his pink-and-black Dodge?

The right to my own life, to not have it circumscribed by Pam's, and the right to be happy in it—this was my dream, though I thought it would be heresy to admit. Pam's life, her happiness, came first and foremost. No one had ever said so out loud, but they didn't have to. I knew that my sister's life held greater value than mine, because every day of her life was hard-fought, and hard-won, and came at such a price.

How, then, was I to prove my value to myself and to the world? How big a mark must I make? Whatever it was that I chose, I knew I must be more than merely good. I must be great. I must be a Star.

I had already joined the Brantford Drama League. Now sixteen, and entering Grade Eleven, I transferred to Brantford Collegiate where they had a good theatre arts program, and promptly landed the lead in a one-act play for the citywide Sears Drama Festival competition. I was nominated for a Best Actress Award, but Noreen, my so-called best friend, won instead. Devastated, I thought about giving up, but my mother wouldn't let me quit so easily.

"That's showbiz," she said. "If you really want to be an actress, you'll have to get used to it."

Then the Glenhyrst Theatre Guild cast me as the lead in William Saroyan's play *Hello Out There* for their One-Act Play Festival. My parents were effusive in their praise, and when my director suggested that I should audition for the Banff School of Fine Arts to study in the summer acting program, they agreed.

Belonging to the drama league and the theatre guild, and being accepted at Banff, gave me a taste of what I hoped to be, separate from my sister. I felt glimmerings of the "me" that I had been before I left ballet school. I began to recognize what a huge part of myself I buried then, to stay home with Pam. I wondered if that's what all my kicking and screaming had really been about. Only now did I feel the deadness I'd carried inside all this time, only now, as I felt that part of myself coming back to life.

The whole family came on vacation to Banff, to help get me settled. I remember the few days we spent together in the mountains before I started school as warm and gentle, some of the happiest we'd had as a family in a long time.

In my sixteenth summer, the "Summer of Love," hippies turned the streets of Haight-Ashbury into psychedelic rainbows.

On my own for six weeks at the School of Fine Arts, I felt psychedelic too, as beautiful as the Oxbow River winding crystal blue and sunset pink before an audience of soaring peaks and sturdy pines. It was a revelation not to feel angry every day, but instead to be at peace with myself and the world.

I returned from Banff and entered the twelfth grade more confident, and with high expectations. The leaves turned, the air chilled. Gregg transferred to a private day school for Grade Seven. My parents hoped this would ward off recent troublemaking tendencies. Jeff went to Greenbrier School for Grade Five, while Pam celebrated another landmark. She began high school at North Park Collegiate.

Since my sister was traveling farther to school and would no longer be able to come home at lunch for a midday physio and mask, organizing her treatments became more challenging. She and Mom or Dad had to get up an hour earlier to accommodate her morning mask and physio. At noon she had a quick lunch in the cafeteria with her chums then headed for the nurses' office to take her pills and squeeze in another mask. Her physio treatments and masks after school and before bed soon had to oblige extracurricular activities, such as football games and sock hops, and an increased load of homework.

More than ever, our routines revolved around Pam.

"We've got to get Pam's treatment in before we can..." "Pam has got to take her mask, or there won't be enough time to..." "We can't do... because Pam will have to miss her treatment."

Their anxiety was palpable. I heard it in their voices, saw it in the weight of their glances. I appropriated their distress. Tension mounted, old resentments resurfaced, and my parents clamped down in an effort to get control.

My newfound, supposedly authentic self disappeared into the wings, while my old self returned with a vengeance, fighting for center stage. I exploded, shouting and stomping in circles around the cherry-paneled family room. Then I ran to my room, slammed my door, turned on the record player full blast, and stood at my window, sobbing to Simon and Garfunkel.

I am a rock, I am an island.

And a rock feels no pain.

And an island never cries.

CHAPTER ELEVEN

*"And no one knows, and never remembers how it was
learned, that there will always be chasms, and across the
chasms will always be those one loves."* — Lillian Smith

By January of 1969 I smoked Craven Menthols, hung out at Tim
Horton Donuts, and thought I was something else. At the very
least, I was trying awfully hard to be something else.

I was a sixteen-year-old virgin, into heavy petting with my new
boyfriend, Sandy. I wore thick black eyeliner, overplucked eyebrows, frosted lipstick, hotpants, and miniskirts. I stuck my paltry
chest out as far as I could without being obvious. Wishing I were
Marlo Thomas or Mary Tyler Moore, I took to wearing a cheap
dynel "fall," a wig that fell straight to my shoulders from a black
velvet headband, curling at the ends into a neat flip. Purchased
with a postdated check, without my mother's permission, I snuck
it out of the house every morning in a brown paper bag, furtively
bobby-pinning it to my scalp in the school bathroom.

Flinging the shiny strands of fake hair from my shoulders and
puffing with mannered gestures on my cigarettes, I sat long
hours at the donut shop with my friends from the drama club,
bragging that someday I was getting out of this town, I was
going to Broadway and hitting it big. I drank innumerable cups
of coffee, extra light with two packs of sugar, and wrote Rod
McKuen rip-off poetry on paper napkins.

Out of the corner
of my eye
i see myself
in that dark corner
huddled, all curled up, afraid
of all the people and the light

but when i turn to face myself
my image disappears
and i stand looking
into empty corners
all the time...

The postdated check cleared the bank prior to the automatic deposit from my part-time job at Woolco. When the check bounced, the bank phoned my mother. I found this out after I was yanked out of history class and hauled down to the nurse's office to take my mother's call. My heart pounded and my hand went clammy on the receiver as I said hello. Having been told only that it was an emergency, I expected to hear that Pam had been rushed to the hospital. Instead my mother began to rant that young women who bounced checks to purchase forbidden hairpieces were headed for a life of crime. I gritted my teeth. My eyes turned hot and wet. She had a good mind to call the police, she said, and send them right over to arrest me.

"Is there anything wrong?" asked the nurse when I hung up.

"It's my sister," I lied.

"Oh dear. I hope she'll be all right."

By the time I got home from school a modicum of reason had prevailed, and my parents settled for house arrest. My reaction was by now, standard.

"I HATE you," I screamed, blasting up the stairs to my room in tears, slamming the door in my usual fashion, this time so hard it blew through the frame and stuck so that I couldn't get back out.

"Good," said my father, surveying the damage from the other side of the door, "you can just stay in there 'til you've had a chance to think things through."

It was Pam who rescued me, prying the door open with a screwdriver.

"I don't know why you bought that stupid wig in the first place."

"Because I'm ugly."

"No you're not. You just think you are."

Later that night, I lay in bed gazing out at the dark treetops as they brushed against the sky, trying once again to make sense of our life, emotions scattered about in my heart like the pieces of a jigsaw puzzle.

It wasn't that my parents weren't good, or that we never laughed and were all completely miserable. It wasn't that they were mean and I was hard done by. It wasn't that Pam's being sick ruined everything.

That's just how it felt.

Summerhayes Industries had been hanging on by a thread since Studebaker, its major client, folded, and I knew my father's livelihood was in danger of collapse. Meanwhile, my mother careened between hope and doom on all fronts, alternating between bouts of bubbling determination and crying jags.

It wasn't that we didn't have tea and speak softly and hug each other and say "I love you." It wasn't that my mother didn't tip-toe to my room to ask me what was wrong or that she didn't look at me like her heart would break. But the bond between my mother and sister was so tight I couldn't breathe. I felt squeezed out, and their intimacy hurt me. And if my mother wasn't with Pam, baking butter tarts, doing her treatments or helping her out with a sewing project, then she was taking care of the boys, or the house, or the yard, or arguing with my father about money. I felt expected to go it alone. At least until I screwed up. I sure did get her attention then. When I had done something wrong—like with the wig, which I got to keep only because Woolco wouldn't take it back—well, that's when she dropped everything for me. And that's when I yelled at her, "You only love me when I'm perfect," and our cruelest battles would ensue.

I was out of hand, my mother said. What was to be done with me?

I asked Grandma and Grandpa Birdsell if I could come and live with them, and Uncle Doug. The day I arrived, however, my small suitcase in hand, my grandmother wrung her hands and paced anxiously.

"I won't have the kind of nonsense here that goes on at your house," she warned me, throwing a disapproving glance at my mother.

I lasted there less than two weeks, not because I misbehaved, but because the house was so small it was untenable, especially when Uncle Doug came home on weekends.

Back at home, the tide of my emotions ebbed high and low with the moon. At their wits' end, my parents sent me to a psychiatrist.

Dr. L. wore Freudian glasses, a drab tweed suit, and an insincere, dentured smile. He had lost most of his hair, and I couldn't help wondering if he had torn it out trying to make bad teenagers like me behave. His face was a smooth mask pulled over sharp, aging cheekbones. He licked his thin, papery lips and asked me in a flat tone of voice to tell him what was wrong.

What was wrong? With me? With Pam? With the whole damn family?

With an air of what I perceived as predatory boredom he waited for me to speak, clicking his dentures, leering at me through the thick lens of his glasses like a bird of prey perched behind his desk, poised to strike at the first sign of neurosis.

"My sister is dying."

"Is she in hospital now?"

The way he said "in hospital" gave me gooseflesh.

"No."

"When was the last time she was in hospital?"

"About four years ago."

"If she hasn't been in hospital for four years, what makes you think she is dying?"

What a stupid question. "She has Cystic Fibrosis. It's a terminal disease."

"Yes, I'm aware of that. But is she sick right this minute?"

What kind of an idiot was this guy?

"She's always sick."

My heart swelled like a bruised fist, and tears rose. I glanced at the framed certificates that floated on the walls behind the doctor, too flooded with emotion to see them or anything else in the room clearly. My mind fastened on the image of Grandma Bill and Auntie Elsie sitting together at tea, knitting and rocking, their laughter frayed and ragged with age, their glances weighty with seven decades of sisterly collusion. How could I make him understand that I was already grieving, that I felt cheated, knowing I'd grow old without my sister? How could I confide to this pasty, tweedy man that I was afraid of death, Pam's death, my death, anybody's death?

"My parents think if I just clam up and do what I'm told and keep my room clean and get good marks in school then everything in our house will be all right. Well it won't."

"Why won't it?"

Dr. L. clicked his dentures, waiting.

"Because."

"Because why?"

My face flushed, my hands went clammy, my brain froze like I'd swallowed ice cream.

Because, because.

"Your mother says you need to calm down. I'm sending you home with a prescription for Valium. And here's an album by that new comic Bill Cosby. Give it to your mother. I think she needs to laugh more."

My visits to Dr. L. in the spring of 1969 dragged on for several excruciating weeks. The Valium made me sleepy at all the wrong times, like in the middle of the school day, but my mother noticed I was "more relaxed" at home. We all had a good laugh at Bill Cosby.

During my sessions with the doctor I sat dutifully in my hard-backed chair, trying to give the right answers to his questions, weeping softly, hoping he might say or do something that would fix the broken parts of me. I didn't know exactly what was broken, except maybe my heart, but I figured something in me had to be cracked or damaged, or I wouldn't need to be there. I felt that the future of my entire family depended on making myself "better," and I was certain I was failing.

During the Easter break the whole family piled into our Country Squire station wagon and drove to Florida. We had done this many times, going back to when we were very small. Such trips had always brought us together. Pam and I always giggled, anticipating the border crossing, watching Dad try to explain all of Pam's pills and equipment to the Customs officials. I looked forward to singing in the car, playing cards and laughing, listening to Mom read American history out of the travel guide as we cruised through the Southern states. I couldn't wait to eat my fill of Stuckey's Pecan Logs, and to smell that Florida air, the fragrance of sand, pool chlorine, mildew, and exotic greenery.

We weren't there two days when Jeff contracted salmonella poisoning. The local doctors, terrified of his CF, told us to get him the hell back home and into Sick Kids. We tore back, driving for almost forty-eight hours straight except for a pit stop somewhere in Kentucky. My father dumped us in the driveway with an admonition for me to look after Pam and Gregg while and he and my mother took Jeff on to Toronto.

"Crozier said if we hadn't gotten him there when we did, it might have been too late," he confided the next morning.

Jeff came home from the hospital after a few days, but his close call filled me once again with dread. I could not take this in my stride, or the ongoing deaths of other CF children, one by one. I had stopped wanting to hear their names, spoken soft and low in our house after clinic visits, when my mother swallowed hard and got up from the table to make Pam an extra mask, or when I stood outside my sister's closed bedroom door, holding my breath so I could hear her sobs, almost inaudible, excruciatingly private.

Pam was sliding downhill. We could see it in the color of her skin, sheer as white voile, and in the bluish shadows that tinged the base of her fingernails. We could hear it in her cough, deeper, rougher, and more dangerous with each and every breath.

Just looking at her reminded me that I was so powerless, so impotent, so futile, so no good and nothing and bad. I woke up angry and went to sleep the same way.

When it became clear that Dr. L. wasn't getting the desired result, he referred me as an outpatient to the psych clinic at the Brantford General Hospital. There, a young female social worker gave me inkblot tests, and asked me to interpret drawings of empty streets and dark houses. I made up the worst stories I could imagine.

She was not impressed.

"Your parents have it pretty rough with two sick children to look after." "You're a smart girl, you should know better." "You know I can't help you if you don't help yourself." "You've just got to learn to accept."

She was overloaded with cases far worse than mine, kids physically beaten and abused, or drug addicted. I was merely troubled and badly behaved.

I pleaded with her, and my parents, to have family therapy, to no avail. My parents had "too much on their plate to get into all that." They were doing all they could. Pam was coping well, and if the boys were fighting with each other a lot, well, boys would be boys. No, it was up to me to change. If there was a problem it was mine and mine alone, and I had better shape up and fix it. Except for my tantrums, I appeared to be an otherwise capable and self-possessed young woman. It shouldn't be too much to expect me to, in my parents' words, "straighten up and fly right."

My parents must have felt ashamed. It was one thing explaining to Grandma Birdsell that they needed help reining me in. It would have been another thing altogether to have the whole world guess that our family was treading water.

In therapy, they would have had to acknowledge their own anger and its consequences, before looking beyond mine to the fear and sorrow there. They would have had to put their own fears, choices, and behavior under scrutiny, *open up the whole can of worms*, as my mother once said. This would have required a great deal of time, attention, and work that would have to be taken away from some other place, specifically I thought, from Pam. It would also have required that they give up the notion of having everything under control, and perhaps relinquish the assumption of normalcy upon which our life was built. It would, as my mother put it, "just be too much."

Meanwhile, hardly a day went by that my dad didn't raise his voice and yell about something or that my mother didn't cry, and that I didn't feel somehow to blame.

My mother had told me I could talk to her about anything, but when I asked a tentative question about birth control, the conversation escalated into full-scale warfare, and I threatened to run away from home.

"Fine," she shouted, sweeping an armful of clothes from my closet and tossing them out the window into the snowy backyard.

I fled back to Grandma Birdsell's, and then moved in with my friend Patti Oates and her family. After a few days, and a phone call from Pam, I returned home to try again.

"Uncle" Rex, my father's good friend and business associate, had always been nice to me whenever he dropped by the house on a casual visit. Now he suggested I come up to his office to talk things over. I jumped at the chance, hoping finally I had found someone who understood my predicament, who saw and understood my feelings.

Instead, Uncle Rex accused me of driving my parents to the edge of divorce. He said my parents would be able to handle their marital problems just fine if they didn't have to deal with the upset I caused. He told me I was ruining the quality of whatever life Pam had left, and setting a bad example for the boys.

Gregg and Jeff, now aged twelve and seven years, were constantly at one another, but that had always been true. In their own way, they were each just as angry as me, but they just took it out on each other. At a loss as to how to deal with it, my mother usually just told them to move it to the basement.

When Uncle Rex was finished with me, I was finished with him, but held my tears until I was out of his office.

That night my childhood dreams returned, quicksand sucking me down, brains riding through the ocean on the heads of pins, pushing me under. I woke up thinking I'd be better off dead. My family would surely be happier without me around. I could go back and ask Dr. L. to put me on the Valium again. I could go into McClures' woods and swallow the whole bottle all at once. The plan turned like a worm in my brain for weeks, with one niggling drawback. What would it do to Pam if I killed myself?

In my sister's name, I vowed instead to try to change for the better. I kept my room spotless, set the table without being asked, made sure to make curfew. I wore my hair off my face as my mother preferred. On field day I burned my lungs out to stay in first place all the way around the track in the 440-yard race, urging myself on by telling myself that because Pam couldn't run, I'd win for both of us.

I threw myself into new theatre projects, and won a Best Supporting Actress Award at the city High School Drama Festival. I organized a Youtheatre program, and involved myself one way or another in every Brantford Drama League production. More and more it was the emotional outlet I found in the theatre, and the validation I received there, that kept me sane and gave me a sense of myself.

My parents suggested I might like to go away to an all-girl private academy for my senior year of high school. Proud of my accomplishments, and sensitive to my interests, they had looked around and found one in Windsor with an excellent theatre program. I dutifully visited the school with them. My better self knew they wanted me to be happy, but my worst self insisted they wanted to get rid of me. Blaming them was a way to hide my real fear of being away from Pam if she got sick.

On the way home my parents made their best effort to paint a bright picture of what life at boarding school could be, while I simmered tearfully in the backseat. Declaring my feelings appeared pointless. By the time we arrived home I was beyond words. My mother moved around the kitchen with desperate cheer, filling the kettle, pulling milk out of the fridge, preparing to make a much-needed cup of tea. Pam popped in from the den.

"How'd it go?"

"Great. It went great!" replied my father.

The conversation continued beyond me, a babbling white noise. I felt a wild disconnection, the searing pain of invisibility. Next thing I knew, I had picked up the teapot and smashed it to smithereens on the floor. That teapot, stout and sweet and made of good clay, had been the heart of our household for many years. We had celebrated and mourned around it at the kitchen table for as long as I could remember. Crawling on the floor, picking up the sharp, scattered pieces, I felt sick, as if I had murdered, knowing the life I had taken could never be brought back or mended.

Forget the genteel, theatre-oriented boarding school. That careless act brought on momentary talk of a home for wayward girls in Guelph. I begged my parents not to send me away, and renewed with extra fervor my promises to be good. As a peace offering, I spent every penny I had to buy a fancy new porcelain teapot from the best gift shop in town.

"It's pretty," my mother sighed, fingering the slender aristocratic spout, trailing with pink roses, "but it doesn't make tea like the old one."

"I know," I said, stifling tears. There was nothing I could do to make things right.

"I don't understand all this anger," my mother fretted, gently stroking my hair. "Where is it coming from?"

How could she not know? I wondered. *And if she didn't know, how could I ever explain?*

It was not a lack of sympathy or intelligence that prevented my mother from understanding my anger. It was the thousand details of her life, and her own pain, blinding her. With all her tender effort, she drained herself *doing*, so at the end of each day there was precious little left of her *being*.

"Donna, is it any wonder you feel empty," a social worker would one day say to her. "You do too much and it's never enough."

Grampa Birdsell called one frozen, snow-blind February morning, asking if he could take me out for breakfast, and I said no, I was too busy with my theatre friends. I came home to a darkened, empty house in the frosty purple twilight, and knew in my bones something was wrong. My grandfather's death punched a hole in the middle of my mother's thirty-fifth year of life, and created a deep, ineffable sadness in her that I had no way to comfort. I blamed myself, knowing how he got out and pushed his stalled car to the side of the road. If I'd been there, I thought, I wouldn't have let him do that, and he wouldn't have had the heart attack.

Shortly thereafter, Pam went to clinic for a checkup one day and was immediately admitted to Sick Kids, her lungs raging with infection; in doctor's parlance, an "exacerbation of her disease." It came from *Pseudomonas cepacia*, a deadly bacteria prevalent in hospitals, a bacteria that loves the warm, wet lungs of Cystics and refuses to die until it has first killed. Ironically, Pam had likely picked it up on one of her clinic visits. For thirty days, my sister lay tethered to an IV while her life hung in the balance.

As precocious, eloquent, and grown up as I fancied myself, I had no language that could translate what I felt, save shouting and tears. My mother and I became lost, to ourselves, and to each other. Our hearts aching and full of need, we tried to find our way back together in the small, quiet moments of the day, sharing small talk and cups of tea. The Beatles crooned in the background, through the stereo speakers in the den. *Let It Be, Let It Be.* Ray Stevens reminded us that *Everything Was Beautiful, In Its Own Way.* A true Pam song.

On my eighteenth birthday, my mother wrote me a letter, telling me she knew things hadn't always been what I thought they should, but that she and my father had done what they could with love and the best of intentions. She hoped they had passed on values that would stand me in good stead, and that I might someday come to realize they loved me not as an image of themselves, but for myself.

When you look at our small remembrance gift, we hope you will think of us fondly and that the unhappy trying times we experienced together will fade from memory.

So—now you are ready to spread your wings—so with our blessings—fly from the nest. May you find the happiness and inner peace you so desire.

I wanted nothing more than to fly, but the debt I owed my mother's pain held me fast, and my sister's need, and my own guilt, and a tiny voice insisting that if I left home, God might punish me by taking Pam.

I sat with my sister on the front porch, short days after her return from Sick Kids. She had cheated death again.

Her skin was like skim milk washed over her bones. Her lips and nails had once again slowly begun to blush a tentative pink. She had just turned sixteen, but the fatigue in her eyes made her look eighty. She lifted a tender white hand to shield herself from the slanting afternoon sun.

My mother's newly planted petunias bobbed and waved in the breeze. The poplars had exploded festively in green. The fresh days of early summer had arrived. Days of decision, for me.

Would I do what my parents wanted? Stay home to work at Woolco scooping ice cream, and then apply for fall admission to the Theatre Department at the University of Windsor? What with Grandpa dying, and Pam being in the hospital, we had probably missed the deadline. Besides, technically I hadn't really finished high school, having shown up at the wrong time and missed my geography final. I'd probably just fight with Mom and Dad all summer anyway.

"What do you want?" Pam asked. Her old-young eyes pene-trated me with a compassion and understanding that she was hardly grown enough to possess. I felt undeserving, though grateful.

"I want to go up north to Orillia and hang out with the Ontario Youtheatre. I did a lot of work helping to get it started, after all. They wouldn't let me be in the first production, because of my being on the Board and everything, and I'm a little hurt about it, but I'd still like to be there. And then maybe I'd move to Toronto, and see if I can get an apprentice job acting in one of the alternative theatres. Mom already said over her dead body."

"What does your heart tell you?" Pam asked.

Tears pushed up through my chest.

"I don't want to leave you."

"You have to leave some time," my sister told me. "We all have to leave some time."

The Girl in the Tree—
Donna Birdsell, 1950

Mom and Dad, Young and in Love

Big Sister, Little Sister

Heather, Gregg, and Pam

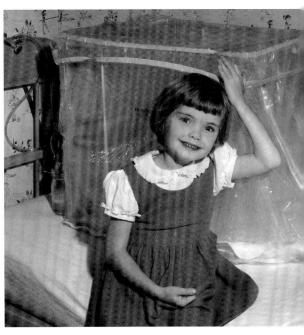

The Ubiquitous 1950s
Pony Picture

Pam Poses for the Brantford Expositor

Family Outing

The Wishing Rock

Pammy at Vicki Young's Birthday Party

Pam and Jeff at Port Dover

mmy, Don't Leave Me

The Girls—
First Day of School, 1965

The Boys—
First Day of School, 1965

The Family, 1966

Pam—
Grade School Graduation, 1968

Pam and Award-Winning Science Project on DNA

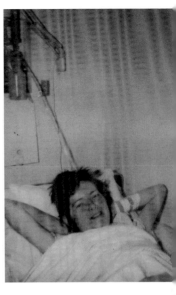

Pam—The Height of 1960s Fashion

Pam and Gregg

Pam at Sick Kids

Bride and Maid of Honor

May 11, 1974

Mom, Pam, and Jeff with Sick Kids Staff

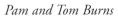

Pam and Tom Burns

Pam and College Roommates

Pam and Gregg at Mom's Graduation from Nursing School

Our Mom the Nurse

The Family, 1975

The Young Actress

Mom and Dad's 25th Anniversary

*Pam's 25th
Birthday Cake*

The Family at Pam's 25th Birthday Party

*Happy at Last:
October 25, 1986*

My Mom and Me

THE RIVER MEETS THE SEA

When Emily is ill there seems to be no sunshine in the world for me. The tie of sister is near and dear indeed, and I think a certain harshness in her powerful and peculiar character only makes me cling to her more...Day by day, when I see with what a front she meets suffering, I look on her with an anguish of wonder and love. I have seen nothing like it; but indeed, I have never seen her parallel in anything. Stronger than a man, simpler than a child, her nature stands alone.

— CHARLOTTE BRONTË

CHAPTER TWELVE

"There came a time when the risk to remain tight in the bud became more painful than the risk to blossom."
— ANAÏS NIN

Writer Toni Morrison says "All water has a perfect memory and is forever trying to get back to where it was."

The Army Corps of Engineers may build dams, dykes, and sluices, may alter flood plains, rerouting the path of water, holding it back in places, controlling the flow. It doesn't matter. The rain comes day after day, and the river rises, flooding its banks, reclaiming its old boundaries.

The rain ends. The waters recede. The river returns to itself. But the river's memory remains, drifting through the currents as real and alive and present as the water in which it flows.

There is no "past tense" in my memory. I taste wild blueberries, I smell the rain, I hear a John Denver song drifting through the aisles at K-mart, and I am there, my heart surging as memory floods its banks. I am inside the moment I remember, and it is just as alive to me as when I first lived it, as tangible as the spoon in my mouth, the damp wind in my face, my hand on the cold metal of the shopping cart. In such unexpected and unsought moments, memory tries to get back to what it knows, reclaims its old boundaries in spite of the dams and dykes I have built to hold it back, defiant of the rerouting of my life.

We may leave the homes we know, the family we love, the friends and lovers who wound us or bathe our wounds. We may try to leave the selves we once were. But we cannot leave memory. Memory lives in our very cells, flows in the water of our flesh, immediate and real, however submerged. It is a fact that our bodies can't tell the difference between memory and present tense. Our bodies react as if the remembered event is happening to us all over again, in that very moment. Adrenalin flows, our heart rate rises, cortisol is released into the bloodstream. That's why it hurts to remember.

If we forget, perhaps memory has made its own choice about what to call forward and what to leave behind. Memory is its own being, holding fast or changing with the years, corrupting and recreating itself. Perhaps it is not in *what* we remember where the truth may be found, but in how we remember.

Memory has a voice, a vocabulary, its own reflective narrative. Epiphany may occur in crisis, but reflection cannot. The reflective voice is useless in the face of calamity, for it is too passive, too intellectual to survive the swirling cauldron of emotion. Whatever reflections I allowed myself as a child made desolate, random appearances in the poetry I wrote, but otherwise that voice was lost. Now I sit by the river, asking memory what it can offer me, moving beyond the vocabulary of crisis and despair, searching for a new voice.

Pam said tell our story. Mother says tell the truth. The story lies somewhere between truth and memory.

The sweetest moments can show themselves suddenly, like bright spots that float before my eyes after the camera's flash, blinding me to my sorrow.

Memories of the joy I know I felt, of maple walnut ice cream and sunshine, and stopping at the Simcoe Dairy on the way to the cottage at Turkey Point are lodged inside the memories of the drowned lady, and the Rescue Game, and Peter Mulder's death.

Memories of tadpole fishing, caterpillar hunts, and croquet games, of backyard Hide and Go Seek played in long, late summer twilights, are stuck in the throat of other memories: my sister's cough shredding the black sheet of night, her mouth an open purple wound, my cries for help echoing down the corridor of time.

The safety of my parents' bed when thunderstorms banged the roof, and the infinite blessing of being carried in my father's arms back to my own room, is swallowed inside the memory of my father pounding his fist on the kitchen counter, *Goddammit,* and my mother's laughter turned to tears.

My mother's busy hands, folding laundry, planting petunias, baking butter tarts. My father whistling a Glen Miller tune, cleaning out the garage, tending steaks on the barbeque. Quiet talks with my sister on the front stoop. My brothers, rolling and tumbling together on the living room rug. Grandpa Birdsell dropping by for Saturday-morning breakfast. Each sweet memory pressed like a leaf inside the memory of a smashed teapot, the frozen earth piled next to my grandfather's grave, and the wreckage swimming in my mother's blue eyes on the day I left home.

The phone booth smelled of pine needles and stale cigarette butts. My mother's voice sent tremors of anxiety through my body and my hand went clammy on the receiver. *Damn, why couldn't Pam have answered the phone?* I had not called home for ten days, since going AWOL, headed for Camp Couchiching and the Ontario Youtheatre Company.

I remained haunted by the image of my sister watching me go, standing in hard silence halfway up the stairs, her face stricken as I faced off with my mother at the front door, pushing, shoving, and screaming.

"Let me go, let me go!"

"You're leaving this house over my dead body!"

"Well then, I guess I'll have to kill you."

I remembered how I had stepped roughly past her onto the front porch, then turned back to face the door, immediately wanting to say, "I'm sorry, I don't want to leave this way." But before I could muster the words, my mother had reached out and grabbed my hand, slapping two twenty-dollar bills into my palm.

"Here," she said bitterly, tears streaming. "It's all I've got."

Then she shut the door in my face.

I ran away to Orillia on a Greyhound bus. It took only a few days before I stubbornly realized that my Youtheatre plans were not going to materialize the way I had imagined.

Now, low on cash and uncertain what came next, I stood chirping with phony bravado into the phone.

"Hi, Mom. It's me."

"Oh. Hello."

Her cool and distant tone cut through me, making me realize that wherever my place was, it wasn't at home, making me forget to apologize about the way I left, or to say that I missed everyone and felt lost and alone.

"It's about time you called," she continued tersely. "You know, your sister's back in the hospital."

My body tingled as if shot through by a thousand pins and needles.

"How long has she been in?"

"A few days."

My heart was pounding now.

"Why didn't you call me? You knew where I was!"

"I didn't think it was necessary. Anyway, you're away doing your own thing. I didn't want to bother you."

I harnessed my tears.

"Well gee, Mom. She was okay two weeks ago. What happened?"

"I don't know, Heather. She just went right down hill after you left."

The lake beyond the phone booth was glassy calm. Lilting voices, piano, and drums emanated from the rehearsal hall nearby. Laughter, somewhere.

"I'm coming home," I said, and hung up.

The Hospital for Sick Children rang with the chaos of life. Emergency was full of tots who had swallowed house cleaner and youngsters who had broken limbs in their quest to climb too far too fast. The cafeteria swarmed with heavy-lidded staff members in white coats juggling trays of runny scrambled eggs and cold coffee.

I stumbled down corridors crowded with tight-faced parents clutching their infants in desperate arms, dodging orderlies whisking children in wheelchairs off to x-ray. The halls were thick and hot with smells of vomit and antiseptic.

Families wept in the chapel while others lined up gratefully at Discharge or sat pensively in the huge, deeply carpeted front lobby, waiting for word from OR and ICU.

I sighed nervously, waiting for an elevator.

"They take forever," a woman said.

When it finally arrived, it was packed with kids, white-faced, hollow-eyed, strapped to gurneys, tethered to IV poles, surrounded by a crush of nurses, doctors, members of the family. I crammed my way on and took the milk run up to 6C, my self-conscious eyes fixed on the floor numbers flashing airless over the door.

I made my way down the yellow hall to the nurses' station, then to Pam's room, poking my head around the door.

"Hi!" Her face lit up. "How ya doin'?"

Pam leaned forward and gave me an awkward hug, being careful of her IV.

"Does it hurt?" I asked, indicating the intravenous. "Whoops, that's a stupid question."

I rolled my eyes. Pam giggled.

Bands of adhesive tape wound around her bruised and swollen left forearm, binding it to a slim, flannel-covered board several inches long. The tape pulled at the downy blonde hair that covered her skin like fine feathers.

"What's the board for?"

"So the needle won't go interstitial."

"What's that?"

"Oh, that's when you're just not careful and you jerk your arm or it gets bumped or something, and the needle slips out of the vein, and the antibiotic drips right into the muscle. You sure know when it happens 'cause it just burns all the way up."

"Does it happen often?"

"More often than I'd like. I don't know what it is about me, but my IVs don't seem to last very long. It went like that on my right arm three days ago." She sighed deeply. "They'll have to come and change this one back again now, but I don't know if they can, 'cause this other arm hasn't quite healed yet."

She turned her right arm up for me to examine. It was puffy, red, and purple. The dried, scarlet pinprick of blood where the needle wounded her was still apparent.

"Sometimes we organize contests to see how long any of us can last before going interstitial," she giggled, "and the winner gets extra cookies or privileges." She regarded her arm thoughtfully for a moment. "Hmm. Maybe next time they can put it in a little farther up."

I wondered how the needle felt resting in her vein, how the tape felt ripping from her arm when they changed the IV.

"It's a real pain trying to eat or brush my hair or anything like that."

Getting Pam dressed or undressed, I soon learned, was a bigger pain. Shirts and nightgowns had to be gently tugged over the IV bag and snaked carefully along the tube leading to the IV'd arm, then up the arm itself, while she poked her head through the neck of the garment and stuffed her opposite arm in the other sleeve. It was a task which took time and patience, often attended by a flood of giggles and a few choice swear words.

"So, what's got you here?"

"The Pseudomonas I picked up in here last spring is acting up again."

"And what's this stuff called that you're on now? Mom told me, but I keep forgetting."

"Carbenocillin. It's supposed to really knock out the Pseudomonas. I'm being a guinea pig. Dr. Crozier said they've run out of drugs that will work on me, so this is an experiment. They've tried it on a handful of kids in England, but I think I'm one of the first to get it here."

"Well now, I don't see any whiskers but you do sort of look like a guinea pig. How does it feel to be one?"

She laughed. "I don't know. If it works, I guess I'll feel pretty good."

We didn't discuss what might happen if the drug didn't work, and we couldn't talk about possible side effects. In those years, clinical trials for new Cystic Fibrosis drugs had to be carried out directly on humans, first, last, and always. Animal models could be created for cancer or diabetes research, but not for CF. Until scientists isolated the CF gene and found ways to create an animal model with it, human testing remained the only option.

"What happened with the Youtheatre?" Pam asked carefully, changing the subject.

"It's a long story."

She defied my answer with a hard stare. I answered her testily.

"I didn't quit because you got sick, if that's what you're asking."

"I didn't get sick because you left, if that's what you're wondering."

Pam closed her eyes. I couldn't tell if she was resting or shutting me out.

A trickle of sweat rolled down between my breasts. The hospital lacked air conditioning. The window gaped, useless, the steaming city outside was breathless and still. A plump, olive-skinned woman wearing a green smock waddled into the room and ran a mop across the floor. She smiled and nodded. The sharp smell of disinfectant stung the air. Moaning sounds floated across the hall.

Pam opened her eyes slowly. "That kid's dying," she said flatly. "I wish they'd close his door."

"Want me to speak to a nurse?"

"Nah. They've got to leave the doors open to get some cross-ventilation. I already asked."

We sat in awkward silence.

"Well, I guess I'd better go and let you get some rest. I'll come back tonight for a couple of hours after dinner if you'd like."

"That would be nice, but you know you don't have to."

"I know."

"Well then, you know the routine. They send the dinner trays up around five-thirty, and around eight I get my mask and treatment."

"I'll be here in time to have a cup of tea with you, and you can tell the physio I'll stay after that and do your treatment."

"Thanks. She'll like that."

I kissed Pam good-bye and walked to the elevator, the taste of her salty skin on my lips. Swinging past the room where the child was dying, I tried not to look. This was the cancer ward, and most of the kids were terminal. Many were bloated beyond recognition, others so frail that their red arteries and bright blue veins almost bled through their skin, transparent as butterfly wings. They lay on their beds, bald, bruised, moonfaced, listless, gasping for wisps of the hot, smelly air. Grief hung like cobwebs in the dim hallway.

Cystics did not yet have their own ward for chronic care. There were still too few of them who lived long enough to warrant it, Pam told me dispassionately.

For six weeks that summer, I visited Pam every day on my way home from the job I eventually landed as a clerk-typist for Pitney Bowes. Frequently, I returned to see her again after I'd gone home for dinner. Scared and lonely, Pam thought I was offering her comfort, but I was also taking it. On my own in the big city, I was scared and lonely too.

After coming home from the Youtheatre, I had cashed in the $300 savings bond from my high school earnings at Woolco, and with my parents' help and tacit blessing, moved to Toronto. I moved in with a group of other rebellious girls at Rosary Hall, a residence ran by the Order of Grey Nuns, a place chosen because our Catholic neighbors assured my parents I would be safe there. Forced to reject the unpaid apprenticeships offered to me following auditions for several alternative theatres, I opted instead for a paycheck from Pitney Bowes.

Pam and I put up a brave front for each other. I affected cheer while Pam tried to appear sanguine. We passed most of the time in idle chat about movies we wanted to see, fabric she wanted to buy, clothes she wanted to sew. The distance my anger had put between us began to close. We mimicked the doctors to each other, made light of the privations of the hospital, told each other morbid jokes, and laughed. We laughed a lot. Other times we just sat, listening to CHFI on her bedside radio. "Raindrops Keep Fallin' on My Head," "The Long and Winding Road," "Cracklin' Rosie."

The silence between us was sweet.

"Gawd," I joked with her. "I think I'm actually getting to like Neil Diamond."

"Uh oh," she smiled. "So, how's work?"

"Blah."

"Maybe you can save up some money and audition for the National Theatre School in Montreal like you wanted to, or that one in England."

"R.A.D.A."

"Yah."

I chose not to tell her that I could have done that anyway, that Mom and Dad offered to help me become an actress, but I'd thrown away my applications to those schools. I couldn't do in Montreal or England what I could do in Toronto. I couldn't be close to Pam.

"Yah, well, we'll see. It'll take a while to save that kind of money."

My sister challenged me with her gaze.

"You're not giving up the way you gave up ballet school, are you?"

"Man, it's hot in here."

"Heth, I know you gave up ballet school because of me. You can't do that to yourself again. You can't do it to me. You need to follow your own dreams and not worry about me."

"How can I not worry about you?"

"Well, all right then, worry about me if you have to, but don't stop doing what you want just because I'm sick. That's not going to help me get better."

"But I want to be around to support you."

"Fine. You can phone me, you can write. We'll see each other on holidays. Mom and Dad take good care of me. Anyway, now that I'm on this new drug, Dr. Crozier said I'll probably be in good shape for quite a long while."

The intercom blared, paging a doctor on call. Footsteps passed by quickly in the hall and then faded. Pam stared at me, wanting to make sure I'd gotten the message.

"Well, in any case," I replied, "no matter what I decide to do, I hope things will be better at home now that I'm not there anymore."

Pam smirked and rolled her eyes. "Not everything that happens at home is your fault, you know."

At night when it was time for me to go, I pulled my chair up close to her bed and for a long moment we held hands tightly, looking straight into each other's eyes and fighting back the tears. Then I withdrew as cheerily as I arrived, laughing through the lump in my throat. Pam smiled and waved, but often as I rounded the door, I caught her out of the corner of my eye, burying her face in the pillow.

My parents visited through the week as time permitted, but usually in the morning, so I only saw them there on weekends when I popped in to say a quick hello.

Neither Pam nor I saw much of the boys. Gregg was thirteen, into popping wheelies on a bike with a banana seat, and Jeff, who was eight, wanted to be just like him.

"I hate bringing them down and putting them through all this," my mother told us, "and besides, they're both going away to camp for two weeks. Pam will probably be out by the time they get home."

The seeds of distance between my brothers and me had already been planted, by my teenage anger, by my leaving home, and by the bond I had with Pam, though I was unaware of it then. I could not have begun to imagine how badly that distance would come to wound me through the far-off years after Pam's death.

When my sister was finally released from hospital in August, I went up to help her pack.

"I guess if you don't get home this weekend," she said, "I'll see you back here in about two weeks."

"How come?"

My sister did not look at me, but busied herself folding pajamas. "I have to come back for heart clinic. Dr. Crozier said I have heart damage."

"What?"

"From the carbenocillin."

My stomach dropped and my brain worked dumbly to filter news it did not want to hear.

"It's a side effect they didn't really know about until now. Congestive heart failure, it's called. My heart was already enlarged anyway, from before I was diagnosed with CF. Remember Dr. Matthews told us that when I first went down to Cleveland? I guess the carbenocillin just made the problem a little bit worse. I have to come down to heart clinic on a regular basis from now on. But my lungs are in beautiful shape." She smiled gamely.

"Well, geez, is this damage permanent or can they fix it…?"

"No, there's not much they can do. They've put me on something called digoxin. The real annoying thing was now we have to make two separate trips down here every six weeks."

"Can't you do both clinics the same day?"

"Nope."

"Shit."

Pam methodically began to empty her nightstand, wearing the same steely aura I remembered after Peter Mulder and Esther Anderson died.

"Listen, don't wait for Mom and Dad to get here. You've

probably got stuff to do and we'll be a while getting through Discharge and waiting for my meds at the pharmacy."

I wrapped my arms around her, wanting to hug extra life into her body, wanting my love to heal her heart, wanting to cry, but knowing she would have none of that. I kissed her lightly on the forehead.

"I'll come home this weekend, then."

"Oh, that would be fun. Maybe I can get Dad to buy some steaks and we'll have a barbeque."

Pam walked me to the elevator and stood waving as the doors closed in front of me. I took a few deep breaths, gritted my teeth against the sting of tears, and empty-hearted, rode the subway back to Rosary Hall.

⌒

Once back at home, Pam wrote to me. She missed me, she said, as did the rest of the family. She remembered a lot of when we were little at the house on Brier Crescent. *They sure were good times...* Dr. Crozier had changed her drugs and she felt better. School was harder this year, but more fun.

Her letters, her voice on the phone, lured me. And my mother's words, echoing through a grimy receiver in a lonely phone booth, all the way down the long, aching summer into fall and winter. *She just went right downhill after you left.*

Most weekends I wore out the railway tracks between Toronto and home. I boarded the train, going over in my mind how I would behave when I got home, how good and grownup I would be, how nurturing and sweet. The snowy farms and forests tumbled past as the train hurtled me away from Toronto and my precious independence. *I'll Be There,* I sang the words of the Jackson 5 to myself, *I'll be there...* The sky grew dark, the farmhouse lights burned bright, and the knot in my stomach squeezed tight. My heart throbbed.

"Brantford, next stop!"

My defenses shot up like a Roman candle the minute my foot hit the platform. They flared in the car as my parents politely asked how my week went, then flashed on and off like heat lightning through most of the next forty-eight hours, until the inevitable storm broke Sunday night in all its fury.

"Goddammit," I screamed as my brothers ran for cover and my sister slunk to her room, stony and sad. "I just can't come home, can I?"

The trouble was, I couldn't stay away.

CHAPTER THIRTEEN

"The question is not whether we will die,
but how we shall live." — JOAN BORYSENKO

For many years my parents dreamed of buying the old Charlton farm out on Highway 24 and turning the big stone manse into a steakhouse. After church on Sundays, we liked to drive out past the place and engage in a lively exchange of pie-in-the-sky ideas about it. So in the spring of 1971, when a For Sale sign went up on a thirty-acre stand of trees down the highway from the farm, my parents bought it, deciding they would subdivide it into estate lots, where Dad would build and sell luxury homes. Summerhayes Industries was in danger of going the way of Summerhayes Lumber, and if that happened, my father would need some way to make a living.

The land was ten miles north of Brantford city limits. Alone. Apart. Too far to run back out and get the quart of milk Dad forgot to bring home. Too far for Pam or Gregg's after-school chums to pop in, or to transport a babysitter for Jeff. A long way for a visiting nurse to come, or an ambulance if needed. Neither friends nor family would be likely to just drop by and say hello. Yet my father insisted he could make a killing on the property. He might be past forty and hadn't made his million yet, but with a little luck and a lot of hard work, perhaps he could still show his mother and brothers, all of Brantford, and the world that he could succeed.

"It will be a fresh start," my mother incanted.

This would be our fifth move in eighteen years. My mother justified it by reminding me of the money they'd made on the sale of each house. "And God knows with the cost of your sister's illness, we've needed it."

Still, I couldn't help but wonder if this frequent uprooting of our family would eventually take its toll. Looking back now, it's almost as if we were acting out the underlying theme of our life: impermanence, an ongoing cycle of construction and destruction. Or as if we were acting out the superstition that changing our dwelling could change our destiny. I can remember wondering, if we were going to move anywhere again, why not Toronto, where Pam would be closer to Sick Kids, and the whole family closer to me?

Out of the tiny wilderness of maple, oak, poplar, and pine, my family carved a place to build their new house. My father sweated over burning piles of brush that he had torn from the earth with hard, gloved hands. He sliced his chainsaw through saplings and thick, aged trunks, bulldozing the amputated stumps and roots into grisly mounds that he set aflame.

The boys, too, chopped and tractored and pulled and burned. Jeff was a pale, wiry nine year old. Except for his build, you would have hardly known he had CF. He grew more like his father in trait and temperament with each passing day. Like his father, he'd grow up dreaming brilliant dreams, implementing fatally flawed plans, laying out tremendous energy, and often ending up bitterly disappointed by the result.

Gregg was almost fifteen, sturdy, with a smattering of freckles across his nose, a charming, crooked smile, piercing blue eyes, and a head full of bristled, brown curls. He was polite and well behaved, still my mother's "good boy," though quietly jealous of the kinship between his brother and his father. And his envy grew, in spite of, or because of, his understanding that Dad made exceptions for Jeff because he had CF. What father wouldn't, if he knew his baby boy could die? Caught between resentment and guilt, Gregg had his share of nightmares. Pam told me how often they found him standing on his bed in the dark of night, flailing in his sleep, shouting at the wall that he was boxed in.

As spring warmed into summer, my father raised the skeleton of the house, hammered down the roof, and nailed up the dry-wall. He hired Nick, and Joe Chato, who used to work with him at the lumberyard, to come and help. Mom drove Pam and me out to the site on my weekend visits. We brought marshmallows and speared them on twigs, roasting them in the flames of the burning brush-piles, giggling, pretending we were little again.

The birds threw up a racket in the elderberry bushes. Pam watched the men work, Dad in his overalls, never so happy as when he was building something. I watched Pam. The grey ash of the end of day curled up and drifted skyward. We stood together, watching, as our father built the place where Pam would die.

My mother had a hysterectomy that winter, at the age of only thirty-eight. She also suffered from sleeplessness, depression, and a lack of concentration, at best feeling overwhelmed and "not quite herself" as she mildly put it. She viewed all this as a personal failure to cope, rather than the physical toll of stress and the consequences of her surgery. Within weeks of my mother's operation, Pam was in and out of Sick Kids for what Dr. Crozier called a "clean-out," a big push of IV antibiotics to quell the relentless Pseudomonas.

Meanwhile, I tramped around Toronto through a January thaw in leaky boots, racing on cold wet feet from Pitney Bowes to Sick Kids and then, having taken my sister's advice to heart, attending evening rehearsals for *The Insect Play* at University of Toronto's Hart House Theatre.

"I'm playing the Chrysalis," I explained to Pam animatedly at her hospital bedside. "That's the stage in an insect's life when it forms a sheath and changes inside from a grub to an adult, and becomes a beautiful butterfly."

"Typecasting," she laughed.

The *Globe and Mail* reviewed my performance. *Miss Summerhaze*, the critic said, misspelling my name, *was at times poignant.*

On closing night the play's director told me I should audition for a new acting school at Ryerson College, right there in Toronto, which hoped to rival the great theatre schools around the world. He was going to teach there, and would give me a positive recommendation.

I was exhilarated, and terrified. Pam encouraged me on the telephone, and on my visits home.

"Maybe they'll say no to you," she said repeatedly, "but if you don't even try, you'll be saying no to yourself."

As the deadline for applications grew closer, my father visited me in Toronto, to "have a talk." We sipped tea in the sparsely furnished living room of the tiny third floor walk-up I'd moved into with three friends from Rosary Hall.

"I can see you're torturing yourself over this. What are you afraid of?"

"Making the wrong decision."

"I don't understand how you can make a wrong decision. Does this have anything to do with Pam?"

I felt harpooned.

"Sweetheart, if Pam thought you were holding yourself back on her account, she'd be very angry."

"I know, but I can't help it. Ever since she got sick last year, I feel bad going ahead with my own life."

"Listen to me. If you're concerned that Pam won't get the chance to do certain things, then why don't you do some of those things on your own and make her proud? She always got such a kick out of seeing you perform in those plays you did in the backyard, and the ones you did in high school. She wants to see your dreams come true almost as much as you do."

"But what if I don't get in? Then I'll be letting her down!"

"Honey, you'll be letting her down if you don't try, and more important you'll be letting yourself down. Look, any decision is better than indecision. Why not just take it a step at a time? All you have to do right now is decide whether or not you want to try out for Ryerson."

"I do."

"Well then, go ahead and try out and do the best you can. After that you'll make your next decision based on the outcome."

I auditioned and ended up one of thirty-five accepted from a field of several hundred. When I showed her the letter, Pam scrunched her fists up over her grin, in a state of utter glee.

"See?" she laughed, very pleased with herself. "I told you!"

The summer before my senior year of high school, my boyfriend Sandy had dumped me for a Barbie doll with big breasts and a country club membership. Thereupon had followed a brief, highly charged, and deeply felt flirtation with a young man named Jeff, who played guitar, sang Bob Dylan songs, and wrote poems full of love and longing. Although I gave myself a library education on the art of keeping a kosher home, the fact that I was not Jewish made our union impossible. So I asked Jerry Jellis to a Sadie Hawkins dance.

At first he turned me down. "I don't want to get involved with you. You're never happy unless you're in a state of turmoil."

Nevertheless.

Jerry had the rugged physique of a football player, with curly blond hair that formed a wild halo over piercing blue eyes and strong, chiseled features. My little brother Jeff nicknamed him "The Strong Man of the Apes." I learned from Jerry how to make a B.L.T., how to peel an orange by quartering just the skin, and how not to compare myself to *Playboy* centerfolds.

"They're all airbrushed," he told me.

I lost my virginity to Jerry in the spring of 1970, somewhere around my grandfather's death, Pam's near-death, and my eighteenth birthday, in a tiny bedroom on a rainy night while Jer's grandmother was out bowling. Our relationship lurched onward from that point, while I discovered that Jerry lived in his own state of turmoil.

"You can't love someone enough for the both of you," Jerry's mother cautioned me, but I persisted.

While Pam was in and out of hospital, and I worked at Pitney Bowes, Jer labored toward his BA at the University of Toronto.

By the time I started theatre school, his sisters were teasing me about marriage.

But there was a young man in my class at Ryerson. He was tall and slender, with long straw-colored hair and soulful green eyes.

"You need to lighten up," the young man told me, tucking a strand of my hair gently behind my ear. Everyone said that, but no one lightened me. Except him.

He adored the Doobie Brothers, and had long, elegant fingers that made fast love to pianos. He drank Canadian Club and Coke, danced with disarming grace, and wore only black. His lips formed a rosy, infinitely kissable pout. He was goofy and sensual and gifted and untried.

"Go with the flow," he always said, a phrase I would eventually come to loathe, but not before the two years I lived with him in secret, typing his résumés, helping him choose audition speeches and making his appointments, vehemently insisting that he couldn't give up acting to play in a rock band or sell fireplaces because his talent deserved better. Not before the other years it would take for *Do you believe in magic?* to become *Oh yes, I'm the great Pretender,* and finally, *If only you'd believe like I believe…*

His name was Rick McMillan, and I would marry him.

~

As I was falling in love, Pam was falling deep into depression. I didn't realize it at first, thinking she was just being moody, indulging in a little healthy teenage rebellion.

"I think it's more than that," warned my mother in one of our semi-weekly phone chats, "but if that's all it is, she'll have to find another way to rebel, because she's lost too much weight, and her cough is horrendous. At this rate she's going to wind up back in the hospital and there won't be much anyone can do."

Pam had been in twice already that year, but for less than a week each time, so I had not been overly alarmed.

"How long has this been going on?"

"Well, if I really go back to the beginning, I guess she hasn't been herself since she got out of the hospital back in 1970."

"Mom, that's almost two years ago! How is it possible I've never noticed anything?"

"She pretty much pulls herself together when you come home, but the minute you're out the door she disappears right back into her room, puts on her housecoat again, and that's that."

"How come you never said anything to me 'til now?"

"At first I thought if we just gave her enough space and time, she'd grow out of it, but I must say she's really gone farther downhill since you started Ryerson."

At home for the holidays, I thought I'd try to straighten my sister out.

Pam glared at me through narrow, furious eyes. We sat alone together in the dark front parlor on Christmas night, our faces lit only by the colored bulbs on the tree.

The entire vacation had not gone well. I had sparred continuously with my father over wanting to leave my roommates and move out into my own apartment. My mother had tried to decorate, bake, and please everyone to perfection, exhaustion, and tears. Pam had spent most of her time hiding out in her room behind closed doors, or sitting glumly on the couch in her housecoat. Gregg, who had just begun high school, spent hours on the new snowmobile, staying as far away from the house as he could for as long as possible, Jeff tagging along in his wake.

Christmas Day at Grandma Bill's house was its usual trying, pronouncement-laced celebration. By the end of the day we were all testy, and tempers had flared.

"Maybe I shouldn't have come home," I blubbered to Pam. "Christmas got ruined, and it's all my fault."

"Oh for heaven's sake," Pam said, disgusted. "Christmas wasn't ruined. Why do you always automatically think anything bad that happens around here is because of you? Stuff goes on when you're not around, you know."

"Like what?"

She looked away and crossed her arms over her chest.

"Look," I said, "I know what happens around here…"

"How would you know?" she cut me off. "You don't live here anymore and you hardly ever come home since you started Ryerson."

"I visit as much as I can, and God knows I phone ten times a week."

"It's not the same. You don't know what it's like since you left."

"Why don't you tell me?"

Pam looked at me uncertainly. She cocked her head and listened to the sounds coming through the wall from the next room, the low hum of the television, canned laughter, the clink of teacups, Dad clearing his throat and blowing his nose.

"C'mon Pam," I prodded gently. "Tell me."

"It's lonely, that's what," she began to sob. "We live so far out of town it's a pain to go to anyone's house after school, or invite anyone over here. I have to be driven all that way and then picked up, or they do, so there's no one around I can talk to or laugh with."

"What about Mom? You always used to talk and laugh with her."

"It's not the same. Mom's always upset, and she and Dad fight all the time."

"What about?"

"Money. They're in trouble trying to develop these estate homes out here."

"Okay, so Mom and Dad aren't getting along. What else is new? And I understand that you're lonely, but that isn't reason enough to start copping out on your treatments and flushing your meds down the toilet!"

Her eyes flashed green lightning. "Who told you?"

"C'mon Pam, who do you think?"

My sister's jaw jutted forward as she looked away. "There's no point," she said.

"No point to what?"

She turned on me, snapping like a dog I'd been teasing. "How would you like it if you were sick all the time, and you kept doing your treatments and taking your pills and it never amounted to anything, you never got any better, and it was getting harder and harder just to stay at the level you are at?"

"I wouldn't."

"Exactly. And anyway, if I don't take my mask now and then or I miss a treatment, it's because I've got better things to do. Just once I'd like to go out to a dance or to a movie with my friends and not have to miss half the fun because of my stupid treatments."

"But you'll get sick doing that. Anyway, that's just an excuse, because Mom said you're not going out and doing things, you're just sitting around moping."

"So what? I'm tired of being a good girl and just doing what I'm told. It's my life, and if I want to mope, I'll mope!"

The way she said mope made me laugh. Pam gave me a sharp look, but I couldn't help myself.

"If I want to mope, I'll mope," I mimicked her. She tried not to smile, but her smile spread and turned to a faint giggle before despair returned to her face. We both sighed deeply.

"I miss you," she said, weeping softly.

"I miss you, too."

"I know you're having a good time with school and becoming an actress and all that, and you come home and go on and on about it, and most of the time I'm excited to hear it but…" Her lips pouted and quivered as she fought to hold back the flood of tears.

"But what?"

"I don't begrudge you any of it, but sometimes it hurts me, and I just wonder if I'll ever get out of this house, if I'll ever get to go to college or have a boyfriend or live on my own. And everyone around here just seems so unhappy right now, and there's nothing I can do about it. I feel like I'm fighting a losing battle."

My sister stared at me through glistening, agate eyes. Her chest heaved up and down, wheezing with each breath while the platitudes I had been saving dried up in my head.

Pam was all I could think of on the train ride back to Toronto. Outside the window, farmhouses flew past in the night as my thoughts churned to the rumbling of the train. Perhaps my absence from home had created a vacuum into which Pam's anger had finally been allowed to emerge. How difficult must it have been for Pam all those years, feeling she wasn't allowed to be angry while I huffed and I puffed and I blew the house down? How painful was it, having to be the sweet little angel when all you wanted to do was smash something?

My anger had certainly caused its share of damage, but Pam's anger was more lethal, because she was turning it in on herself, with consequences to her own well-being.

Pam was never far from my mind as I settled into my new, very own apartment early in the New Year. With my parents' help, I had chosen a furnished studio with a kitchenette on the ground floor of a tree-shaded Victorian stone house on Bernard Avenue in Toronto. Within a week of moving in I received a housewarming gift from Jeff, a handmade macramé to hang over the stove. Aware of my penchant for walking out the door and absent-mindedly leaving the stove element on HI, he had printed "DON'T FORGET TO TURN OFF THE HEAT" on a piece of paper and pinned it to the plaited brown hemp. I smiled at my ten-year-old brother's concern.

A few nights later, smug and cozy, I snuggled down on my couch to watch a made-for-TV movie. The story concerned a troubled young woman who ran away from home, leaving a younger sister behind to deal with her well-meaning but demanding parents. By the end of the movie, after everyone in the family had gone through hell and back, the parents came to better understand the needs and motivations of their insurgent daughter, while the young woman finally figured out that her parents loved her more than she gave them credit for.

I saw for the first time the hole my own absence had left in my family. I also realized that my sister wrongly blamed herself for the turmoil between my parents and me, and for my leaving home.

I leapt bawling from the couch and dialed my parents' number. The line was busy. As soon as I hung up, my phone rang. It was Pammy.

"I don't believe it. I just tried to call you, because I saw this movie."

"We saw it too! That's why I'm calling." Her laugh bubbled through the phone, though I could tell she'd been crying.

"I'm sorry," I blubbered. "I never understood. I thought you all just wanted me out of there, that you'd all be happier without me."

"Well, we're not happier. We miss you, all of us. I thought you left because of me," she said, breaking down in tears again, "because of my being sick and all the trouble it's caused."

By the time I hung up the phone, I had spoken to my mother and father, and even the boys. We exchanged heartfelt apologies and soothing words. We told each other how much we loved one another.

I went to bed thinking I'd arrived at a new place of *complete* clarity. But clarity can be fleeting, and life must teach us the same lessons again and again.

Half of my visits home were warm and sweet, and the other half still ended badly. Pam disappeared quietly to her room and shut the door, spilling tears onto her pillow. The boys split for the back woods. The whole family was sullen and exhausted as I left to catch the train. Two hours later, apologies were made and love earnestly professed by all over the phone.

During the week, Rick actively courted me, squandering his student loan to spoil me with lunches and dinners, and taking me dancing. I saved the plastic twizzlers and paper umbrellas from my Singapore Slings as souvenirs of our romance, soaking up his attention like watercolor on paper.

I was thriving in my acting classes, I was in love, and I danced to the radio in my tiny kitchen singing along with Three Dog Night, "Joy to the World." But at the end of the day my joy felt like a sharp reproach to my life as Pam's sister. I paid for it in nightmares, frequently dreaming that a stranger was coming through my window with a knife.

I wanted my dreams to lead me away from death. I wanted my life to be larger than the one Pam's disease had us trapped in. I wanted to be calm and wise, strong and fearless, gifted and famous enough to have the power to wave a magic wand over life, the way famous people seem to do. I wanted to be able to save my family from their pain and sorrow, not add to it, and I wanted to do it all NOW.

I couldn't take all the time I needed to grow up. My sister was dying.

CHAPTER FOURTEEN

"Dreams are made if people only try. I believe in miracles…
I have to…because somewhere the hurting must stop."
— TERRY FOX

Mist rises from the glossy waters of the Hudson River on a steamy August morning. I am here to see it. A wife, a grandmother, a daughter of aging parents. A surviving sister.

I read the words of the ancient poet, Rumi:

The morning wind spreads its fresh smell.
We must get up and take that in,
that wind that lets us live.
Breathe before it's gone.

I am here, living and breathing. I am here eating blueberry pie, sipping iced tea, and for a moment it feels sinful to be so alive. Until I remind myself that this is how Pam would want me to feel. She would want me to revel in the warmth of the sun, the taste of her favorite dessert, and even the sultry humidity that once made it so hard for her to breathe. She would want me to live and grow in all the ways she imagined I could. To live for myself, not for her. Yet I still can't help being aware that I am living a life Pam never got to live.

So I try to never take my life for granted, to live consciously, holding nothing back. Yet there are moments when I'm frozen in fear. Fear of not getting this life right. Fear of not holding it precious enough. Fear of failing Pam.

What would Pam say to that, if she was here? She would purse her lips and roll her eyes and look at me in mock disgust. Then she would laugh. She would tell me for the millionth time that the only failure is in not trying. She would remind me not to give up. She would say it's silly for me to feel this way—she wouldn't have lived the life I'm living anyway, because this life is mine. Her eyes would sparkle with compassion as deep as the river before me, and she would touch her hand gently to my cheek.

One has no time to reflect in a crisis. So, as much as we grow through the day-to-day trials and challenges that life presents, a lot of growing up, it seems to me, takes place in the aftermath, sitting by the river, in reflection. This wrestling with my feelings never ends, but that's good, because it means I'm fully human and alive. I am healing. I sit alone by the river, where it meets the sea, listening to my heart, communing with God. The morning wind spreads its fresh smell...

I couldn't have been more proud when Pam turned eighteen.

"Old age, for a Cystic," she joked.

She was among a handful of teenagers that we considered living miracles. Patty Murphy and Darlene Bunyan, Pam's close friends from her young days at Crippled Children's Camp, were among them.

It was 1972. My sister had reached what would be her full height, five feet, three inches, and weighed a robust, for her, 85 pounds. Though still fighting despair and occasionally skipping her meds and treatments, she had begun meeting with

Bernadette Ferry, a social worker at the CF clinic. Bernadette, she told me, was helping her sort through her feelings.

"It might be a good idea for you to talk to someone too," Pam suggested. Memories of high school and seeing Dr. L. made me cringe.

Her plans to get a summer job evaporated with her checkup in late May. Dr. Crozier wanted her in for at least ten days. She had her first bronchoscope. The doctors stuck a tube down her throat without anesthetic and scraped away at her lungs.

We'd been warned of all the possible complications. Excessive bleeding, infection, injury, heart rhythm disturbances, any of which could be life-threatening.

I couldn't be there during her surgery, for I had gotten a full-time summer job as a receptionist at the Actor's Equity Association, but I bolted from work and hightailed it to the hospital the second the clock hit five.

Pam sported dark circles under her eyes and her voice was raspy. My mother's eyes bore the hollow, red-rimmed stare of someone who hadn't slept all night, then had been up at dawn to drive from Brantford to pace her daughter's tiny, empty hospital room, praying.

"I can't talk much," Pam croaked, "my throat's really sore."

"That's okay," I said, kissing her cheek, "you know I can talk enough for the both of us."

"Well listen," said Mom, "now that Heather's here, I'll leave you two girls to yourselves and get back home to Dad and the boys."

She gently brushed back Pam's sweaty bangs and planted a soft kiss on her forehead. Pam grabbed my mother's hand and stared up into her face, managing a small, grateful smile.

I walked my mother to the elevator. We fell into step together, our rhythm identical. At five feet, seven inches, my mother stood two inches taller than me. I was a size six; she was a size twelve. Her hair was short and curly. Mine was long, and pulled back straight into a ponytail. I saw the world in 20/20 vision while my mother wore glasses, but my face was a younger version of hers, my eyes were just as blue, and in our mannerisms, the harmony of our stride, and the timbre of our voices, there was no mistaking that I was her daughter.

Perhaps it was because we were so much alike, not only in trait but in temperament, that we were often at odds with each other. Perhaps that was why I had to work so hard at rejecting my mother in order to become myself. If it weren't for Pam, I thought, we might be closer. If it weren't for Pam, we might never be close.

"She's in more pain than she's letting on," my mother told me. "None of us can really know how hard this was on her. They gave her a local so she wouldn't choke on the tube, but she was awake for the whole thing. Normally they put them right under, but in her case they were afraid they might lose her because the anesthesia would have repressed her breathing and slowed down her heart."

My mother lost her brave front for a moment, and tears glistened in her eyes. "I honestly don't know how she got through it."

I reached out and embraced my mother fully. She leaned toward me slightly, chuckling self-consciously, holding her purse between us while patting me on the back with one arm.

"I'll try to get back up tomorrow," she said, "but if not, I'll be here the next day."

"Don't you worry," I instructed her. "I'll call you later and let you know how she's doing."

"You know," she said, "it's really good for her that you're here."

My mother stepped into the elevator and smiled gamely as the doors closed. I knew it was good for my mother that I was here too, and it pleased me to know she felt she could count on me. I knew she would hold herself together now, at least until she got home and made a pot of tea. Then, with my father sitting next to her at the kitchen table, sighing, and the boys having fled outside, she would let go and have a long, hard cry.

I hurried back to Pam's room and sat up on the bed with her, holding her hand. Her breath was shallow and raspy, her eyes mossy and moist. Just trying to imagine her pain made my own lungs burn. The soft rock of CHFI drifted from the radio. "Lean On Me." The hospital world bustled outside her door. I looked in her eyes and she gazed back into mine. No words were needed. She was still here, and I was with her.

Later that summer, Pam packed up her pills, her mask, and a newfangled machine called a Percussor, ready to head off to camp. The Percussor gave her new freedom and the opportunity for cherished independence, for it was mechanically able to pound her chest, replacing the need for hands-on treatment.

The camp, called Teen Ranch, was not for "crippled children" like the one she had gone to before, but a place for "normal" kids that taught horseback riding, with an emphasis on spiritual ethics. Pam had attended the camp the previous summer and learned how to ride and muck out a stall. I could only imagine her in the barn, trying to hold her breath against the smell of manure, coughing, but patient and fastidious in her task. She had revisited and deepened her relationship with God at this camp. This time, she took Jeff with her.

"He'll love the horses, of course," she said one night before she left. We were sitting out in the screened porch, sharing a pot of tea and a plate of butter tarts after her mask. "But I want him to learn what I started to learn there last year."

"And what did you learn?"

"Now don't think I've gone all born again and religious," she winked, "but I've discovered that as I search for a deeper truth in God, I'm finding an even deeper truth in myself. It's giving me back my confidence."

She paused for a moment to see if I was taking in what she was saying, then went on.

"Teen Ranch taught me that attitudes can create a ripple effect. So I've decided I want to make some waves," she giggled, "the kind that will help others find a good attitude, even while they're having problems. So for instance, that means if I view doing my treatments as beneficial to me instead of hating them, I can set an example for younger kids with CF when I'm in the hospital, and I can make a difference that way."

We all went to Teen Ranch Rodeo. Pam grinned widely from her horse as the campers and counselors paraded past. Jeff's skill at barrel racing and steer roping turned out to be nothing short of amazing. Watching him, understanding how huge an accomplishment this was for both of them, Rick and I were somewhere between tears and laugher, hooting and whistling, clapping, and hugging each other.

Later, Pam dragged me into the barn to show me how she could curry a horse. Wheezing and panting, she stroked the horse's flanks with the greatest of care, murmuring softly to the animal. The dust of the barn made her cough, but she grabbed a heavy shovel with her spindle arms, chucked horse manure, and then in her fastidious, patient manner, spread fresh straw.

Pam had just graduated from Grade Twelve. With her remarkable sewing skills and her love of textiles, she had long dreamed of a career designing and manufacturing clothing, but Dr. Crozier and the CF clinic staff succeeded in discouraging this ambition, citing the lint she would be exposed to and forced to breathe in such a working environment. After coming home from Teen

Ranch, she decided instead to work with young children and "use whatever time and energy I have to make a difference."

There was that phrase again. Make a difference. It was all she wanted to do, and it did not seem such an impossible dream.

She made application to the Province of Ontario for a Rehabilitation Grant, to finance two years of college in an early childhood education program. Such grants were routinely given to "handicapped" persons to continue their education.

The Rehab Board turned her down.

"We can read between the lines," said my mother. She handed me the curt and formal letter from the province, and as I read, she squeezed the life out of a dishrag and wiped the counter furiously. "The government doesn't think Pam will live long enough to make it worth spending the money on her," she complained.

Pam and I sat at the kitchen table, glumly nursing cups of tea while my mother attacked the kitchen and Rick attacked the new organ in the living room.

"I spoke to a woman on the Board. She said they think Pam should simply stay home and, as they put it, enjoy whatever time she's got left. They suggested she might apply for disability insurance."

"So what are you going to do?" I asked my sister.

Pam shrugged and pursed her lips. "Jane Nixon wants me to go into Grade Thirteen with her at Paris District High in the fall. She said we'll have a blast. She wants me to join Pub Club with her. She said a few beers now and then will put a couple of pounds on me for sure." My sister smiled self-consciously.

"Miss Goody Two-Shoes drinking beer?" I teased.

"Yeah, well, I can work on my marks a bit, and then maybe I can reapply for the rehab grant again next spring. Who knows, maybe I'll be in better shape by then, or the people on the Board will have changed. And anyway, Jane wants me to help work in the election!"

Trudeaumania was on the rise, the Liberal Party on the march, and Jane's father was running for office. Pam and I liked Trudeau. We had put a Liberal sign next to Dad's Conservative sign on the front lawn, and giggled all afternoon waiting for him to come home and see it.

"What the hell...?" he gasped, and we laughed even harder.

The Unsinkable Pammy Brown, as I called her, took the Rehab Board's advice and applied for disability insurance, going through a whole new rigmarole of filling out forms and going to interviews. Once again, she was turned down.

On my next visit home Pam showed me the rejection letter, explaining to me that life-threatening congenital diseases were not included in the *Family Benefits Act*.

"If I was in a wheelchair, or missing a limb, or had injured my back lifting something at work, they would give me disability. But they won't do it simply because I can't breathe."

She had ripped off a letter back to them, detailing her confusion and concern. Ever the actress, I suggested that if it got her a case review and another hearing, she should go in a wheelchair.

Pam smirked. "Yeah, I know, but that's not the point. They should give it to me because of my real disabilities. Why should a person in my condition have to fake being sick?"

"If I was famous," I told her, "I'd call a press conference."

"Ya right," she said, and we both laughed.

The trees and fields surrendered to fall. The late afternoon sun set the leaves and stubble ablaze. My mother wrote to me that Jeff had built a stock car with a lawnmower engine on it, painted it orange, and entered it in the Labor Day Parade under the name Cheese Whiz.

Gregg had tried for his beginner's driving license and signed up for driving classes. He was looking forward to getting his license the minute he turned sixteen in December, so he sold the mini-bike he'd been getting around on and found a part-time job bagging groceries at Loblaws to save up for gas and insurance. It was hard to believe that my brother was already in his second year of high school. I felt as if I hardly knew him.

My mother wished I would come home more often, although there was no place for me to sleep except the foldout couch in the den, and nowhere for me to change my clothes except the bathroom. When I asked my father why he built a house without a room for me he answered, "Because you left." I asked my mother and she said, "I don't know, Heather. Your father and I were busy just trying to make ends meet and raising two sick children. We couldn't look sideways or backwards or too far down the road, so I guess we just didn't think of it. I'm sorry."

I didn't know how to come home to a place that had no place for me, but I came as often as I could, at least two weekends a month. Once in a while, Rick came with me. He slept on the foldout couch while I bunked in with Pam. He hung out a lot in the living room, away from the uncomfortable sights and sounds of Pam's masks and treatments, hiding out from my family's open displays of both temper and affection, which were completely foreign to him. Much to Pam's delight, Rick was fond of playing the organ. We listened from the other room, sipping tea.

"That's kind of Rick's approach to life, isn't it?" my mother asked me one day. "Just letting his fingers dance lightly over the keys?"

"What do you mean?"

"I mean he never really commits. He never really digs his fingers into those low notes and makes a big, deep sound. You know, Dum Da Da Dum!" My mother intoned Beethoven's *Fifth*, miming the dramatic action of a concert pianist.

My mother was asking me to look deeper, but I didn't want
to. If I looked at Rick any deeper, I would have seen him for
what he was, and not what I wanted him to be. It was the same
with Pam asking me to look at God, or to get counseling and
look at myself. I'd had enough of facing reality. I wanted the-
atrics and flights of fancy. I wanted life to come easy for a
change. I wanted joy, but I was still too young to know that real
joy comes from the inside, not from external sources, and that
we ourselves must choose it.

By the middle of October, Pam was back in the hospital. Dr.
Crozier was disturbed by her weight. She had dropped below
eighty pounds, and continued to lose ground. Her body was
using all its energy to fight the Pseudomonas infection eating
away at her lungs.

For fourteen days Pam was fed by a plastic tube that snaked
up through her nose and down into her stomach. The procedure
was called hyperalimentation. I could hardly pronounce it, much
less watch her go through it. Bags of creamy white food supple-
ment were hooked up to the tube on an IV stand and poured
into her round the clock. The tube chafed her throat and
blocked the mucus she tried to cough up after her treatments. I
gagged every time I visited her, while she stared dispassionately
out the window or at the wall next to her bed, stoic and silent.

The hospital discomfited Rick. Occasionally he waited for
me in the emergency waiting room, playing the coffee table with
his fingers as if it were a piano. When he came up to the ward
with me, self-conscious and restive, I could see that this was way
more reality than he wanted to deal with. He made a good show
of it, getting Pam to laugh, but I knew he didn't want to live at
the depths I was being forced to. It was hard to forgive him for
that, and not to envy his ability to live on life's surface.

My mother wrote that Grandma Bill thought Dad was working too hard trying to keep the business going. Mom chatted

about the chili sauce and "Heavenly Rhubarb Jam" she was doing down, and how she wished she had the money to send me on a London Show Tour. She asked me to take care and remember they were all thinking of me every day.

I try to say each morning, Today is the day the Lord hath given me, she wrote, and I ached with love for her. Not long after, Mom phoned to tell me it looked like Dad was going to lose the business. Grandma Birdsell had found her a job as an orderly over at the John Noble Home. She would work there part-time, as well as start a night school course in geriatric nursing at Conestoga College.

"Just in case…" she sighed.

The black dog of depression had been nipping at her heels all year. She closed another letter to me with a poem she had written:

I
Am but a shadow
of the woman
I once thought I would be
Heather,
Be a tree
And stand
In the sunlight

My father tried hard, worked harder than anyone I knew—up early, off, home late, even on the weekends when I visited, optimism and despair warring in his eyes, calloused fingers gripping his teacup, deep sighs pushing down the tears he wanted to shed.

I didn't know, and I still don't, why things always unraveled for him. He worked the phone, made cold calls, spent nights and weekends at the plant, hammered crates and pallets on the line with his men, drew up plans, got bank loans, signed everything including our house as collateral.

His brothers and mother still didn't think much of him, and he was still trying to prove them wrong. His mother-in-law wondered where all the money was—the fine life on easy street that being a Summerhayes was supposed to have brought her daughter.

"It's the Liberals," he said, "and what they've done to the damned economy. It's Trudeau."

The Conservatives had lost the election, but it would have been too late for them to help my father's business anyway. The economy was bad and people owed my father money, which meant that he owed money too. Forced to declare bankruptcy, Mom's part-time job became their only source of income.

"I am down but not out," he said. "I'll sell real estate."

In a town where houses weren't moving but people were— out and away. Massey-Ferguson, Brantford's largest employer, had closed its doors. There was not much left in my hometown but empty storefronts and a slow housing market. My father, having been self-employed, could not collect unemployment.

I realized that my father's talents were in his hands, in the way he could make a perfect join or lay a hardwood floor. At theatre school we were working on scenes from *Death of a Salesman*. The requiems for Willy Loman made me think of my own father. He was a salesman, like Willy, and as Arthur Miller wrote, a salesman "got to dream." Like Willy, my father rode on a smile and shoeshine, and when people stopped smiling back, it was an earthquake.

I thought of the houses my father had built as his living testament, and the Cystic Fibrosis Foundation.

The foundation had grown to fourteen chapters across Canada. The clinic at the Hospital for Sick Children, funded by the foundation, was performing cutting-edge clinical and genetic research. Hundreds of children's lives were being extended, and might possibly be saved.

"Be proud of that," I urged him, but he shrugged his shoulders as if it were nothing.

"How can you be proud of doing something that had to be done?" he asked me matter-of-factly. "Your mother and I only did what had to be done."

Witnessing Pam's slow demise, my father's bad luck, and my mother's hard choices, I tried to stay above it, like Rick. I was afloat on a sea of unbearable sadness for my family, and I used Rick, and theatre school, like a life raft.

Taking Pam's advice, I began private counseling with my psychology teacher, Ron, who was also a qualified therapist.

After several talk sessions, Ron suggested I explore primal therapy, the latest trend. The theory was that deeply buried childhood memories lay at the root of all emotional difficulties. Primal therapy was supposed to be a fast route to that source.

So it was that I found myself shivering on the thinly carpeted floor in Ron's tiny concrete office, my head filled with a white wind, an icy white wind that was whirling all through me, as if my body was a wide-open space.

"It hurts, it hurts…"

I wanted to curl up and cover the place where it felt like an ice pick was stuck behind my breastbone.

"Try not to move," whispered Ron, "stay open to it." His voice was like a soft wave, lapping on a shore.

My teeth chattered as I lay on the floor, legs and arms open, allowing Ron to talk me back through my life, into a cold river of memories all but forgotten.

"Tell me what's happening to you," he whispered. "Tell me what you see."

I was back in the room I shared with Pam when we were little.

I could see Pammy, and my mother. My mother's voice was soft as she began to speak, pulling me back through the vortex of time.

I wanted to get out of the room in my mind, I wanted to get out of Ron's room, but I couldn't go anywhere, I couldn't move, I was drowning in the memory of ballerina wallpaper, and the white wind raging at the window, and my mother wanting to tell me something, something that felt like it would kill me. The memory came and went in my head, as if I was watching it on TV and having trouble with the reception. My body began to convulse in sobs while waves of terror swept through me. *Don't worry Pammy, you won't die alone. I will be your Protector, and we will die together.* A strangled shriek rose out of my throat and echoed off the cement walls of the office. I could not cry hard enough.

"I know in my head I can't die with her," I sobbed, sitting up to grab a handful of Kleenex, "but in my heart..." I gasped for breath. "I don't want to die. But I don't want to live without her."

Here was the bottom of the well, the depths I'd been so afraid of. The memory I had been pushing down for almost fifteen years had finally resurfaced.

Late on a Friday afternoon in early December, Rick and I arrived to spend the weekend and to celebrate Jeff's eleventh birthday. We also celebrated the news from Dr. Crozier that my little brother was in such good shape he could stop the physio treatments, pack up his tent, and even go off digestive enzymes for the foreseeable future. His prognosis, we were assured, was excellent. Could he live fifteen years? Twenty? How impossible that seemed, in spite of the doctor's confidence. We didn't know of anyone with CF who was alive and well over the age of thirty.

I stood at the window, staring out across the snowbound field behind the house on Highway 24, searching for a small boy in a snowsuit. Jeffrey would be on his way home from school any time now.

My mother had made tea. The cinnamon scent of fresh baked hermit bars tempted me to leave the window, but I stood and watched, looking for my brother as my mother had instructed me to do. When I saw him, I aimed to open the window and yell at him to hurry up.

The stream that flowed past the bottom of the front yard wore a thin layer of ice. On the ridge above it, a number of gaunt black trees huddled like refugees in the wind. The low-slung schoolhouse lay beyond them, across the field, a dark stamp on the horizon.

"There he is!" said Rick, pointing.

I strained my eyes in the descending twilight. There he was indeed, awkward in his snowsuit, running, stumbling, falling, jumping up again, dancing, waving his arms at the snow whirling around him like fat chunks of cotton falling from a gunmetal sky. His mouth was moving, as if he was talking to himself.

"What's he doing?" Rick laughed.

I opened the window to shout at him. A gust of cold air shot into the back of my throat, knocking the breath out of me. A patch of sound drifted in on the wind, the voice of a child, my brother.

"He's singing!" Rick exclaimed.

We stood together in the open window as the wind rushed in, listening, watching Jeff come up on the ridge of trees. He threw his arms out to the side as if he were performing and the trees were his audience. He leapt forward and slid all the way down the hill on his bottom, his arms still outstretched, his voice strong and sweet.

"To dream the impossible dream, to fight the unbeatable foe, to bear the unbearable sorrow, to run where the brave dare not go..."

He tramped defiantly through the stream, breaking the ice, oblivious to the soakers he must have been getting with every step.

"This is my quest, to follow that star, no matter how hopeless, no matter how far..." Jeff plowed his boots into the soft, deep snow, trudging his way up the front yard. "...and I know, if I'll only be true to this glorious quest, then my heart will lie peaceful and calm when I'm laid to my rest..."

When Pam dreamed, she dreamed of being normal, of doing the things her friends did, going places they went. She dreamed of finishing high school, changing the mind of the Rehab Board, and going off to college to study early childhood education. She dreamed of living on her own, finding true love, and maybe, well, who knew?

My mother still dreamed of becoming a nurse, though the path to that dream was more circuitous than she'd imagined. She had begun attending Conestoga College during the day, studying to be a Registered Nursing Assistant. She worked nights and weekends at the John Noble Home, shopping for groceries, cooking, doing laundry or cleaning the house at odd hours, squeezing her life into and around every small crevice of time. She dreamed of the day when she'd graduate, of a good paycheck, security, and somewhere off in the distance, a vacation by the sea. In her spare time, gazing out the kitchen window at the wind-tossed trees, she dreamed that the dreams of her husband, and those of her children, would come true.

My father dreamed of the day he'd make his fortune, the day he'd be able to lay the world at my mother's feet, and the day that his brothers would finally respect him.

He was on the road every day, trying any way he could to make that dream a reality, nabbing real estate listings, showing houses and commercial properties. In his spare time he was on the phone to god-knows-who, trying to get "deals" going, or he was outside in the bush behind the house with chainsaw, shovel, and hand wagon, clearing more of the property, dreaming of the homes he wanted to build there, and sell.

Gregg dreamed of being a policeman, of helping people, but also having authority and control. He dreamed of having his own family, and time to play with his children. He said his home would be full of laughter and fun. His kids would have a special padded room where they could bounce and play and throw themselves around and make noise and never hurt themselves or disrupt the household.

Jeff dreamed of owning a horse and a dog, his own true companions. He dreamed of the day when he would not be left out or left behind by the other members of his family, the day when his mother wasn't too tired, his father wasn't too busy, his brother wasn't too scornful, Pam wasn't too sick, and I wasn't too far away.

Sitting together on the edge of her bed, Pam and I stared out through the window into the white winter wonderland. I told her about watching Jeff cross the field of snow, singing "The Impossible Dream." A shock of recognition and dismay rippled softly through her eyes. She bit her lip so as not to weep.

"I'm scared that when I die, he'll give up on his own life like Peter Mulder did after his brother Brian died," Pam told me.

There are small, quiet dreams, and gaudy, Hollywood-sized fantasies. There are dreams that get deferred, others you simply outgrow, and once in a while, dreams that come true.

There are other dreams, though, that grow in the deep places, rooted in terrible longing. These are the dreams that surpass all others. The impossible dreams.

Love without sorrow. Time without measure. Life without Death.

CHAPTER FIFTEEN

"Being deeply loved by someone gives you strength;
loving someone deeply gives you courage." — LAO TZU

An early morning in April 1973. A freshly graded country road.
A light spring rain. Neil Diamond on the car radio. "Song Sung
Blue." Pam was smiling, singing along in her slight, wheezy
soprano as she drove herself to school.

As the car headed over a rise, the tires swerved gently in the
bed of soft gravel and dirt. Pam braked. The car swerved slug-
gishly in the opposite direction. She braked again, her heart
beating faster. The tires would not grab the mushy road. The car
continued downhill, picking up speed. She was losing control.
Panicking, she braked again, hard. The car veered and left the
road, airborne. The world turned upside down.

Pam heard a crunching sound as the car landed on its roof.
Time slowed like warm taffy. The windshield imploded, showering her with glass crystals. The car slithered through the long,
wet grass that grew in the ditch beside the road. It sailed through
the gap between a telephone pole and a post and wire fence bordering the farmer's field, coming to rest three hundred feet from
where it left the road.

Pam hung upside down in her seat belt. The world was suddenly still, quiet except for the sound of softly falling rain and
her own rapid, wheezing breath. Carefully, she unhooked the

belt, slid down to the ceiling of the car, jiggled the door handle, and kicked the door open. She crawled out onto the soggy ground and sat, resting her elbows on her knees with her head in her hands. She did not know how much time passed before she heard the far-off cry of a siren.

Pam called Dad up to the hospital. She had a bump on her head, and a few minor cuts and bruises, but was otherwise okay. On the way home, she and Dad stopped back at the scene. Dad took pictures with his Polaroid, recording the deep scar in the road, the chute of flattened grass, the abraded telephone pole, the mangled wreck piled next to the fence.

I came home as soon as I could, and she showed me the photos.

"I didn't even cry," she exclaimed. "I guess I was in shock."

"You could have been killed."

"I know, but that's the best thing! When I was sitting at the side of the road waiting for the ambulance, I realized that God could have taken me right then if He'd wanted to. But He didn't. It wasn't my time. Do you know what that means?"

I shook my head no.

"That accident told me that I can die just like anyone else. It can happen anywhere, anytime, anyhow, not necessarily from CF. I could slip on a banana peel, or get hit by a bus!"

I smiled at her as if she'd gone soft in the head, and she tried not to laugh, waving her hands at me.

"No, seriously. It means I'm still alive for a reason. I have a purpose in my life that I haven't fulfilled."

"How did you figure all this out?"

"I don't know. It just came to me. Maybe that bump on the head knocked some sense into me. All I know is that I don't feel afraid anymore, of dying from CF I mean. And I'm finished with sitting around and moping, waiting for it to happen. Your time is your time, and there's nothing you can do to prepare for it, except to live your life well. From now on, that's exactly what I'm going to do."

Come June, Pam graduated from high school with honors and took a summer "job" working as a full-time volunteer at the Andrew Donaldson Development Center, a school for mentally retarded and multiply handicapped children. Mary Stafford, her supervisor, quickly became a close friend.

Like the kids at Crippled Children's camp a few years earlier, these children also had a profound effect on Pam. Their limitations were so severe that hers felt diminished by comparison. Yet because of her own physical circumstances and emotional struggles, she found that she had unique gifts of strength and insight to share.

"I feel needed," she explained to me, "and their love is absolutely unconditional, full of such joy. We could all learn from them."

She gave me a book of poetry that Mary Stafford had passed on to her, *Tears of Silence* by Jean Vanier.

"Read this," she instructed, tucking it into my hands before I left to catch the train one Sunday night, her eyes full of portent.

As I read, the dark shapes of the countryside flying past outside, I realized why the poems spoke to her, and how they spoke *for* her.

to evolve
life does need security
in the mother
in the father
in the home
with friends

but above all trust in the spirit
against all assaults of fear and anguish
against all the unknowns
against anything that might destroy
the flowering of my life

She soon brought me other inspirational writings, including the life stories of paraplegic Joni Eareckson, and disabled Olympic hopeful Jill Kinmont. I reciprocated with Richard Bach (*Jonathan Livingston Seagull*) and Kahlil Gibran.

You would know the secret of death. But how shall you find it unless you seek it in the heart of life?...For life and death are one, even as the river and the sea are one...And what is it to cease breathing, but to free the breath from its restless tides, that it may rise and expand and seek God unencumbered?

Even as death began incrementally to close in, Pam's instinct was to open up completely to life. At the age of nineteen, my sister resolved to push the limits of her prognosis further than the doctors told her she could go, further than most Cystics had gone, testing her physical abilities against the time she wanted, and needed, to fulfill her spiritual growth.

She decided to go for her degree in early childhood education, and reapplied to the Ministry of Community and Social Services for a rehabilitation grant to help finance her college tuition. This time, the review board agreed to give her a grant on one condition—that she could get a college to accept her. They asked for, and she provided them with, a list of every college to which she would apply. When each college turned her down, one by one, we all felt suspicious, devastated, and not at all surprised.

This is when my mother insisted that Pam quit being so amenable to the Board and apply to a college that wasn't on the list. Sheridan College, in Oakville.

"Why don't we just get in the car and go?" she urged my sister one afternoon.

Pam walked in to Sheridan without an appointment, gripping her high school transcripts in her clammy palms. As luck would have it the ECE director was in, and agreed to an on the spot interview.

"I was totally up front about everything," she told me excitedly that night on the phone. "I said I might have to miss a lot of school because some days I'm just not up to it, and other times I might have to go in the hospital, but I promised to never fall behind in my work."

"And what did she say?"

"She said she was sure I'd make Sheridan College very proud."

Rick proposed, and I accepted.

No one was happy about it. Even my best friend Debbie Grover said she wouldn't stand up with me, much less attend, the wedding.

Pam tried to reason with me.

"I just want to make sure you don't give up on being an actress just because you're getting married. Some women end up throwing their dreams away for a man even when they don't mean to."

"Well, I'm not most women, and you've been listening to too much feminist propaganda. Anyway, as I understand it, being a feminist means you can have it both ways, marriage and career, so Rick and I have vowed to not let marriage get in the way of either of our careers."

"Oh." Pam pursed her lips into a wry smile.

If I had any doubts, I ignored them. I loved Rick as truly and deeply as I knew how, and believed that his love for me was strong enough to help me survive Pam's death.

We set the date for the following year, May 11th, 1974, and went about the business of looking for summer jobs. I ended up waitressing at Harvey Wallbanger's, a restaurant in Toronto. It was a far cry from being the leading lady in the musical *Silent Edward,* for which I had auditioned. The role had gone instead to my best friend Deborah. Adding insult to injury, Rick was starring opposite her on the summer tour. While they were in rehearsal, I sulked a great deal of the time, repeatedly cranking up a song from *Funny Girl* on the restaurant's player piano, singing out loud whenever I could get away with it, "I'm the greatest star, I am by far, but no one knows it…"

"Who do I think I am, trying to become an actress anyway?" I blubbered to Pam over the phone.

"You're just feeling sorry for yourself," scoffed Pam, "and you give up too easy." She cautioned me that if I thought about quitting or got mad at my colleagues every time I lost a part, I would very quickly have no friends and no career.

I complained to her that I didn't want to go back to Ryerson now that I was getting married, because I didn't want to spend two more years in school. Now that he had his Actors Equity card, Rick was going to quit school and try to keep working professionally, but I didn't know where that left me.

"Now listen, I have a suggestion, and don't get upset when I say this. Why don't you come with me to Sheridan College? They have a theatre course."

I sighed dramatically.

"I knew it!" she laughed. "You think that just because it's a community college it won't be any good. Well you might be surprised if you'd just consider it. It's only a two-year course and I'll bet they'll give you credit for Ryerson and let you right into the final year. Maybe that's all you need to build up your confidence. And if you come to Sheridan, we can see each other almost every day!"

I had to admit she was convincing.

"Hey, you're only nineteen years old. Where did you learn to give such good advice?"

"I don't know," she laughed, "maybe from my big sister."

I did not return to Ryerson, and instead entered the second and final year of the theatre program at Sheridan College. I would be able to graduate with a certificate within a few months, and get out into the world as an actress.

Within a week of starting the program, however, I wound up in the hospital with a raging fever, a monster headache, and glands in my neck as large and hard as walnuts. Rick was still out of town with *Silent Edward*. Alone and frightened, I called my mother from a phone booth in Admitting, asking her to come right away. "And bring Pammy!"

"Nobody's touching me until my sister gets here! She knows all about IVs. I don't want it to go interstitial. I don't want anybody giving me anything until my sister gets here!"

The floor nurse, unimpressed by my use of the term "interstitial," went ahead and stuck in the needle hooking me up to the IV. I lay in bed as if mummified until Pam arrived about four hours later.

"How the heck did you end up like this?" my sister asked, examining my IV needle, and flicking the bulbous tip of her index finger at the connection between the IV bag and tube.

The nurse came in to take my temperature. "Ah," she said to Pam, "you must be Dr. Summerhayes. I'm so glad you finally decided to do rounds. Your patient's been very uncooperative."

"I'm sure that will change after I've had a talk with her," Pam giggled.

"Good," said the nurse.

I stuck my tongue out as she left the room, making my sister laugh.

"How do I sleep with this thing in my arm?"

"You just close your eyes, silly."

"Yeah, but won't it move and go interstitial?" (I loved that word.)

"Well," she said, shrugging her shoulders and smiling, "maybe it will and maybe it won't. If it goes, they'll just pull it out and reinsert it somewhere else."

"Thanks a lot."

I spent the next few days in misery as my symptoms responded slowly to the medication. I thought about Pam as I ate the unpalatable hospital food, and suffered fitful, interrupted sleep. I learned what it was like to have no control not only over my body, but also in practical matters. The medical staff conversed with each other at the foot of my bed as though I were invisible. They treated me like a good child or a bad child, depending on how I complied with their instructions, given to me as if I were indeed a child. I wept for the need of company on days when no one came, and exhausted myself entertaining visitors when they did come, and I didn't feel up to it. Ten days later I went home realizing that as much as I thought I'd appreciated what Pam went through at Sick Kids, I'd never had a clue.

While I continued on at Sheridan, Rick took a job singing backup and playing keyboard and drums in a rock band. He toured northern Ontario, working smoky dives in small, scruffy towns, flirting with the local girls, pretending he was one of the Doobie Brothers.

Deborah Grover, or just Grover, as I called her, was back at Ryerson Theatre School, but she and I spent weekends together, attending dance classes and practicing audition monologues.

Outside of the fact that she didn't think too much about my marrying Rick, our growing friendship proved to be a cherished gift.

During the fall and winter of 1973 and spring of 1974, my sister boarded weekdays with a family near Sheridan College, going home only on weekends or when she didn't feel well. She bought a little used car to ferry around in, though it had "pissed her off" when the bank insisted Dad co-sign her life-insured loan. She palled around with two good buddies from her class—Rosalie Simms and Deb Sheperdson—going to movies, bowling, ordering in Chinese food.

She and I enjoyed seeing each other at school, occasionally lunching together in the cafeteria or sharing an afternoon cup of tea in the student lounge before going our separate ways.

We had a great chuckle when she confided that she had gone on The Pill. At nineteen, she had still not developed breasts or had a period due to complications from her CF.

"I told Dr. Crozier it was about time I became a woman," she giggled, "and he agreed. So he put me on it!"

"Is it working?"

Pam's starch-white face turned crimson. She bunched her fists below her nose like she always did when she was excited, and her eyes sparkled merrily as she nodded yes.

Her letters home to Mom and Dad were evidence of her new-found perspective on the family, born of her new independence.

...I'm sitting here listening to the beautiful film music on my radio and remembering so many wonderful things of home. Such things as your warmth, love, thoughtfulness, stubborness, concern and willpower are all with me always and I feel help me so much in learning to begin life on my own.

I know that seeing your children reach out on their own is a pretty wonderful thing, but somehow it is both difficult and depressing for both sides, as well as exciting and adventurous. In a way I feel comforted in realizing this and knowing that you are with me in experiencing these feelings.

I think of everyone so often and find myself praying more and more for strength, courage and direction to help us all live through our trials as a family, and still find a light shining at the end. Do you know what I mean?...Keep your spirits up now! I'll be home next weekend (only six more days).

*Remember now I like you, and love you all too. Here is some-
thing important I am learning to be true.*
    "One must love himself in order to show he truly loves others."
Here is my love, Pam

Pam wanted us all to love ourselves and each other as she loved
us. She wanted us to reflect less on our circumstances, and more
on our internal essence, but the world was too much with us.

Dad had secured some loans to develop the property behind
the house, and Pam laughed affectionately at the big dollar signs
he got in his eyes every time he talked about selling the lots and
contracting himself out to build the houses. She admired his
ambition, but wished he could see that his worth as a man did
not depend on his making a million dollars.

Mom had gotten her Health Care Aide certificate from
Mohawk College, and was now working nights and weekends at
the John Noble Home. Pam was proud of her, yet she wished
Mom would take more time for herself. She worried about the
price Mom might pay for her achingly high self-standards.

"What can we say to her?" Pam asked me, and I just
shrugged. We knew that if we said anything, Mom would
respond by pausing for only a second in the midst of ardently
wiping the kitchen counter, or ironing her uniforms, or writing
out checks to pay the bills, her whole body pumping with adrenalin, and ask us without a trace of self-pity, "What other choice
do you think I've got?"

"Mom wrote to me," I told Pam. "She says she and Dad are
getting along better, but she wishes she didn't get so easily discouraged. She thinks that's what comes between them."

After discussing our parents, our conversations turned to our
brothers. Gregg was Pam's hero. He had been since they were kids
and fought a boy named Gordon Beardwood for Pam's honor.
Gordon, a year older and physically larger than Gregg, often

teased Pam to tears. One day, Gregg responded by pummeling and wrestling with the bully for nearly three hours after school.

"He was practicing to be a policeman even way back then," Pam giggled. He had his eye on applying to Sheridan College for security and law enforcement.

Pam was most concerned about Jeff, a concern I shared. In spite of his obvious intelligence, he was struggling through Grade Six.

"Mom was always there for the three of us when we were Jeff's age," she reminded me. "We could come home from school for lunch, and she always had a snack waiting for us in the after-noon, and we had each other to play with, or friends close by. It's very different for Jeff with Mom working and going to school at the same time, and them living so far out in the country. We're both here, and Gregg is busy with his own life as a teenager, and you know Dad. He probably comes home late from meetings and falls asleep watching Archie Bunker in *All in the Family*. I think Jeff leads a very lonely life, and I'm afraid of what trouble that might lead to."

"What can we do about it?"

Pam shrugged her shoulders and stared glumly into the dis-tance. I sighed, equally dumbfounded.

My sister's instincts were correct, as Jeff would admit to me many years later.

"You guys couldn't be there for me like you were for Pam," he said. "At clinic, the doctor would ask me how the family was coping, and I'd tell him that Mom and Dad and you were all coped out. There was always something going on. Pam had a medical crisis, or Dad's business was in trouble, or Mom was studying for exams or working. The day-to-day relationships were a struggle. And many times I'd come home from school, and Mom and Dad were at the hospital, and there was just a note or a babysitter, and I'd worry all night. And then Mom and Dad would come home tired and anxious. And I could see that all you and Gregg wanted was to get the hell out of there."

He grew up feeling like an outsider in his own home, his child's nose pressed to the glass of our busy grownup lives, experiencing a sense of disconnection that would eventually drive him down a dark road. This, despite the fact that, as Gregg would contend, "Jeff always got everything he ever asked for."

Whatever Jeff got in the way of goods or attention—his own horse, new skis, etc.—was probably more in compensation for what he wasn't getting from parents who were overextended in their own physical and emotional lives, or at times simply absent. Given the demands of the family's daily routine at that juncture, it was likely easier to just say yes to Jeff, rather than wrangle with him when he wanted something. It may also have been more expedient to bail him out of a tight spot, instead of taking the time or energy to confront and resolve the issues that put him there. So while it may have been true that Jeff got most of what he asked for, none of us were able to give him all he needed.

And how was a young, lonely boy to reconcile the paradox of his life, afraid his own disease could take a bad turn at any moment, yet well enough to feel guilty about his health relative to Pam's?

Pam sensed this, as she sensed whatever was at the heart of each of our ongoing dilemmas. She badly wanted the power to change things for the better, and to support each of us as she felt supported by us. Yet, she was wise enough to know that she had only the power to love, and to encourage love among us. She would put all her faith in that power.

As each member of my family continued to struggle with their identity and purpose, our bonds of love were tested by distance, and difficulty. We each needed to find our way out emotionally intact, not just in the normal sense of moving beyond family boundaries, but also beyond the margins of the life Pam's disease had transcribed for us. Yet we also needed to stay close. How were we to do this?

With love. Always with love.

Gregg bought a poem for me at the mall that Christmas, printed on mottled parchment, suitable for framing. Someone else might have found it a little "schmaltzy," but I was moved to tears. It said it all, I thought, for everyone in the family.

People
so seldom say
I love you
and then
it's either too late
or love goes
so when I say
I love you
it doesn't mean
I know you'll never go
only that I wish you didn't have to

CHAPTER SIXTEEN

"The most authentic thing about us is our capacity to create,
to overcome, to endure, to transform, to love and
to be greater than our suffering." — BEN OKRI

Love was the anchor that held Pam fast in the swift, rising water. She believed that family support was paramount to her survival, and to ours.

> *...Thank you for talking to me and putting up with me on the weekend. I know I was pretty bad. You helped me face myself anyway, and even though I say you don't understand, you always seem to. I couldn't live without the family encouragement so much. It helps me through from one bad time to the next.*
>
> *The boys show me their love and affection in their own special way too. Gregg really has so much love and concern for me I think. This is making me cry again, but at least it's a happy cry.*

On her bad days, Pam cried for fear of not keeping up. Her failing body wasn't up to long days in the lecture hall followed by late nights of study, and the many required hours of work placements in daycare centers. Exposure to the children posed another threat, for even the healthiest of student teachers came down with colds and coughs.

Pam and her classmates were on notice that, based on their performance, only a certain number of them would be invited back to complete their second year. My sister felt she had it in her mentally and emotionally, but she was frightened by weight loss and overwhelming fatigue, the disturbing length and bone-chilling depths of her coughing spells, the murky color of the mucus she coughed up, the blurry chest x-rays and lousy clinic reports.

It was not fear of death. Pam was afraid of unused life.

"If I can just get my body to cooperate," she'd swear. "If I can just make it through to the end of the school year, then at least I can say I did that much."

Every day was a fight to stay out of the hospital. She was among the first wave of Cystics to reach adulthood. All bets were off now. There were new goals to be set, new limitations to adapt to, and new questions to consider about her quality of life.

Would she possess the energy to cook, clean, and care for herself if she lived alone in her own home? What about sex, marriage, procreation? It had recently been learned that most CF males were sterile. Could she bear children? If she could in fact conceive, what risks would pregnancy pose? What effect would it have on a fetus carried by a mother low on oxygen and loaded with drugs? Who would commit to marry and have children with someone whose main aim in life was holding death at bay?

Given her starved appearance, and loud, frequent bouts of coughing, how would potential employers react? What of her need to take masks throughout the day, or possibly take more frequent sick days than other employees, or leave work for occasional hospital stays of two weeks or more for serious treatment of chest infections. Would employers hire someone whose life expectancy was so short as to be unknown?

And what about longevity? Her chest infections were now reasonably controlled with massive doses of antibiotics. Over the long term, what new physical problems might present? Her heart was already enlarged, her lungs had been severely deformed by scar tissue, and her immune system had been compromised by prolonged use of the very antibiotics that were extending her life.

Every time my sister breathlessly climbed a staircase, or admired a cute guy in the school cafeteria, or passed a test on the way to her diploma, these questions stuck in the back of her mind. They prompted weekend fights with Mom and Dad, and the tearful, apologetic letters home. They caused doubts that plagued her sleep and kept her awake in the small, dark hours of the morning as she lay alone in bed.

These same questions spurred long conversations between the two of us, over the phone, at school or at home on weekends. Such talks left me anxious, either incapable of fully enjoying my own life, or so gung-ho that all my efforts were stamped with the mark of desperation. My success at school, my impending marriage, my whole promising future, begged every question my sister had to ask about her own fate. Any insecurities or fears I had about my prospects were trifling by comparison, but did that mean they were less important?

We advised each other to take each day as it came, or to use our mother's well-worn proverbs, to "put one foot in front of the other and just keep going," or to "cross that bridge when we come to it."

We sent each other encouraging poems and proverbs, yet all the poems and proverbs in the world couldn't alleviate the burden of conscience that came with comparing my life to Pam's. The only way to live with myself, or so I thought, was to live in part for her. I had hoped to have outgrown that sense of obligation by now.

We had a wonderful time choosing the gingham for the bridesmaids' dresses Pam would sew. The wedding shower she threw for me had us both flush with anticipation and joy. I hoped that my wedding would be a much-deserved blessed event for my family and create a memory so fine that it would glow forever in the dark. I hoped to forge a marriage so strong and happy that Rick and I would be the sun to which our families and friends could turn their faces.

The morning of my wedding dawned to a cloudy sky the color of the seed pearls on my wedding gown.

Pam trundled out to the kitchen with me, so we could steam my veil. It was made of three-quarter-length double-layered netting, adorned with lace appliqués. The veil was to be held in place by a delicate pearl crown, chosen because Rick's pet name for me was "Princess," and because the lady at the bridal salon had suggested if someday we had a little girl, she could wear it to her first Communion. I had promised Rick we'd raise our children Catholic, so that sold me.

My mother had made tea, and the leftover water was still steaming in the kettle. I removed the lid and turned the element on HI to keep the water boiling.

"C'mon," I said to Pam, "let's do this right here."

"I don't know if that's such a good idea," she countered, taking one end of the veil in both hands while I took the other. Gingerly, we moved it back and forth over the steam.

"Be careful you don't drop that veil and let it hit the element," my mother cautioned on her way out to the garage.

"We won't," I answered testily, turning my head in her direction.

My mother closed the door and I returned my attention to the veil. Pam and I gasped in unison. As I watched my mother leave, I had inadvertently allowed one side of the veil to drop a few inches. Right in the front of it, on the left side, was a hole an inch in diameter, edged with black. My stomach lurched. My sister stared at me incredulously. We barely suppressed the urge to laugh.

"Don't tell Mom," I begged Pam. "She'll say it's a bad omen."

"Don't tell Mom? How are we going to hide it from her?"

We thought of calling Uncle Doug and Aunt Gloria to see if I could use her old veil, but realized it was probably too late.

Pam took my veil and walked calmly to her sewing box, then disappeared into her bedroom. I followed, watching fitfully over her shoulder as she carefully snipped the burnt edge from around the hole, cut a length of fine white thread from a spool, licked the end of the thread, eyed the head of the needle, carefully threaded it, and then delicately sewed the two sides of the hole together.

We both stood back to admire her handiwork. The thread made a thin, puckered scar on the transparent netting. Pam made a pursing sound with her lips as she tried not to laugh. I covered my mouth with my hand and mumbled, "Oh my God!"

Finally we figured out we could remove two lace appliqués from the back of the veil and move them to the front, where one of them would cover the scar.

"There," she said only a few moments later, beaming, holding the veil out to me in her hands as if it were my life. "I fixed it!"

At the church I stood nervously in the vestibule, listening as the strains of Bach's "Ode to Joy" floated through the air. Pam grinned at me, and my bridesmaid, Bonnie Jellis, told me to take a deep breath. I held it instead. The door opened before me with unseen hands. A sea of heads turned toward me. I peered down the aisle toward the altar where Rick was waiting, stiff in his tuxedo and ruffled shirt, smiling wanly.

"You see?" said Bonnie, winking. "He's there!"

My father took my arm. Pam grinned at us both, and then turned and walked ahead. I took a deep breath and stepped forward into my new life.

A reception at home under threatening skies ensued, replete with a buffet served by the Rebekah Lodge, to which Grandma Birdsell belonged. Later that night, Rick and I headed back to

Toronto in a driving rain, and onto a Jamaican honeymoon marred by Rick's fear of flying, his overindulgence in dark rum, and a devastating fight caused by my own overblown expectations of what a honeymoon should be.

"You guys just need a little time to get used to married life," Pam commiserated with me when we returned home.

I could only hope she was right.

⌒

There was blood everywhere, my mother told me. It was splattered all over the cement floor and the plastic wrappers on the sheets in the storage room of the bedding and linen department at Sears, where Pam had taken a part-time summer job as a salesclerk. It was hot and humid, mid-August, when the tall corn drowsed in the fields around the mall, and even the air conditioners in the Sears appliance department couldn't stand up to the thermometer. Pam's chest always got bad in that weather, full and tight and suffocating.

I sat in the tiny galley kitchen of my newlywed apartment, clutching the phone, shivering as my mother's voice poured through the receiver.

"Is it Pammy?" Rick mouthed, hovering nearby. "Is she all right?" I couldn't tell from the expression on his face if he was afraid for her, or afraid he would have to comfort me and wouldn't know how. I turned away to concentrate on the sound of my mother's voice, that familiar polite calm that always told me all hell had broken loose. My sister had, in my mother's words, "blown a lung."

Sears was having a pillow sale, and Pam had been running up and down all day in the heat. She was helping a customer when she started to cough and couldn't stop. She barely made it to the storage room before she hemorrhaged. The store had called my father to come and get her. When he finally brought her home, my mother said, they both walked into the house white as sheets.

"Was that when you brought her up to Sick Kids?"

"No. She refused to go. She practically shouted at your father that she'd be all right, and to leave her alone."

"So then what happened?"

"We told her we'd let her rest overnight and see how she was in the morning."

They didn't have to wait that long. Just after dinner, while they were still sitting at the kitchen table having tea, Pam started to cough, violently, and couldn't stop. With a dark, belching sound the blood came again, bright red.

"It was all over the place, the floor, the table, the walls. I thought we were going to lose her right then and there. It just froze me."

Goosebumps came up on my arms. My teeth chattered. "What did Dad do?"

My mother's voice cracked. "He just lost it." She began to weep. "It's the first time in all these years I've seen your father break down."

My father had fallen to his knees in front of my sister shouting "Pammy! Pammy!" as her blood spattered his shirt, his hands, his face. "Oh no, oh God no, please no," he choked as tears streamed down his ruddy cheeks.

"I called an ambulance but they told me it was going to take thirty minutes to get here," my mother continued.

"That's crazy!"

"That's what your father said. He said we could have her halfway to Toronto by then."

By that time, she told me, Pam's spasms had begun to subside. "I ran a tea towel under the tap and tried to clean some of the blood up off Pammy and your dad. He just stayed down on his knees; I couldn't get him to move. He kept holding Pammy's hands and stroking her hair."

My mother started to cry again, and as I sobbed with her, my shivering stopped.

Pam had walked out to the car under her own steam, refusing to be carried. She lay down in the back seat with a blanket and pillow, and my parents tore out of the driveway, the gravel shrieking and spitting beneath the tires. They had her at Sick Kids Emergency in less than an hour. Auntie Elsie got someone to drive her out to the house to look after the boys.

"What caused it? Was she coughing too hard?"

"The doctor told us it's because she doesn't have enough Vitamin K in her system. All the antibiotics she's taken over the years have destroyed the natural flora in her stomach. That's the stuff that helps make Vitamin K, which clots the blood. So the doctor explained to us that every time she coughs now, it's like skinning her knee. The coughing creates an abrasion in her lungs, and it bleeds. He called it a 'hemoposis.'"

"Why didn't you call me right away? I could have met you at Emerg."

"We didn't want to upset you until we knew exactly what we were dealing with, and by the time they got her settled in a room, it was too late at night."

"What if she'd died and I wasn't there, Mom?"

"Heather, she could have died in the storage room at Sears and none of us would have been there."

"Then why didn't you call me first thing this morning?"

My mother sighed. "Heather, I haven't got the energy to get into this with you right now. I'm worn out and so is your father."

"You know, you always do this."

"Do what?"

"Wait to call me until she's been sick for a few days."

"She hasn't been sick for a few days, this just happened. We were at the hospital all of last night, and as soon as we knew she was stable, we just got in the car and came home to get some rest. This is the first chance I've had to phone anybody."

"I could have been there to support you last night. I could have gone to see her this afternoon!"

"The doctors said Pam can't receive visitors today anyway."

"I think I'm more than just a visitor," I complained weepily.

My mother sighed deeply. "Oh my darling daughter. Of course you're more than a visitor, that's not what I meant... Look, they didn't even want your father and me to visit or else we'd have been back there this afternoon. You can go first thing tomorrow. I know she'll be wanting to see you."

"Okay," I sniffed.

"Now they'll be giving her blood transfusions, so I want you to be prepared for that. They have to give her blood very slowly over the next few days because of her heart failure."

"Heart failure?"

"Yes, you remember, from all those years ago when they gave her the carbenocillin."

"Of course I remember, and she told me it damaged her heart somehow, but nobody ever said anything to me about heart *failure*."

"Well, whether anybody told you or not, or whether it just never registered isn't the point now. She has heart failure, and she's had it for a long time."

I held on to my breath, held on to my own heart so it wouldn't fly to pieces.

"I have to go now, Heather," my mother said. "Your father and the boys need their supper, and I've got a paper to write for school and then I've got to try and get some rest before I come back to the hospital tomorrow."

We said our good-nights and I love you's, and hung up. Rick appeared from around the corner.

"Is everything all right?"

"She always does this. She always waits until Pam's been in a day or two before she calls me. I hate that, why does she do that?"

"Come here," he said, holding me close and hugging me. "It's all right, it's all right."

"You don't understand!" I moaned, pulling away. It was not all right, and there was nothing he could do to make it better.

Twelve days later Pam was allowed to go home. She had only two weeks to convalesce before starting her second year at Sheridan, during which time she packed up and moved into the apartment she had rented with Deb and Roselee, her buddies from the previous year at school.

My mother, who thought she was overdoing it, was terrified to let her go, and called me to say so.

"Mom, she made the Dean's Honor List last year. You know Pam. She's not about to quit now, no matter what."

"But what if what happened at home this summer happens again? Will those girls know what to do?"

"Mom, you can drive yourself crazy with what ifs. And you know what Pam always tells us—you can't control life by being afraid of it."

My sister's damn-the-torpedoes attitude that autumn inspired me to take my own risks.

I auditioned for the St. Lawrence Centre Theatre Company in Toronto with a speech from *The Jewish Wife*, a piece I had no business doing, neither being Jewish nor even close to the age of the character. Perhaps the artistic director saw me as more audacious than naïve, for the theatre actually hired me as a full-time acting apprentice.

Rick and I spent much of our first autumn as a married couple apart; I remained in Toronto rehearsing and performing while he plugged along with his rock band, touring northern Ontario.

Gregg began his last year of high school, looking forward to his eighteenth birthday and edging closer to his lifelong dream of becoming a police officer. He had also fallen in love with Janice Phillion, a sassy, voluptuous, blonde sixteen year old.

Jeff entered seventh grade.

My father diligently pursued a number of business ventures that invariably evaporated into wisps of smoke, sometimes along with the money he'd invested. There was a moment or two there when Pam and I worried that our parents' marriage might finally implode. Through it all, my mother wept and vacuumed, made lunches and dinners, wiped the countertops and washed the floors, did the laundry and worked eight-hour night shifts as a nurse's aide to help pay the bills. She kept our family together in the simplest, strongest, and least appreciated of ways. For a time she flirted with the possibility of attending nursing school, a dream that Pam and I vigorously encouraged. In a letter to us late in September, she explained her decision.

Dear Heather and Rick,
Today finds me more at peace with myself and the world than I have been for a long time. It became beautifully apparent to me within the last few days just who I am at this time in my life and just where I fit in terms of my family life. Firstly, I am aware now more than ever how very thankful I am for my beautiful family. You are all so precious to me. When I think of my children, I think in terms of the qualities of character they individually and collectively possess and I am overwhelmed with gratitude for their very being. None of you are cruel or vindictive, haughty or proud. Each of you are honest,

ambitious, resourceful and above all loving. As I grow older it seems to me that to love, not just your family but to embrace the world as much as we can is so important.

I did not lightly change my mind to enter nursing. For the past few years we all have been in such turmoil. To add 2 more years of pressure seemed more than I can bear to submit us all to. Mind you, I am not giving up my intent for further education, but merely changing the path by which I hope to find my way!

For the present, I am going to work part-time at something, and go to Mohawk [College] and take Sociology each Wed. night for the winter. This will allow me to contribute a small amount to the household, which is still very much on an uneven keel economically, and to continue to keep my mind active and learning. It will also permit me to enjoy my husband and family with some measure of ease without the pressure of continually meeting a pressing timetable.

I know that all of this in no way spells an end to our many unsolved problems here at home, but it is at least a beginning. Some people go through their whole lives and are never able to see themselves in terms of their place in this world. At least I've made a start!

We at home are all thinking of you both. It's nice to know you are so happy together. I look forward to hearing that you are enjoying your work Heather, and that Rick is successful in his musical venture.

Gregg is now working at Jack Frasers and really likes it. Jeff has joined the Brant Aquatic Centre and hopes to be in the St. George Arts and Crafts Assoc. this winter. Pam is really enjoying the apartment and the companionship of the girls is so good for her morale.

I'll close now and hope to hear from you both soon.
God Bless, Love, Mom

My mother was forty-four, but looked several years younger. Her hair, which she now colored from time to time when she got around to it, had barely begun to gray. Her statuesque figure had softened into the plumper curves of a middle-aged woman. She complained that she was getting fat.

"You're as beautiful as the day we met," my father grinned.

"Oh Doug, for heaven's sake!"

"Well, all right, maybe the sands have shifted a bit, but you're still a beautiful woman."

"Oh girls," she lied. "I just hate it when your father goes on like that."

The circles under her eyes had darkened with fatigue, but the few worry lines on her forehead did not mirror the load of anxiety she carried. Though she had a habit of fretting, she was still vigorous and purposeful, a regular swashbuckler when she had to be.

I was beginning to see my mother through different eyes. She didn't laugh enough, but when she did it put the whole world to rights. She took others at face value, and continued to do so even when people let her down. I understood why she could be so demanding: because when she saw the best in you, she expected it from you. She was honest, and honorable, and always hurt and amazed when the world around her was not.

Her heart was the heart of our family, a battered heart, physically taking the brunt, as we would someday learn, silently absorbing the blows. It was in my mother's heart that we could always find our own.

September 30/74
Dear Mother,
This morning I had my class in "Child in the Family" and we had one of the best discussions yet. After thinking about it all

day I wanted to write and tell you and dad how lucky and great I feel it is to have a family such as ours.

This is a class where we can really discuss events that have happened to our families and how we hope to bring up our perspective [prospective] families. This morning we were talking of emotional honesty and dishonesty.

I discovered much to my surprise, that we do have a much more loving family tie than many other families. Most of the girls said that they find it very hard to say "I love you" to their mother or father or even the rest of their families. Many of them actually had little or got little affection from their parents or family simply by saying those few words once in a while. Even Deb admitted that she found it hard.

It is this type of discussion that makes me so thankful we, as a family, are not inhibited or do not feel childish to reassure the others of our love and care for them by repeating these simple words as we go out the door or before we go to bed; or even to offer each other a simple hug or kiss just because we want to and not just for a special occasion.

Boy, we may not have a lot of things other family's have, but we sure have something that's worth a lot more to me. Have a good week now, OK? See you on Thanksgiving!

All my love…from your daughter, Pam

CHAPTER SEVENTEEN

*"Hope begins in the dark, the stubborn hope that if you just
show up and try to do the right thing, the dawn will come.
You wait and watch and work: You don't give up."*
— ANNE LAMOTT

Pam kept notes on her condition, scribbled on pieces of scrap
paper and the backs of envelopes. I did not know this until we
found them among her possessions, after she died. They made
me think somehow of the corners she used to hide in when she
was little, needing a place to work her feelings out and cry in private. The old Duncan chesterfield she'd crawled behind... "Am I
going to die, Daddy?"

This was how she summed up the bare bones of her life at the
end of 1975, the year she turned twenty-one:

- *flu in Jan. – never recovered fully*
- *tipped failure – showing in next six weeks*
- *lacked energy – ? day, then slept*
- *up at night wheezing can't breath*
- *heart racing & palpitate – depressed*
- *some puffing in ankles and knees*
- *almost certain feeling heart – chest fine*
- *Feb. visit – told doctor – REMARK: serious "Have you
  fallen in love?"*

- *Confirmed "NO" – immediately – heart clinic*
- *ECG, x-ray and exam*
- *Confirmed Cor pulmonal – R.S. [pulmonary hypertension, right side]*
- *Digitalized and diuretics – low dose – activity at tolerate*
- *didn't say much – home to apt. & cry*
- *just coming to big 21st birthday*
- *think, last – end of the world*
- *graduating – can I work? – questions*
- *improvement in months – high spirits, energy to burn, new person*
- *finished [school] year – stable*
- *summer – lung collapsed – obstruction R.S.*
- *IV antibiotics 7 weeks – heart shift to right*
- *remained fairly stable – home – holidays – steady but slow improvement*
- *Nov. Pneumothorax L.S. upper*
- *healed next 3 mths. (up) steadily – bargained*

By this account, whatever mountains Pam thought she had been scaling with Cystic Fibrosis turned out only to have been foothills. After the hemoposis, her disease became a sheer rockface as her lungs began literally to fall apart, abscessing, collapsing, rupturing, and bleeding. Over the twelve months of that year, she spent seventy-one days in the Hospital for Sick Children.

Cor Pulmonale R.S. meant pulmonary hypertension of the right side. In other words, her right lung was so full of fluid that her heart could barely pump blood through it. This, in turn, worsened her congestive heart failure; her heart was losing its full pumping capacity, so there was a danger of blood backing up not only into her lungs, but also into other organs such as her liver. Her blood pressure fell; her abdomen, legs, and ankles swelled, her liver enlarged, her heartbeat was at times rapid and irregular. She had shortness of breath on exertion, and even lying flat in bed.

The lung collapse she referred to was called an atelectasis, a total obstruction of the air passages in her right lung. Bronchoscopes, all done without anesthetic, brought only temporary relief. Her pneumothorax constituted a collapse of the upper left lobe of her lung caused by an abcess, which resulted in the rupture of air sacs, and pressure from free air in the chest between two layers of her pleura (the thin membranes that cover the lung). Pulmonary edema (the lungs filling with fluid) and lung infection resulted. Ultimately, her right lung failed utterly, and her heart shifted into its cavity on the right side of her chest. For what remained of her life, she would have only her ravaged left lung to breathe with.

Part of me was always with her, part of my heart, my mind. My focus was split during rehearsals. I lost sleep agonizing about her condition. I exploited my creative energy thinking up ways to cheer her, finding gifts to bring her, baking food to take to her. I didn't know how else I could help keep her alive.

Pam was thrilled to see me featured as a young actress on the rise on the front page of the arts section in the *Toronto Star* Sunday paper. My own excitement was tempered because my desire for fame and recognition now seemed crass.

Moving back and forth between my world and Pam's left me reeling. For several hours every day I occupied the realm of pretend and make believe, costume and scenery, ambition and ego. Later at the hospital I was confronted by harsh reality, though I made believe there too. I made believe that what I saw didn't scare me. I made believe the kids would all get better, that Pam would get better.

The young children on the CF ward staged races with their IV poles. They gathered at one end of the hall near the elevators and yelled "Go!" Running, pushing their poles ahead of them, they jumped on when they'd gotten up enough speed, squealed and careened around nurses carrying plastic trays full of meds. It made me laugh and broke my heart.

Pam changed her own IV needles. She had become proficient, as had many of the CF teenagers and young adults, though technically it wasn't allowed. She winced with pain as she absorbed the pounding of her treatments even after her lung collapse. When her veins turned to mush, the nurses had to invent new places to put her IV. She struggled for oxygen, for energy, for faith and endurance, climbing through time from one moment to the next, like a fish fighting upstream.

What was my life compared to that?

Late that spring Pam suffered another, if quite different, assault on her heart. Tom Burns, a young man with CF whom she had met at Sick Kids, openly declared his affection for her.

I perused my sister's first love letter as she sat next to me on my parents' living room settee, her eyes dancing, her smile hidden behind the fists she bunched giddily over her mouth. She had flagged me down the instant Rick and I arrived at the house, home for the weekend to celebrate my twenty-third birthday.

"... When I think of you Pam, I think of a very wonderful person, who has done and is doing some pretty terrific things with her life. I think it is important that you realize that the CF plays a very small role in my feelings. I do not think of you as Pam Summerhayes with CF, but rather as Pam Summerhayes, attractive woman..."

"Pam, this is wonderful!"

My sister shrugged her shoulders as I returned the letter.

"I don't know if I love him," she said. "I mean, I love him as a friend and all that, but I don't know if I love him romantically."

Tom Burns was tall and pale, with dark wavy hair, intense

brown eyes, and a sparse mustache. He had a world-weary air about him, accentuated somewhat by the concavity of his chest, and the rising curve of the spine near his shoulders, which was a hallmark of an adult with severe CF. He was a year or so older, and worked as a medical photographer.

"How do you feel about his having CF?" I asked her.

"Well, I guess I always kind of hoped I'd interest someone who didn't have it because, well, you know it's hard to think of having a relationship with someone when you both face an uncertain future. But, it's not that I wouldn't have a relationship with another Cystic…"

She chose her words carefully.

"I really like Tom, he's a good person and all that, but he's very serious, you know, and I'm a little frightened of him being too needy. I've got to be careful about how much I can give, realistically, 'cause I've got my own stuff to deal with, like my heart for instance."

"What?" I teased. "You don't want it to get broken?"

"You know what I mean. My heart's not getting enough oxygen on account of my lungs being in such bad shape, so it has to work harder to pump blood to get the oxygen into the rest of my system. But it's working so hard now that I get tired real easy, and sometimes I even start going into failure. The digitalis is supposed to help that, but there's only so much I'm allowed to take. And Dr. Crozier's put me on Lasix, but that really upsets my electrolytes." Lasix was a diuretic that helped get rid of the fluid that built up in her lungs due to congestive heart failure.

"It makes me have to pee about every five minutes, but if I don't take it, my chest just fills up and I can't breathe and my ankles and hands swell and everything."

"Remind me what electrolytes are."

Pam smiled patiently. "Your electrolytes are your sodium and potassium. They're supposed to be in balance with each other, and if they get too far out of whack, you can go into shock or get kidney failure."

"Oh charming."

"So, anyway, I'm not doing too well on that score at the moment, and it's all I'll be able to do to get through my finals and find a job in the next month, never mind starting a relationship. And besides, I don't want someone loving me out of pity. Or maybe he's just settling for someone with Cystic Fibrosis because he thinks that's as good as he can get because of his CF, you know, not because he really loves who I am."

"Pam, you know better."

Pam shrugged her shoulders, sighed, and gazed out of the bay window to the trees in the front yard, shimmering with the new green life of spring. The sound of trilling birds filled the thoughtful silence before she spoke again. "I guess loving anybody is a risk. And God only knows life itself is a risk. I guess if I'm not willing to take the risk, and then I'm not really living my life." She turned to me again. "What do you think I should do?"

"When I was deciding whether or not to marry Rick, you told me to follow my heart. I think you should take your own advice."

Pam's hazel eyes turned green as they filled with tears. And then she laughed.

Tom courted Pam through the spring and early summer, while she continued to sort through her feelings about making a romantic commitment in the face of death. Looking for a metaphor to give her, it struck me as the sort of decision that young couples had historically struggled with in wartime. And there was no question that she and Tom were engaged in a war with as mortal an outcome as any between nations.

For a Cystic, being twenty-two was like being eighty-two in a normal lifespan. As Pam put it to me, you knew that you only had so much time left, so you had to decide how you really wanted to spend it, and not waste your time and energy on things that you didn't consider important.

"I wish everyone lived more like that," she said.

I agreed. None of us really knew how much time we had left, so what was the point of doing anything you didn't feel with your whole heart?

Acutely aware of this, my own goals and commitments took on a religious fervor, while I proselytized to friends and colleagues that they should feel likewise. What came out of Pam's mouth as philosophic, however, sounded didactic in mine. "Shoot From The Hips Summerhayes," my friends called me. "Don't ask Heather what she thinks," they half-joked, "'cause she'll tell you."

Grover tried to counsel me. "You're so intense, Heather, some people find it hard to take. You act like everything's a matter of life or death."

"But it is, it is!"

She smiled, and took my hand.

"I know," she said, with great compassion. "I know."

I did not attend my sister's graduation from college in early June, and now I can't remember why. What could I have been doing that was so important? Did I have a matinee? Or did the college restrict attendance to parents only? I should have called in sick. I should have fought the college. These are the kinds of choices that, in hindsight, teach us what's really important.

It was July before we got around to officially celebrating Pam's twenty-first birthday, and her diploma. She had made the Dean's Honor List. There was early corn and late strawberries. There was whipped cream and vanilla cake, lemonade and chocolate chip cookies—even though Pam's dear friend Darlene Bunyan had died a few weeks earlier. There were balloons and streamers and flowers—even though Pam was in excruciating pain and had been for three days.

Pam hid it so well that only my mother knew, and even she didn't realize how bad it was. Three days earlier they had gone to see Dr. Overholt, our local family physician. Mom told me he literally punched Pam's left kidney where my sister told him the pain was. She winced but did not cry out or speak. She'd already been in the hospital for two weeks earlier in the year. She did not want to go in again, and she did not want to cancel her party.

Dr. Overholt diagnosed a kidney infection and sent her home with a prescription. Not until the last partygoer went home did Pam give in to her agony, and have Mom and Dad take her up to Sick Kids. My mother phoned me at the Simcoe Summer Theatre where Rick and I were appearing together in a new play.

"It's an abcess," she told me. "Her right lung has completely shut down."

"How bad is it?"

"It's bad, Heather. It's real bad."

⌒

Rick and I drove silently through the sunlit morning past fields of tasseled corn and purple-blossomed tobacco while Melissa Manchester begged tunefully on the radio for *one more try*. I gazed out of the car window toward the green horizon, pressing back tears, telling my sick heart to go bury itself. It wasn't just because Pam was in dire straits.

There was a seventeen-year-old girl in the theatre company with whom Rick had been flirting openly. I caught them together alone backstage. He flashed me a supercilious grin as she sat draped on his lap. Later, when she injured her arm in rehearsal, Rick insisted he drive her to the hospital. They were gone for hours. Apparently the small-town emergency department had been unbelievably busy.

He swore nothing happened. I wanted to believe. I needed to. Not just because I loved him. Pam could die any day now, and I was in enough pain already.

⌒

My mother studied for her Registered Nursing Assistant final exams, continued to work part-time as a nurse's aide, and of course, took care of the boys and Dad. I stayed at the hospital with Pam for several hours every Monday and Tuesday, but Wednesday through Sunday Rick and I were both at the theatre in Simcoe. This left Pam alone more than any of us, especially my mother, could bear.

My mother wrote to her:

Dear Pamela,

I want you to know how very much I will miss you this week, but that I will be with you in spirit every minute. So many people have called to let me know they are thinking of you and hoping you would have the courage and patience to see this through and come home really well healed this time.

I am thinking in my heart of hearts that your recovery is going to take a fairly long time. Dad and I are quite prepared for this and accept it—we want you to feel that we are not anxious or fearful but just concerned that you yourself will take the time for a complete recovery.

During the next few weeks your rate of progress will reveal itself to you and you no doubt will have many questions in your mind. Please share them with us and let us love you and support you in every way we can without taking your independence away from you, because I know it is so very precious to you.

*Do not be afraid to assert yourself with the health care
team when their procedures are mediocre and unnecessarily
painful. You are a young adult who has sufficient to bear
without added discomfort.*

*...I have every confidence we will all make it together and
come September perhaps my horoscope will prove true and
things will take a turn for the better.*

*I am leaving a little prayer with you that I wrote this
morning. It is what is in my heart—keep it close to you.*

*You have given your Dad and me the real meaning of
courage, humility, quiet strength and love; we shall always be
grateful for that come what may.*

God Bless and Keep You My Lovely Daughter

Love Mom

Pam lay in her tiny room, second down from the nurses' station, listless and tearful, staring at the green wall next to her bed.

In from Simcoe on my day off, I sat opposite her next to the
wall at the end of the bed near the door, on the edge of a hard-
backed chair, not knowing where to look or what to do. My
mother had told me that Pam was fighting for her life. The lung
collapse had forced her to relinquish the dream job she had
recently landed with a daycare center. She had fallen into a deep
depression, which the doctors said could adversely affect her
prognosis.

"Losing the job was bad enough, but Tom had tickets to take
me to see John Denver at the Canadian National Exhibition,"
Pam wept. "It's the first time he's ever sung here, and by the time
he comes back again it may be too late..."

Pam took great solace in music. John Denver was her idol.
"Sunshine on My Shoulders" was practically her theme song.

"Won't they even let you out to go to the concert on a day
pass?"

"No."

"Not even for a couple of hours? What if we can arrange for a nurse to go with the two of you?"

"They won't let me leave this bed as long as my lung's collapsed."

I reached for the Kleenex and handed her a fistful. She blew her nose and gazed at me pitifully. "They keep trying to fix it, but it won't stay inflated for more than a few hours and then it collapses again. I'm probably never getting out of here."

"Don't talk like that."

Pam jutted her jaw forward, turned her head away and grew steely-eyed. The sides of her mouth pulled down and her nostrils flared as she tried not to cry again.

I have to do something, I thought, I have to do something. I know!

"You'll never do it." Pam's voice startled me. I looked up to see her grinning. She had absolutely read my mind.

"You just see if I don't," I said. I got up smiling and kissed her good-bye. "And I'm off to do it right now."

I raced home, put John Denver on the stereo, grabbed several sheets of paper, and sat down to write.

I wrote about Pam's history and condition, her present circumstances, and the almost spiritual joy that she received from his music. Would he be able to come and give a short concert at the hospital while in town, as Tony Bennett and Ella Fitzgerald had once done, so my sister could attend?

Next I called the reporter who had interviewed me for the *Toronto Star* and explained the situation. He told me how I might get the letter to John Denver's representative at the C.N.E.

Rick and I had to return to Simcoe for our weekend performances at the summer theatre. We stopped into the hospital on the way out of town.

"Okay," I told Pam. "I've written John Denver a letter and this guy Gino Empry said he's going to pass it on. It doesn't sound like he'll be able to get over here to the hospital, but my guess is he'll send you an autographed photograph or something. It's the best I can do. I hope I haven't let you down."

"You haven't let me down."

"Well, I'll call Mom after the show on Sunday night to find out if you've heard anything."

The entire cast joined Rick and me at a local pizza joint after our Sunday evening performance, crossing their fingers and giving me the high sign when I excused myself to go to the payphone to call home. My mother burst into tears the minute she heard my voice.

"What is it Mom? Did something happen to Pam?"

"It sure did," she said. "John Denver telephoned your sister."

⌇

After thirty-five days in the hospital, Pam went home. The call from John Denver had turned her around. She so enjoyed telling me all the details of the call.

"He must have thought CF caused a speech impediment, because I was stuttering so badly, I was so nervous. But I managed to ask him to dedicate a song at his evening concert to all the nurses and doctors at Sick Kids, who are doing such a good job taking care of me."

"And?"

"He said he would. He said he'd dedicate his third song, and I asked him what it was going to be, and he said..."

"No!..."

"Yes!…"

"Sunshine on My Shoulders!"

He also gave her a mantra: whatever it was she wanted, she had to "Go For It!"

Her lung collapsed again two weeks later, and she was re-admitted for a further eight days. She would put in sixteen more days at Sick Kids in December. She moved back into our parents' home with orders to "take it easy." Dr. Crozier put her prognosis at six months.

Unfortunately, we all still had to forge ahead with our own lives. Gregg had left home and inaugurated his studies in security and law enforcement at Sheridan College. Mom had graduated from the RNA program with the Award for General Proficiency. Not resting on her laurels, and with little celebration or ado, she forged pragmatically ahead with job hunting. I had begun rehearsals for my second season at the St. Lawrence Centre, and Jeff had entered his final year of grade school. Dad was busy ferreting out new business ventures.

Pam spent a lot of time alone. All of her friends had moved away to graduate school or begun new jobs. The visiting nurses checked in on her, and Mom and I called her several times through the day, for we were haunted by fears that she'd be caught on her own with a lung collapse, a hemoposis, or acute heart failure. She refused hired help, and in any case, we couldn't afford it.

The isolation was difficult for Pam to bear at first, not because of the solitude, but because everyone she knew was active out in the world.

My thoughts were always with her. During rehearsal breaks, I sat wondering what she was up to, instead of studying my lines. I imagined her sitting by the window, watching the leaves fall from the trees, crying because she felt so alone. I considered leaving the company to spend a few days a week at home with her, but when I made the suggestion she told me I was being ridiculous. I tried to offer her hope and strength, but it was usually me who ended up bawling while she reassured me that everything would be all right.

She spent the winter reading *Man's Search for Meaning*. She found her own philosophies articulated in Viktor Frankl's book, validating what she had come to believe through her own experience.

"We may not be able to choose our circumstances," she quoted to me, "but we can choose our attitude toward them. Everything can be taken from you, but you still have a choice how to respond."

Viktor Frankl reinforced Pam's thinking that the sort of person she became had more to do with her own inner decisions than the situation in which she found herself.

Pam agreed with Frankl that the way she bore her suffering could be a genuine internal achievement. *"It is this spiritual freedom—which cannot be taken away—that makes life meaningful and purposeful."*

Pam wanted to change her personal tragedy into triumph, making her life a work of art in and of itself, as one might take bits of broken colored glass and create a beautiful mosaic. Sharing these ideas with me in our long talks, enacting these concepts in her life, she taught me that when we are unable to change a situation, we are challenged to change ourselves.

My sister could no longer believe in a body that constantly betrayed her, so she turned to her spirit, which now seemed ever more tangible, and trustworthy. She could no longer look out to the world, so she looked further inward. Her illness, by definition, had always forced her to live in that liminal time and space between this world and the next. Now, it demanded that she live there ever more deeply. It became incumbent upon us to enter that liminal time and space with her, recognizing what was sacred and eternal, and seeing clearly what really mattered, each of us facing the truth of our own personal situations.

Christmas was coming. Pam sat with needle and thread as snow fell on the frozen stream and softly graced the pine boughs. Tenderly, her slender fingers smoothed the soft gold cotton she had chosen to make a quilt for me. She unraveled the measuring tape, considering the many inches, and carefully marked the fabric. She lifted the shears and slowly, meticulously, cut the cloth. Over the next several days, she patiently trimmed, hand-stitched, and ironed.

Miles away, in Toronto, I threw my windows open to the cold. Sleet was falling on the sidewalk. I removed the lampshades and turned the trilights up to their brightest wattage. I spread newspaper on the living room parquet, and knelt before Grandma Birdsell's old wooden hope chest, rescued of late from her backyard shanty. I put John Denver on the stereo, vacuumed the chest's innards, donned a pair of rubber gloves, dipped a brush in paint remover and stroked the surface of the wood with great affection. The finish creased and bubbled up. Fumes stung my eyes. My lungs ached as I inhaled. Flecks of remover splattered and burned the exposed skin in tiny spots on my wrists and cheeks. Lovingly, I sanded, oiled the hinges, varnished and polished, imagining the look on my sister's face when she unwrapped it.

On Christmas morning we exchanged our handmade gifts.

"This is to keep you warm," she smiled.

I smiled right back.

"This is to fill with hope."

On the last night of 1975, the Canadian Cystic Fibrosis Foundation raised $700,000 during the first ever twenty-four-hour New Year's Eve Telethon for CF Research, under the stewardship of foundation president Mary Corey, the young mother of little Jenny Corey, who had CF. Jenny was a robust five year old, a miraculous example of the new generation of Cystics who had been treated with the latest research right from birth. The image of Jenny that night, a spunky, rosy-cheeked little gymnast, dared us to believe that the word "fatal" might soon be stricken from CF vocabulary. To hear Jenny laugh was to hear the faint voice of hope whisper softly in our hearts that other unspeakable word, "cure."

Although my parents' role in the hands-on administration of the foundation had been peripheral for some time, our family also appeared on the Telethon. Rick stood watching off-camera as my parents, brothers, and sister crowded together onto a white couch under the hot studio lights. I knelt on the floor at Pam's feet.

"Coming to you live from CFTO Studios in Toronto..." My father was introduced as the founding president, my mother's contributions to the foundation were acknowledged, and the announcer rhymed our names off in turn as the camera panned. My brothers fidgeted and gazed self-consciously into the lens. When it came my turn, the announcer introduced me as a local actress. I smiled broadly beneath my Mary Tyler Moore flip, for a fleeting, stupid moment secretly hoping that I might catch the eye of some producer out there in televisionland who would "discover" me.

These thoughts evaporated the second my sister's face appeared on the monitor. Pam sat primly, smiling with embarrassment and delight, replying to the famous question, "So, what's it like to live with Cystic Fibrosis?"

"Well," she coughed politely, "there are days when it's very hard, but I try to keep a good attitude, and with some of the new medical breakthroughs, it's getting better."

"Pam will be twenty-two in March," my mother broke in to tell the announcer proudly. The studio audience applauded. Pam, even more than Jenny, was living proof that those research dollars could make a difference.

"Just look at those phones light up!" the announcer smiled. "And there they are, the Summerhayes family!"

The audience applauded again. We all smiled once more for the cameras, spirits soaring as the dollar totals changed swiftly on the giant, lighted board.

Later, beneath the cold and starry winter sky, we all returned to spend the night at my apartment in mid-town, our hearts warmed with the hope offered by the Telethon and a New Year.

We could not imagine how far that hope would have to carry us.

CHAPTER EIGHTEEN

*"Your pain is the breaking of the shell that encloses
your understanding."* — KAHLIL GIBRAN

January 10/76
Dear Heather,
*I don't know if this small piece of paper can hold all of the
loving thank-you's I have to write on it, but I'll give it a try.*

*I originally set out to write a note of thanks to you and
Rick for all the nice visits we were able to have when I was in
the hospital this past year. Believe it or not, I always looked
forward and enjoyed having you come. You usually were able
to give me a laugh or two, which did much for my spirit, even
tho' you may have been bored at times. Now admit it, it must
have been at times, eh?*

*Anyway, even though you and I are opposite in many more
ways than one, I think that I can say our hearts are closely
knit together with love! And may they always be—I pray. You,
like the rest of the family, but in your own special way have
given me more than you think, and in many ways which you
won't understand.*

*Please don't continue to punish yourself because I am sick.
It has no blame on you or anyone else.*

I have enjoyed the earphones immensely. It was certainly a

perfect [Christmas] gift since I listen to my stereo a lot. The
sound quality through them is beautiful.
 It was so good of you to have us down at New Year's. I
don't know how good a sleep we all got but we did enjoy it!
The apartment was looking pretty nice.
 Dr. C. give me a fairly good report. I'm not clear, but I
sound a little better. Luckily, I got him in a good mood.
 Mom started work today up at Paris Willet Hospital. She
will be working 3-11 part-time. I think it will do her good.
We sure have gotten a fair bit of snow here. Everything looks so
beautiful when it is white...

Unfolding the brief, delicate pages of my sister's letter, this winter day so many years after her death, I wail long, loud, and deep,
just as I did the first time I read it. *Please don't continue to punish yourself because I am sick. It has no blame on you or anyone else.*
Those words, tucked so casually in the middle of a newsy thank-
you note. Words of warning and absolution, of epiphany, words
that left me feeling painfully exposed. I did not know what to do
with those words. I remember calling my sister, sobbing.

"Heather," she counseled, "you've been doing this to yourself
ever since we were little. You have to stop now. You have to forgive yourself. It's not your fault. It's no one's fault. Please, I can't
carry this anymore, and neither can you. It's a waste of energy,
and time."

Her words fall through memory, fall through the snow on
the Hudson River, fall softly, fall stinging, into my heart. We are
having record cold temperatures. The river is freezing over, a
luminous, icy swath between me and the far shore. Naked trees
across the way in Riverside Park gather snow in their arms as if

wrapping themselves in mink. I dry my tears. Gently, I finger my sister's handwriting. I smile.

Everything looks so beautiful when it is white.

Dr. Crozier had advised Pam to put her life in order and enjoy what time she had left.

"You know what I'm going to do?" she asked me. "I'm going to Go For It, like John Denver said. I'm going to apply for disability pension, and I'm going to volunteer part-time at the Paris Day Nursery."

"Oh Pammy, is that a good idea? What about what Dr. Crozier said about taking things easy?"

"To hell with that. I'd rather have six good months of feeling useful than a year of sitting around feeling sorry for myself."

Pam was as good as her word. After a restorative trip to Florida with my parents, she returned and immediately applied for her disability pension. Within six months she was no longer volunteering at the nursery, but working part-time. Remarkably, she remained reasonably stable for an entire year, with only intermittent illness and no hospitalizations.

Inspired by the recently published book *On Death and Dying* by Elisabeth Kubler-Ross, Pam also began to work closely with Bernadette Ferry, the CF clinic social worker, and Mary Linda, another social worker in Brantford, in an effort to come to terms with her mortality.

At Pam's urging, my mother and I also read the book.

"We've been going through those five stages of death over and over since the day Pam was diagnosed," my mother observed wryly.

Pam's health remained modestly stable but precarious. The lion's share of our vitality still had to go toward supporting her efforts to survive. This meant there were times when we were myopic to the needs and feelings of both our extended families, and could afford little time or patience for affronts and dilemmas that seemed marginal to us in light of the life and death issues we grappled with daily. It is the nature of long-term catastrophic illness that the legitimate needs of family and friends go begging. It is also natural that to some extent, the ill person appears to be canonized, and the caregivers martyred. This can produce a strong, simmering brew of resentment in the extended family, and apparently it did in ours. Distance continued to grow between us and my father's family, and there were murmurings of discontent from Uncle Doug and Aunt Gloria, on my mother's side. They were all tired of Pam's frequent medical crises, of the way each emergency threw our lives into disarray, or perhaps took focus from their own triumphs and calamities. As my aunt would repeat to me years down the road, "We kept waiting for her to die, and she didn't." Perhaps by that she meant she thought we had overstated Pam's case. Clearly, she and my uncle did not understand the context in which we were then living.

By April of that year, for instance, Pam knew that her dear friend Patty Murphy was losing ground to a bad chest infection. One night Pam called to check in and encourage her, as Patty had done for Pam so many times through the years since they met at Crippled Children's Camp. Patty's mother answered the phone.

"Can I speak to your mother for a moment, Pam?"

My sister told me that she felt the blood drain from her face, knowing instantly in her heart what Mrs. Murphy was going to tell Mom. At the age of twenty-seven, Pam's friend was dead.

"Pam was in no shape to go to that funeral," my mother told me. "But she made your dad take her anyway."

"When my friends die," Pam told me afterward, "I ask myself

what I can take from them and use for myself. Like with Darlene, and now Patty, and even with Esther way back, each friend had something of value that I admired and gave me strength, and I figure if I can make those qualities part of my own self, then it's a way for them to live on. And now that they're gone, I have to keep fighting. I know they'd want me to, to sort of carry on, not only for myself, but for them, and for all the kids coming up behind us who are watching to see how we do, and how we die."

Rick and I were spending long periods of time apart while he toured with Young People's Theatre, or appeared at the National Arts Centre in Ottawa, and I remained in Toronto at the St. Lawrence Centre. By the spring of 1975, he had moved to Stratford to be a member of the Stratford Festival company.

In a whirlwind weekend, we gave up the lease on our apartment, Rick moved our furniture to Stratford, and I took up housekeeping with my friend Deborah Grover in a tiny, frigid, studio apartment on Rose Avenue. Thereafter, Rick and I communicated by phone nightly, but saw each other infrequently. I used my days off one week to see Pam, and one week to see him, alternately.

This already untenable situation became more difficult for both of us in the weeks after Rick made a sudden and devastating discovery.

He had been visiting his parents in Beaverton on his day off, and gone rummaging around in a storage room looking for some old high school artwork he wanted to bring home and show me. Pawing through one of the boxes, he had found what looked like a birth certificate, and a letter to his mother from a priest, discussing a baby. Hastily he had copied down the name and dates from the birth certificate, and sped to the St. Lawrence Centre in Toronto, where I came offstage to find him unexpectedly, standing in the hallway, shattered and numb.

Rick had been adopted, and never been told.

He decided for the time being not to confront his parents, but many nights that first summer after I'd finally moved with him to Stratford, I woke in the darkness to find him sitting up in bed with tear-stained cheeks, staring at his hands.

"Who am I?" he cried.

I held him then, but he could not be consoled.

As Rick struggled to assimilate the shock of his adoption, my sister fought to expand the bounds of her life, and I stretched my heart in a fine line between the two.

In a bold move, Pam left home and went into a studio apartment close by the spot where she planned to open The Three Bears Daycare with two colleagues in the fall. My parents were fearful, but supportive.

She joined the Big Sister's Organization, and proudly invited her Little Sister Michelle for weekly visits. Happily settled, she looked forward with great excitement to the summer, and Gregg's forthcoming wedding to Jan.

Our brother had been dating Janice Phillion for two years, and though barely out of their teens, they were each eager to begin a life together. Gregg was just twenty, and Jan eighteen. My mother felt disquieted about the coming nuptials, mindful of her own youthful commitment. She had already cautioned them once, asking that Jan return a promise ring Gregg had given her, and give it time.

"If I had it to do over again," she had often told Pam and me, "I wouldn't have married so young."

Only weeks before the wedding, my mother confided her mounting concerns to Grandma Birdsell. Mom had been running herself ragged—trying to prepare for the wedding while working twelve-hour night shifts at Memorial Hospital in Cambridge and, haunted by the fresh specter of Patty Murphy's death, racing back and forth to Toronto to visit Pam, who'd recently been admitted to Sick Kids with a chest infection. Emotionally and physically, my mother was close to exhaustion. She broke down and wept as she spoke to her own mother about her fears for Jan and Gregg.

"It's got nothing to do with Jan. She's a lovely girl. They're just so young, too young, and I'm afraid for them."

As far as I have ever been able to piece it together, my grandmother later called Uncle Doug and Aunt Gloria in a state of high anxiety, insisting that Doug call my mother to talk her into stopping the wedding. The nature of that conversation will be forever open to debate, but the outcome remains indisputable. Given my mother's raw state, my aunt and uncle's brewing resentments, and whatever overblown misperceptions my grandmother threw into the mix, irreparable damage occurred. Sharp words drew blood.

June 18, 1977, dawned sunny and full of expectation. This was the day Gregg married Jan.

Pam grinned triumphantly, pale and wan beneath a picture hat, an IV heparin lock on her wrist, her dress hanging in soft folds from her bones as she started up the aisle of the church. She had read Dr. Crozier the riot act, insisting she be released from the hospital on a day pass to fulfill her role as bridesmaid. Tom Burns had picked her up that morning, and would whisk her back that night.

Gregg stood at the altar, grinning at his sister, beaming at his bride. Yet this was also the day when Uncle Doug and Aunt Gloria estranged themselves from us, forever. This was the day when Grandma Birdsell began to blame us for that estrangement; when a tiny, black seed took root in her heart and started to grow. This was the day we would begin to pay for our all too human failures as a family in constant crisis.

I can say only this: if we failed our friends or family, or even each other, it was a failure of attention, or perhaps comprehension, but it was never, not ever, a failure of love.

CHAPTER NINETEEN

*"The world is full of suffering; it is also full
of overcoming it."* — HELEN KELLER

My sister's notes to herself, prompted by conversations with her
social workers Bernadette and Mary Linda, reveal her anguish as
she attempted to centre herself into stillness and fight despair.

- *mixture of happy & sad*
- *happy – alive, healthy, active*
- *farther ahead than ever believed I'd be 3 yrs. ago*
- *friends supportive*
- *seen friend cystics deteriorate & die even when they better
  than me – leaves me wondering*
- *not afraid of death – settled*
- *friend died cancer – January*
- *get school off ground [Three Bears Daycare]*
- *need new friends & close relationship*
- *feel lonely often*
- *feel need of someone to share my love, thoughts & time with*
- *feel need of close relationship with male*
- *someone to laugh, cry, talk with*
- *something inside of me not being presently satisfied &
  reaching out for comfort, perhaps because I can no longer
  retreat home for security or companionship*
- *at a loss where to go*

- *sister's relationship questionable?*
- *Nurse in hospital said "My, you really are a problem child, aren't you? If not one thing, it's another"*

Why didn't you talk about it in the hospital?
- *want to help in confidence – had other things to work out*

How do you feel about the situation? [our parents]
- *feel compassionate & understanding of both – torn & heavy heart*
- *helpless – watching 2 people I love so much being hurt deep inside – effects on Jeff – helpless*

Do you feel responsible?
- *yes & no – naturally extra strain on relationship & themselves due to chronic illness in family – I wonder if stayed together sometimes because of me*

Goals – to feel more content again with what I am able to do rather than discontent about what I can't do
- *to perhaps learn to "let go gracefully" of some desires or abilities not able to accomplish*
- *to maintain a level of self dependence in living each day but depending on other people when needed*

"Sister's relationship questionable." It was. Rick and I were foundering. I was certain he'd fooled around on me while I was away at the Manitoba Theatre Centre working on *Night of the Iguana*, so I did a little fooling around of my own.

Pam had talked me into going—I hadn't wanted to be so far away from her in case she got sick, and of course, she went into the hospital the first week I was there. The night she called me I had a wailing good cry, lit a Craven menthol cigarette, and poured myself a huge glass of sweet red screwtop wine. Long into the night I sat at my window, sipping the wine, dialing Rick's number in Toronto where he was working, counting the number of rings, hanging up, lighting another cigarette, inhaling deeply, dialing again, staring outside into the brittle darkness, forty degrees below. The last of the wine tasted bitter. The radiator pumped out scalding heat around my knees while below-freezing cold knifed through the pane of glass, stiffening my fingers as I dialed one last time. No answer. It wouldn't be the last time I called and his telephone went unanswered well into the night.

I detached myself, not from Rick or Pam, but from the heartache of a dubious marriage, and the anguish of having a dying sister. It wasn't a conscious choice. I simply let myself be a little wild, unencumbered, light-headed, and light-hearted.

It sickened me in the aftermath when I realized that cheating and lying were anathema to my nature, that I really loved my husband, that I hadn't found any healing or even fleeting joy in my actions, but only wounded my husband, and sabotaged my future with him.

My parents were holding on to their own marriage with their fingernails. Jeff had bought himself a horse with money he'd earned from cutting lawns, and chopping and selling firewood. When my parents fought he hitched a ride or hiked to the nearby stable where he kept his horse, and remained there, sitting in the hay, sometimes having a good cry, until he thought things might have calmed down at home.

My sister's note on the card she sent for Rick's and my fourth anniversary was very telling:

I didn't know whether to send 1 or 2 cards but I figured one or the other of you would each see it sometime, if not together...

A letter she sent to me a few days later had this P.S.
You want some advice from me. Well, I'm staying out of
your decision.
All I want to say is what I've found.
"Consider all the possibilities and problems very carefully
first; but in the end you must listen to what your heart tells
you." I would suggest that one evening you go some place
inspiring alone and just sit there and think and talk with God.

I spent most of that summer away from Rick in Toronto,
rehearsing scenes for acting class, shooting commercials, doing
some fruitless theatre auditions, and spending my spare time in
the company of a new friend, Brenda Devine.

I had met Brenda through the Centre for Actors Study. She
was a kindred spirit on more than one level—her beloved sister
Carol had been a lifelong, severe diabetic who was prone to
seizures, had lost an eye, and now desperately needed a kidney
transplant.

My closest friends all came from difficult, painful backgrounds: Grover had been abandoned by her father at age three,
leaving her to be raised by a mentally ill mother who was frequently institutionalized; Rhonda's sister suffered from paranoid
schizophrenia serious enough to have thrown her entire family
into chaos. These women attracted me in part because of their
courage and ability to create wholeness where their lives had
been broken. It was also a relief and a comfort to be with friends
who did not view my perpetual grief as an overreaction or need
to dramatize.

Brenda and I saw each other almost every day. We spent
afternoons in the tiny front yard of her tiny house drinking
Mexican coffee in the sun, sharing ideas and dreams about our
future as actresses. As twilight descended, we moved inside,
poured ourselves large glasses of wine, and analyzed the men in

our lives. After dinner we worked on our scenes for class, brewed fresh pots of strong coffee, opened a bottle of Metaxa brandy, peeled the cellophane off new packs of cigarettes, and wept together for our sisters.

I told Pam about Carol, who lived in Newfoundland, and Brenda told Carol about Pam. Our sisters became pen pals, and began talking to each other long distance on the phone. We made plans for Pam to visit me for a few days in July when Carol was scheduled to come to Toronto to have her kidney transplant. Brenda had been okayed as her donor.

"I'm so jealous of you," I told my friend. "You get to save your sister's life."

Gregg was accepted as a constable with the Ontario Provincial Police.

He and Jan rented a townhouse in Mississauga, just west of Toronto. Jan worked full-time for the *Mississauga News*, and Gregg began his shifts as a rookie, working highway traffic. Once in a while I went out on the commuter train to have dinner with them, and Jan and I shared girl talk. I enjoyed my new sister-in-law immensely; she had a dry wit and a great sense of humor.

Gregg and Jan were not planning to have children right away, but Jan confessed that if she became pregnant, she'd be thrilled. They had discussed the possibility of having a CF child. The genetic counselors at Sick Kids couldn't tell them anything they didn't already know, but looking at Jan's background, there seemed a pretty good chance that she was not a carrier. Since childhood, Gregg had only wanted to accomplish two things with his life—to be a policeman, and a father. Jan had always wanted to be a mom. For them, it was not a question of if, but when.

Rick and I had begun to talk about children, as couples often do when they're in trouble and are looking for a way to cement their relationship. The idea seemed doomed, however. Rick complained loud and long how ugly he thought pregnant women were, and I was terrified of passing on the CF gene, or having, then losing, a child. And we'd have to be together far more often than we were, if we were going to get pregnant.

I remained in Toronto for Carol and Brenda's kidney transplant. Brenda's kidney started working the very minute they sewed it into Carol's body.

"She peed!" Brenda said excitedly when I visited her in the hospital. "She peed right there on the operating table!"

"You have no idea," laughed Carol, quarantined in a room on a separate floor, "how wonderful it is to be able to pee! People take peeing far too much for granted!"

I ran messages back and forth between their rooms as they recovered, wishing medical science would reach the point where I could give Pam a lung and say, "She breathed, she breathed right there on the operating table!" and Pam could say, "You have no idea how wonderful it is to be able to breathe! People take breathing far too much for granted!"

The water lapping gently at the shore, the stately trees, the spider-webbed cabins at Lake Couchiching were all just as I remembered from my foray seven years before, when I'd run away from home to pursue my dreams with the Youtheatre. Now I was back to visit Pam, who had come to volunteer as a nursing assistant and counselor at a summer camp for Cystics, run by the CF clinic.

On a day off, Rick and I had driven up to visit his parents. Because Beaverton was only a short distance from the camp, we stopped in on the way. Dozens of bony, hacking children ran amok on the campground, running, hanging from trees, making cannonball dives off the dock to see who could make the biggest splash, whooping like Indians and wearing yellow T-shirts that read Catch a Smile at Couch. Pam greeted us, grinning widely, and took us on a tour, bubbling over with excitement as she showed us around.

"It looks like you're having a ball!"

"I am! And that's not all!" Pam grabbed my hand and pulled me aside, giggling. "I'm in love."

"What?"

"Sssssh!" she whispered. "I don't want anyone to know. I want you to meet him, but don't let on anything."

"What do you mean, don't let on?"

"He doesn't know I'm in love with him yet."

We wandered down to the edge of the lake, where a group of young boys were raising havoc in the water, swimming back and forth to a raft offshore, pounding their skinny chests like Tarzan and bellowing, pushing each other from the raft, laughing.

A handsome, thin, bespectacled young man with sandy-colored hair and a charming smile casually approached us. I guessed him to be in his late twenties.

"Hey Pam, how's it goin'?" he asked.

My sister blushed ten shades of red.

"Great," she said, trying to be nonchalant. "My sister's here visiting me."

"Ah," he nodded shyly.

"Uh, Heather, this is Fred Tapping. Fred, this is my sister, Heather. She and her husband are both actors."

Fred extended his hand to shake. "How do you do?"

"Fine. It's a pleasure to meet you. Look's like you've got your hands full here."

"Yeah, well, that's okay. A lot of them don't get to be this loose at home, you know; their parents can be quite protective. So we let them go a little overboard here."

We exchanged further pleasantries, and Fred excused himself.

"Isn't he wonderful?" Pam asked as she walked us back to our car.

"He's wonderful. He's nice and he's good-looking and everything. So, when are you going to tell him how you feel?"

"Soon. I'm just working up my courage. And it's hard to find a quiet moment around this place."

Pam did not get a chance to tell Fred Tapping that she loved him. She was rushed from the camp by ambulance to Sick Kids a few days later wearing her yellow Catch a Smile at Couch T-shirt as they wheeled her into Emerg. She was in severe pain from arthritis in her joints and gout in her feet. And, as my mother put it to me, and Dr. Crozier had put it to her, with one lung completely shot and not much left of the other, Pam's congestive heart failure continued to be life-threatening. This time, he wouldn't even give my mother a prognosis.

"All right then," I chirped, showing up at Pam's door, "put on your rally cap!"

Pam's hospital room was cramped and green. It was furnished with a bed, a metal nightstand with one drawer, and a cupboard. In the corner, next to the door, stood a large white porcelain sink crowned by a tall curved silver spout, backed by a small mirror. Next to her bed stood the ubiquitous IV pole with its paraphernalia of bags and tubes. Over the coming days, they would aggressively ply my sister with antibiotics to fight infection, Lasix and digitalis to combat heart failure, and potassium-magnesium compounds to stabilize her electrolytes.

Anticipating that Pam would be in for a long haul, we instantly went into "make her comfortable" mode. I decorated her room with colorful art posters from the Stratford and Shaw theatre festivals. Mom brought her favorite blankie from home, her clock radio, a hotpot to make soup or tea, and a few other items to make things cozy. The staff allowed us to bring baking or homemade dinners up to the ward, and the nurses kept it for her in the meds fridge. We negotiated a microwave to heat such food on the days when the hospital menu wasn't to Pam's liking. I gave her a stained-glass suncatcher with a pastoral scene—a stream, a tree, and rolling hills—to hang in her window.

When Pam got out of bed she sat up in a large padded easy chair with a foldout leg support, the type I always associated with men in smoky dens watching football games. It was covered with a white flannel sheet trimmed with green stripes, and sported a pillow to support her back. It was a stolid, comfortable place from which to ponder the busy hallway—a throne from which to hold court during visits. Pam was Queen of the Ward, resting easily in the authority and wisdom earned through the trials of her illness, at twenty-four—an almost mythical age for a Cystic—one of the oldest surviving patients in the Toronto clinic.

She had secrets of survival to impart to the little children as they gathered around her feet, which they did often.

"I know there are times when you just get so discouraged," she told them, "because of doing the same thing over and over every single day and not seeing a great deal of progress; just sort of maintaining all the time and not really improving and getting instantly better like people often expect to. And you sometimes bargain with doing your treatment because there are always better things to do—to go out, to be the same as everyone else and do the same. So you tend not to do this and not to do that, or maybe just cut down on this and cut down on that, and often it doesn't work." She would giggle knowingly. "Let me tell you, I've done it myself, so trust me, you can get away with it for a while, but it doesn't work in the long term, really. So you must do your treatments every day without fail, even when you are tired, and take all your pills and never, ever skip them. But the most important thing is to learn to open your eyes to every new day and smile, and appreciate all that is around you, your family, your friends, and thank God for another day of life."

Staff dropped in after shift to have tea. Parents came to visit her as well, and she encouraged them, assuring them of the strong need for family support, love, and understanding.

"There are families who don't give it, you'd be amazed," she told me. "I think that's why some kids die, you know." Her eyes glistened as she spoke. "They have problems at home, pressure in the family partly from having CF. And they get all this attention and their sisters and brothers have such a hard time coping with it, and their parents fight a lot, and it's depressing, you know, and I think they finally just lose the will to live. Another friend of mine just died, and I think that's what happened to her."

"You could be describing our family," I admitted, beginning to tear up. "Are you trying to tell me...are you...?"

"Oh for heaven's sake no, that's just my point. We've had a lot of problems in our family, but there's a lot of love there too, and I feel it. That's what I'm trying to tell you. I can honestly say, I have so much love flowing from my family and friends toward me, I know that I will never lose my will to live."

I stayed in Toronto the entire two weeks Pam was in, visiting two or three times a day. She craved food. I brought her Swiss Chalet chicken, blueberry pie, macaroni and cheese in microwavable containers, homemade strawberry jam, and frozen yogurt for the two of us to share.

Pam sat in her big easy chair, gesturing for me to sit on the bed if I wanted to. Awkwardly, I hiked my hip up onto the high mattress and dangled my legs over the edge, always feeling like I was breaking some kind of rule. Every time a nurse came by I jumped off, which made Pam laugh. Then I'd climb up once more and perch uneasily over my sister, who leaned back into her chair, arms on the armrests in a meditative pose, her soft smile squished by her newest accessory, elastic straps holding oxygen tubes in place.

We chit-chatted about ordinary stuff—how lovely the roses were that Grandma Bill had sent from her garden; how Grandma Birdsell couldn't find anyone to cut her lawn to suit her, so she had done it herself and hurt her back.

In quiet moments, Pam spoke of Fred Tapping.

"I wonder if there's any point in telling him how I feel. Who'd want me in this condition? And I don't know if I want to put someone through the risk of loving me and then losing me if die."

"Pam, we're all taking the risk of loving someone and losing them when they die, every one of us. Besides which, who says you're ready to die? They're going to patch you back up in here good as new."

My sister gave me a dark look, and went on.

"I told Mom she should go ahead and go to nursing school this fall. Did she tell you she was accepted?"

"Yeah, she told me, but she's been talking lately about changing her mind and backing out."

"That's since I've been in here. She's afraid of my getting too sick and her not being able to take care of me if she's in school. But I told her she's built her whole life around taking care of me, and when I'm gone there's going to be a big hole there, and she'll need something to fill it. So I said she had to go for it, like John Denver told me. It was her dream to become a nurse, and I want to know that when I'm gone she'll at least have her dream—that my being sick didn't take that away from her."

She went on to talk a little about camp, friends who'd sent her notes and cards. Her attitude had changed toward the hospital staff, she said, after seeing them at camp. She saw how the campers and the staff dealt with each other more from a human being level than she'd ever seen on the ward.

"I really see now that they care with their hearts—the staff, I mean. They care as people, not just because they are supposed to care because they work at what they do. So now that I'm in the hospital, I don't see the nursing staff and the doctors staff just as nurses or doctors doing their duty. They're coming across to me as real friends, and that's important, because I need that friendship now when my other friends can't be here to encourage me."

These hospital friends included her physios, Ellie Wanamaker and Inese Krastins, her head nurse, Carol Sheppard, and Bernadette Ferry, the clinic social worker.

Pam smiled. "'Course it's a little harder being friends with Dr. Crozier or Dr. Levison. But I'm working on them."

Pam felt she still had a lot of unfinished business, and this latest episode convinced her more than ever that she needed to begin working it through, whether the rest of us were ready or not. In the hard, dark hours of early morning she lay awake and faced her demons. In the afternoons, when I visited, she was ready to talk.

"Gregg was in here the other night."

"Oh yeah? How's he doing?"

"He had his first fatality."

"Oh no."

"Yeah. This guy was on his way home from work, and I don't know what happened, whether he rammed into the back of a truck and flipped over or what, I don't know. There were actually a couple of accidents Gregg told me about, and I'm probably getting them confused, but in one of them Gregg said the force of the impact smashed the car so bad they basically had to pick this guy out of his trunk, and he'd been decapitated, and there were shards of glass sticking in him and everything. Gregg seemed pretty upset about it."

I winced. "Did he have to go to the house and inform the relatives?"

"I think so. It made me feel pretty bad when I thought about him going through that. And imagine the poor family. Imagine saying good-bye to someone in the morning and then never seeing them again."

"Yeah. And what if you've had a fight the night before or something? Or even if you were just in a rush and hadn't given them a hug or a kiss good-bye?"

We sat in mournful silence for a moment, thinking of the nameless dead man, his wife, and kids, if he had any, or his parents.

"What are you thinking?" Pam asked.

"Honestly? I'm wondering if it's better to go like that guy in the car accident, just all of a sudden and it's over, and there's no long-drawn-out suffering, or if it's better to…you know, know that you're dying and have time to say your good-byes."

Pam stuck out her bottom lip and shrugged her shoulders. "Like me, you mean?"

I blushed.

"I know what you mean, and I've been thinking about it a lot myself lately."

"And?"

"I think it's better to have the time to say good-bye, and make sure you don't leave behind any regrets."

"So," I took a deep breath, "do you have regrets?"

Pam sighed and looked away sadly, choosing her words carefully before she spoke.

"No. I just think we need to resolve some of the stuff about us being jealous of each other growing up. I was always jealous of you because you were so healthy and you could do so many things I couldn't, and I know one of the reasons you were always so angry was because of being jealous of me, because I got so much attention."

My heart was beating very fast and I felt short of breath as Pam went on. "I always felt guilty knowing it was because of me that you were so angry."

"Well, I always felt guilty about being so angry. But I was mad about your being sick. I was never mad at you."

"Yes you were. You had to be. Heather, it's okay. There've been times I've been mad at you, too. It's only natural, and it's better for us to just admit it and get all that out of the way."

The room seemed smaller, the paint on the walls greener. The sounds of street traffic below, the bustle in the hall, all melted into silence. I could feel the strong pulse of blood in my stomach, as if I was being kicked from the inside.

"My anger ruined your life," I blurted, tears suddenly streaming.

"That's nonsense, your anger didn't ruin my life anymore than my being sick ruined yours."

I slid down from the bed and knelt in front of Pam, putting my arms around her.

"Oh Pammy, you didn't ruin my life. If my life is ruined, it's my own damn fault for behaving so badly."

Pam started to giggle through her tears. "Now I'm confused. What's going on here? Either we've ruined each other's lives or we haven't!"

Both of us laughed now as we wept. I stood up and grabbed a bunch of tissues from the box on the metal nightstand, dispensing a few into my sister's tender, club-fingered hands. We each blew our noses and laughed some more as I jumped back up on the bed.

Pam was ready to change the subject.

"Did you know there was a Mennonite girl brought in here by helicopter yesterday? She fell off a thrasher and it severed her arm."

"Oh my god!" I sniffed, still wiping tears from my cheeks.

"Yeah, but they packed the arm in ice and brought it in with her, and they reattached it last night with that new microsurgery they're doing now."

"Holy cow!"

"They say it went well. There's quite a buzz about it all over the hospital. It will be a few weeks before they know whether the operation takes or not."

"What happens if it doesn't? Do they amputate her arm again?"

"I don't know. I guess they'd have to. It'd be better than walking around like this for the rest of your life," said Pam, flapping her arm crazily at her side, laughing. "I'd say take it off and give me something that works!"

We tumbled laughing on her bed.

A few days later, I climbed the dark tunnel of steps out of the subway into blinding sunlight. The sky above was white, dancing, filled with doves, dazzling white doves, dozens of them crowding the sky above University Avenue, streaming and swooping in the air over the cars and the trees and bright gardens planted in the median of the roadway.

No, they were not doves, they were paper airplanes. Flying in from the vault of heaven, hordes of gleaming white paper airplanes, soaring through the canyon between Mount Sinai Hospital and the Hospital for Sick Children. My heart soared with them.

I flew through the doors in Emerg and raced up the seven flights of stairs rather than wait for the elevator, excited for Pam to see the planes. Perhaps from the vantage point of her floor, we could figure out where they were coming from.

The hall leading to her ward was unusually empty, and there was a sound of great commotion coming from down the passageway around the corner, exactly where I was headed. As I turned past the nurse's station and entered the second corridor, I saw a small forest of IV poles amidst a throng of children letting loose torrents of squealing laughter. I walked straight past my sister's room, drawn by curiosity.

"What's going on here?"

The children turned their shining faces upward and opened a path for me to approach. There at the end of the hallway, next to an open window, sitting beside a tall stack of white paper, was Pam, grinning madly, folding paper airplanes.

⌇

Pam went home permanently leashed to a large oxygen tank. For short forays to the mall she wore a purse-sized oxygen tank slung over her shoulder. Before her release, an oxygen salesman had visited her room, bearing pamphlets advertising the different models of tanks.

"Look at this," she giggled, showing me a color brochure of a family picnicking in a setting reminiscent of the Swiss Alps, one of the members sitting happily on a blanket next to an oxygen tank. "In the first place," she said, laughing, "if someone had to be on oxygen, how are they going to climb up a mountain to go on a picnic and then sit there with a tube up their nose eating fried chicken and potato salad?" Now she was howling and holding her sides. "And in the second place…" She did not get to the second place, for she was laughing so hard she launched into a coughing fit. Her phlegm was pink.

Mom and Dad wanted her to move home. Her colleagues at Three Bears felt uncertain about her being able to continue working. She defied all of them, moving from her studio apartment into a one bedroom for fire safety, so the oxygen tank could be kept in an area separate from the kitchen stove. She ordered a second tank for work at Three Bears, and sat tethered to it as she read to the children in circle, the tubes hooked over her ears, pressed against her pale, grinning cheeks, and tucked into the tiny nostrils of her pug nose.

"I know I have to accept things as they are, not as I want them to be," she told me, "but I'll do it on my terms, and in my own time."

Her sense of time running out meant that she wanted to accomplish more, not adjust to less. She and her "Little Sister" Michelle baked cookies, planted flowerpots for Pam's balcony, and attended Big Sister special events.

My mother, honoring Pam's request, had begun nursing school. She was forty-five years old.

"What's a woman your age doing in nursing school?" a young fellow student asked on her first day. "You'll be nearly fifty by the time you graduate!"

"I'll be nearly fifty anyway," my mother replied.

My parents' marriage was slowly mending.

"We've struggled this far together," my mother said, "we're not about to throw in the towel." In fact, my mother said, now that she was back at school, she had grown to depend on Dad. Frequently he drove her to work or to class, ran errands, and generally pulled things together in much the same way she had done all these years.

Dad bragged that he had become a grocery shopper extraordinaire, and Mom said it was true, laughing affectionately at how my father spent hours driving all over the county searching for the best cheese and the best produce at the best prices.

"Oh heavens," she said, "He's taken over nearly everything at home. He won't let me near the dishwasher. He said he's the only one who knows how to load it right."

I was heartened by this, and by the fact that I was finding a place where I fit comfortably with my mother and my sister. Pam was heavily dependent on my mother, but also needed to be her own woman. My mother was devoted to Pam's care, but needed to know when to step back. I was often able to facilitate the delicate balances between them.

Pam went back into Sick Kids from December first to the fif-teenth. Winter always had its way of wreaking vengeance on kids with CF. The ward was packed.

With my sister in the hospital, my mother wrote her first set of nursing exams in despair. I pictured her in the car on her vis-its up to Sick Kids and back, staring out the passenger window, wondering where she would find the time, the sleep, the money, the strength, the heart. My father, tense behind the wheel, offered mindless chatter, then sighed, and then fell into a deep silence.

He stood restlessly in the hospital hallway outside Pam's room, nervously wiping his nose side to side with his big cotton hankie, adjusting his glasses, and attempting with halting, stop-start utterances to exchange a discourse with anyone who might be willing. I once saw him carry on a one-sided conversation with an immigrant lady who worked there mopping floors. She spoke little English but nodded patiently, pushing her mop in circles as my father rambled on.

Christmas was an effort, but the effort had to be made. When Pam was released, I came up from Stratford to help her and Mom with the baking. My mother festooned the mantle over the fireplace with green felt, twinkling lights, and holly. The house smelled of wood smoke, peach brandy, and cinnamon, and it rang with the voices of the Mormon Tabernacle Choir, more melancholy than joyful.

Rick held Pam's hand and entertained her at the kitchen table while she had her mask. I had come so close to losing them both in the past year.

Who would I be without them? What would my life mean? There was Pam, who would have given anything to declare her love to Fred Tapping, to have it reciprocated, to have a marriage and a life—and here I was with all of that and nearly throwing it away.

"You're going to need Rick when I'm gone," Pam counseled me. "You've got to pay less attention to me and more attention to your marriage."

On New Year's Eve, I resolved to triage my priorities. My marriage would come first. Pam would be second, and my career third, just fitted around the corners and into the nooks and crannies of my life. With enough love and energy, enough prayer and tenacity, I could make it work, "God Willing and the river don't rise…"

CHAPTER TWENTY

"Do not fear death so much, but rather the inadequate life."
— Bertolt Brecht

I once stood with Rick on the dock in Beaverton, gazing out across the water while a squall blew in from the other side of Lake Simcoe. Sunlight poured down all around as the dark edge of the storm moved slowly toward us, at first just a black line on the far shore, then a giant smudge of sooty cloud in the near distance, then a hard gray wall of rain inching relentlessly closer, moving like a scalpel through the glassy water, until finally it slapped the shore with a cold, hard rush of wind flinging sheets of icy droplets that shredded our skin like pinpricks, like straight razors.

If Pam's death was an approaching storm in 1979, life was a transistor radio playing pop tunes on the beach while we tossed Frisbees, listened to John Denver songs, and kept a wary eye on the horizon.

Each morning at the Three Bears Daycare Centre, the children's laughter gave my sister a surge of renewed energy.

Her partners in the daycare, Judy and Janet, were frightened by the progress of my sister's disease. In spite of Pam's dedication, discipline, and commitment, and the hours she continued to put in there, they felt threatened by the uncertainty of her condition.

Pam returned to work in early January blissfully unaware of

this, anticipating the joy of being with "her kids," doing meaningful work, determined to pace herself as she convalesced, but giving all she could.

It was not to be. One day, without warning, Judy and Janet sat Pam down during the lunch hour and blurted, "You won't like this, but we've got to say it—we don't feel our partnership is working out."

Pam reeled, blown away by their cold list of small but carefully itemized objections to the manner in which her deteriorating health was adversely affecting the daycare.

"It would relieve the strain," they said.

"On who?" Pam managed to whisper.

Her chest heaving with mounting panic and the effort to breathe, she tried to argue that she was contributing to her capacity. She reminded them that they had entered into the partnership on the full understanding that she would not be able to pitch in a full share of the physical load.

"The only way to do this is to buy you out," they continued undeterred.

"Can I still come in and read to the kids in circle?" Pam was close to tears.

According to the notes Pam jotted down after, Janet sat quietly, nibbling at a sandwich, while Judy just sighed and looked at her watch.

Pam felt the hurt as sharp in her body as any lung collapse.

"I need some time to put this into perspective," she said, gathering her wits. "I've got a lot of feelings about this I need to settle."

She showed up for work again the next day, but right away realized it was a mistake. Afraid things might start to get ugly, she left, feeling resentful and angry.

"I'm going to get a lawyer," she reported to Mom. "I have to protect myself…"

Losing your reason to live is far worse than losing your capacity to do so. Feeling that you no longer have anything meaningful, however small, to contribute to the world, can cause a psychological hemorrhage as painful and fearsome as its physical counterpart. You bleed Will. Spirit drains out of you. I saw this happen to Pam.

"I wish they would just let me stay a while longer," she wept. "At least until I'm ready to decide for myself that I can't do it anymore. It wouldn't really cost them anything."

No, it wouldn't.

"I want to hunt these women down and muckalize them," I fumed to Pam.

She chuckled half-heartedly. "Wouldn't do you any good."

The next few weeks were as painful for Pam as any time in her life, as she and the lawyer negotiated a settlement.

Meanwhile she went over all the updated books and accounting with Judy and Janet, explaining how to organize the daycare's finances. I was astonished by her equanimity, and generosity.

The most difficult day came when she finally returned to the daycare to personally explain to the children and their parents that she was leaving due to her ill health. My mother said she'd never seen Pam so low.

"This has completely knocked the stuffing out of her. I don't know how, or if, she'll be able to get over it."

Pam wrote more notes to herself, sorting through her feelings.

- *adjustment large*
- *support from: parents and family*
- *reassurance: friends and V.O.N.*
- *guidance: med. Team in T.O.*
- *listening: Doctor and family*
- *understanding Social Worker at Family Services*
- *on Disability under Social Services*

- *still don't want to believe at only 25…*
- *incredible emotional working through to accept*
- *heart weak—desire to live*

We kept in touch by phone. She told me repeatedly she was trying to find some way to replace this loss with other means of fulfillment that would help her maintain a positive self-image. In spite of her best efforts to sound upbeat, her voice was hollow with despair.

To lift her spirits, we threw a huge party for her twenty-fifth birthday. Grandma Birdsell decided that something along the lines of the wedding Pam would never have, was in order. A head table, speeches, toasts, and flowers. We rented a banquet hall and invited EVERYONE. Mom went shopping with Pam and purchased a blue floral chiffon dress that floated softly on my sister's skeletal frame.

It was a bittersweet affair, crammed with friends from public school and college, members of the Sick Kids staff, her "Little Sister" Michelle, Tom Burns and the Coreys with their young CF daughter Jenny, Bob Ivey, who had worked with my parents on the CF Foundation twenty years before, and several aunts and uncles. Even her ex-daycare partners, Judy and Janet. Pam's secret love, Fred Tapping, was too ill to attend. Doug and Gloria didn't come either, though we'd asked Grandma to invite them.

There were gifts and laughter, memories shared out loud, and of course there were tears. Photographs show my sister drooping like the pink rose pinned clumsily to her tiny right breast, her eyes red-rimmed and teary behind a pair of large, square spectacles, all the light she had left inside her escaping through her smile.

She disappeared repeatedly, creeping back and forth to an anteroom to take oxygen while the rest of us sipped our sparkling wine. Then she reappeared, and like a bride, moved about the room spending a few moments with each guest. She smiled graciously, gulping air into her beaten lungs as surreptitiously as possible, stifling her cough with a hand placed genteelly over her mouth, leaning against chairs or tabletops to prop herself up. When the time came, she struggled to her feet once again, and from her place of honor at the center of the head table, thanked everyone, not only for the party, but also for the life she'd had.

A few days later, this letter appeared in the editorial section of the *Brantford Expositor*:

A while ago I was honored with a beautiful birthday celebration. To share this time of great joy and happiness with me were family, friends and many caring people who have been a part of my life. Every one of these people were genuine, beautiful and inspiring personalities.

The restaurant handled this occasion most graciously; the meal was very good and the atmosphere most pleasant. But what made this occasion most delightful was the opportunity to share my full 25 years of life by feeling so loved as well as being able to share my love in return.

The spirits of these people and many more I have had the pleasure of experiencing throughout life are perhaps why I have been able to overcome a life-long incurable illness.

If we take the chance and opportunity of seeking out beauty in the world about us, every moment of every day can be treasured. I have learned that no matter what misfortunes or joys one may be faced with – life will surely go on...with love.

I counted on my life going on with love. With Rick's encouragement, I auditioned for the Stratford Festival, hoping to both live

and work by my husband's side. It would be the best of both
worlds. We were both excited about the lovely house he had
found for us to rent, with a large yard on a tree-lined street not
far from the Avon River and a ten-minute walk from the theatre.
We had forgiven each other our excesses and failings of the previous year and vowed to make a fresh start. Rick seemed committed and caring, surprising me with flowers, entertaining me
with his cartoon drawings detailing the adventures of Poop and
Pep, two little characters he had based on us. We were content-
ed, affectionate, dare I say happy? Our friends remarked that we
couldn't seem to get enough of one another.

When I didn't get a job at the Festival, I decided to try to be
content with being a good sister that summer, a good daughter,
and a good wife.

I threw a fifth wedding anniversary party in our home, inviting almost the entire theatre company. I spent days shopping,
cooking, and preparing the house, filling the place with yellow
roses like those that had graced our wedding. I had a cake specially made and decorated, which we cut while posing for our
friends' cameras. Rick looked as wan and uncertain as the day we
married, while I gazed at him adoringly as if for a Hollywood
publicity still.

Pam could not attend my anniversary party, because she had
been rushed up to Sick Kids six days earlier. Her latest crisis cast
a shadow across my twenty-seventh birthday as well. I felt just as
sorry for myself as I did for her. *"Can't I just once plan something
special without Pam getting sick?"*

But there was no room for such thoughts. My mother was in
the home stretch of her first year of nursing school. Having pretty much vowed to be there for Pam when she couldn't, I often
did double duty at the hospital.

At least three or four days a week I rose at dawn, then rushed
to fix Rick bacon and eggs, and organize his lunch and dinner. I

made sure to leave him a little love note tucked somewhere as a surprise. Then it was off to the 8 a.m. train and a two-hour ride into Toronto.

At the hospital it was mostly silent spaces and idle chat. Sitting. Staring out the window. Cranking the bed, fluffing the pillow, pouring a glass of water. Helen Reddy on the radio. *"I'll be your candle on the water..."*

I helped Pam do her physio, gave her massages, or ran errands for her. Once in a while I slipped away to have coffee with Brenda or Grover or Rhonda, and have a little cry. With the best of intentions my friends exhorted me to stay focused on the big picture.

"Look down the road where there's hope," they'd say. I blessed them for that, but what they didn't understand is that in this kind of illness there is no big picture, and there is hope only in the moment. There is enough terror there too, without looking all the way down the road.

Back on the train for the two-hour ride home, I looked forward to some loving time with Rick. Before I could really settle in with him, however, I first had to call my mother to report on Pam's welfare. By the time I got off the phone, Rick had been sidetracked by a *Star Trek* rerun, and I just wanted to cry.

I put on a good show, but my life was ruled by fear. Fear of getting pregnant. Fear of Rick leaving me. Fear of not pleasing my parents. Fear of not being pretty or talented enough to get another acting job. Fear of Pam dying and leaving me alone with all this fear.

Not working was excruciating. If I wasn't acting, I reasoned, I was nothing, if not to myself then certainly to the other actors I met with Rick in the bar after his rehearsals. My prayers were soon answered, however. With less than a month left before the June opening, the leading lady in the Festival's musical took ill. With no time to find a replacement, the director bumped the understudy up into the role, and put out the call to replace the understudy.

At noon that same day, my phone rang. A friend in the company exhorted me to grab my tap shoes, show up at the rehearsal hall, and declare myself available. I did just that, auditioned on the spot, and was asked to stay for the afternoon's rehearsal. Within hours I had a signed contract to perform in the musical through the end of October.

Once again, my excitement was tempered when Pam went back into Sick Kids, less than a month after her release from a twenty-day stay. An electrolyte imbalance had become so serious it threatened her life with kidney failure. I had second thoughts about working, as I realized I was once more going to be pulled in two directions.

Within days, our brother Jeff was also admitted with a chest infection and intestinal obstruction, a condition that doctors were beginning to see with some frequency among Cystics as they got older.

Jeff was now sixteen. He had not been hospitalized since his second diagnosis in 1964. He was naturally upset that his disease had taken this sudden turn. To complicate matters, he was admitted to the ward only hours after another young CF patient had died. The patient's father was threatening to sue Dr. Crozier and the Hospital for Sick Children, although the girl had not been brought in for treatment until she was too far gone to be saved. The mood on the ward as Jeff checked into his room was one of anger, confusion, and depression.

This reinforced Jeff's notion that he had just taken his first step on a path toward his own death. His CF had been mild up to that point, so he'd never had to come to terms with his illness in the way Pam had done. He was an active teenager, used to playing hockey and riding horses with little or no thought for his health.

They put Jeff in a room down the hall from Pam. For the entire two weeks that he was in, he rarely came to visit her.

"I always have to go see him," Pam complained, "and I'm not doing it anymore, because even when I do he hardly speaks to me."

When Jeff walked past her room he kept to the far side of the hall, without a look or a wave. He remained antisocial with many of the other CF patients as well, as if by keeping his distance from them, he could prevent himself from "catching" their mortality.

Jeff's attitude toward my parents' visits ranged from indifference to irritation. Feeling like the family outsider, he had built a lot of walls around himself. He resented our concern and support, mistrusted it, and experienced it as an intrusion.

My mother struggled with doubt. She repeatedly insisted to me that she was a bad mother, a bad wife, a bad daughter, and a bad student, doomed to failure. I reassured her as best I could, promising to be there for Pam and Jeff so she wouldn't have to worry.

"It's what Pam's living for," I said, "to see you become a nurse."

I juggled my timetable through Rick's and my opening nights, and our subsequent performance schedule, to be at the hospital in Toronto as much as possible. I'd never gotten my driver's license, so I had to depend on the train. I spent more time there than I did almost anywhere else, back and forth, back and forth.

As might have been expected, one night I hit the wall. I arrived home from Toronto in the late afternoon, just in time to grab a bite and make the 7:30 half-hour call for my evening show. The house was a mess. The garbage, which I had asked Rick to take out before I left that morning, was still stinking up the kitchen. There was no food in the fridge. I went upstairs to take a shower, and there was no hot water. As soon as the cold water hit me I blew, howling, crying, and bashing the walls with my fists. Rick came running.

"What's the matter?"

I stood in the pink-tiled shower goosefleshed and dripping. "There's no goddamn hot water!"

"You can have a shower at the theatre, for Christ's sake. There's no need to get bent out of shape."

"That's not the point!"

"What's the point?"

"You, that's what! I'm carrying the whole damn load for both of us! I'm working and paying half the rent and doing all of the cooking and cleaning and grocery shopping, and I've got all this stuff going on with Pam and Jeff, and you can't even fucking take the garbage out or get dinner or make sure there's enough hot water!"

Rick fell to sleep that night with his back to me. I lay in the dark, silent and tearful.

A couple of days later I was meant to go again to visit Pam and Jeff. I wouldn't be able to see them over the weekend because I had matinees, and I wanted to spend my day off on Monday making things up to Rick for the fit I had thrown.

I woke to the sound of a heavy rain, feeling as if I hadn't slept. I called a taxi to take me to the train station; I would buy myself a coffee on the train. It took every ounce of my strength to climb the steps into the station. I had never felt so tired, beyond tired.

I bought my ticket and proceeded outside to the tracks. The train stood steaming in the warm summer rain. People were boarding; they jostled past me. I felt odd, disassociated, like a cardboard cut-out in a world of wind-up toys.

"All aboard!" called the conductor.

He lifted the stepstool from the platform and jumped up onto the train. He looked at me quizzically. His lips moved. Was he talking to me?

The great dark wheels of the train began to screech and turn. For a fleeting second I imagined throwing myself beneath them. I stared up at the faces of the people gazing back at me through the windows of the train, thinking dumbly, *why aren't I up there with them?* The rain pelted my head and shoulders as I stood rooted, the ticket growing flaccid in my hand. A suffocating dread swept over me, a drowning feeling familiar from my childhood nightmares, when I dreamt of giant brains on pins pushing me beneath the ocean.

I stood that way for a long time, watching the train disappear into the horizon, barely able to breathe, tears and rain streaking across my face.

After finding my way home from the train station I made somewhat hysterical phone calls to both my mother and Pam, each of whom urged me to seek immediate help. I was grateful when Dr. Ough told me to come right in. He listened thoughtfully as I poured out my tale. I must have seemed like a frightened child, for he spoke to me as if he was calming down a little girl who'd just woken up from a nightmare.

"And what is it you're most afraid of?"

"That Pam is going to die." I wept spontaneously.

"Let me reassure you," he said. "People don't die suddenly most of the time, even when they're really sick. It takes a while, and it's a process, and there are signs along the way, and if you know what those are, you can have time to prepare. For instance, people start to sleep a lot."

"Pam's doing that."

"Then that is a sign. Has she got anything living in her room?"

"What do you mean?"

"For example, does she have any plants?"

"Yes, she had plants and flowers and has her radio playing all the time."

"Well," he said, "that's a good sign, because when someone nears death they begin to cut themselves off from living things."

"She's been discussing her funeral arrangements with Mom," I blubbered.

"I see. Well, that's probably very wise."

"But at the same time she's insisting that while she's in the hospital, you know, she says, 'I don't want the shades drawn and I don't want the lights out and I don't want to be up to my neck in sheets. I want a bright room and I want people coming and going. I want everything to continue as normal. And I don't want people coming in here and breaking down in front of me.' Last week Mom came in and broke down crying in front of her and Pam said 'I don't want you to do that in front of me anymore. There is no reason to cry.'"

Dr. Ough passed me a box of Kleenex and I blew my nose.

"It sounds as if your sister has a pretty good handle on things," he said, "maybe better than you."

"Yeah," I smiled, "I guess she does." I chuckled weakly. "Last week her bedpan fell off the table and clanked on the floor and I said, 'My God, I thought it was Skylab falling,' and we laughed so hard…and if she does get angry or frustrated or anything, she'll usually say so right out, or she'll write it all down on a piece of paper. Like one night, she told me, she was mad about her situation and the way it's so hard on the family, and we're all trying so hard and going through so much on account of her, and she was angry about Jeff getting sick too, so she said she just wrote this five-page diatribe on her anger. She told me that by getting it out of her that way, she could spend more of her time with us laughing."

Dr. Ough cautioned me to be careful not to anticipate Pam's

death too much, or let my mother's reactions upset me. I must take my cue from Pam, he said, and if she was not distressed, I must ask myself why I felt that way.

I sniffed and nodded.

Then he warned me how the stress might affect my marriage, as if I needed a warning.

"No doubt Rick is feeling the strain too, but it is outside the realm of his experience, and he probably doesn't know how to help you. So, you know, if you get in a fight over the laundry, for example, how to fold the sheets, it's not really a fight about laundry. It's because you have so much anxiety over what's happening to Pam." As long as Rick understood that, and I let him know I was grateful that he allowed me to blow off steam, Dr. Ough said it would probably be okay. Rick needed to be nurtured, he advised me. I shouldn't ignore what was important to him, or make him feel that his problems were less than mine.

I let a few days pass before I went back to see Pam and Jeff. My brother was on the mend. His intestinal obstruction had moved so he hadn't required surgery, and his lungs were clearing up nicely.

Pam had been busy. Following the death of the young girl earlier in the month, the kids on the ward had held a bitch session, where it had been made clear that both the patients and staff had a lot of mixed emotions and unanswered questions about living with, and dying from, a chronic-terminal illness like CF. Pam had decided to answer some of those questions herself, in a video interview she and her counselor Bernadette had put together.

"Wanna see it?"

She grinned and jumped down from her bed, pulling her IV pole along beside her. I followed her to the nurses' station to pick up the videotape, and then down along the hallway to a classroom full of empty desks. I drew the blinds as she installed the tape in a TV/Video machine. Her thin body was electric with nervous excitement as she shuffled over to turn off the lights and grinned, instructing me to sit down.

Music swelled as the TV screen came to life revealing Pam, wearing her yellow Catch a Smile at Couch T-shirt from CF Camp. A nervous smile flickered across her otherwise sober onscreen face. Bernadette, round-faced and sweet, with straight honey-colored hair and large, square eyeglasses, gave a preamble, and then began to ask Pam a prearranged series of questions.

Pam and I sat together in the dark, watching her image on the TV screen as she spoke about her childhood, and laughed at her early notion that being skinny was more painful than the thought of dying. She recounted her realization at age ten that she was going to die, the struggle she had waged to overcome negative thinking, to maintain the discipline of her treatment regime, and the difficulty of losing her friends as they died. Then she began talking about her own death.

"My biggest thing I had to settle was the fact that I will be losing the people that I love, and that they will be losing me. And that's really the hardest thing is losing... thinking that you're going to lose the love, rather than losing your life, because that's what you always sort of think of as what you're gonna miss. And I always used to think, well, it will hurt them so much and it hurts me a little beforehand to see them go through some pain. But at the same time I'm realizing more and more that it's by going through this pain that we're experiencing how much we love each other, and the fact that we have meant a lot to each other. And I think if we, if I can make this a positive experience for me and help them to know that although it is frightening, that because they love me, it makes it less frightening."

I quivered. "You're not going to lose the love," I wanted to shout. "I'll love you forever." But I kept still, realizing that my sister was acquainting herself with Death, if not making friends. Did she expect us to do the same? I glanced at her, but she sat aloof in the desk next to me, staring pointedly and purposefully at the TV monitor.

> *"I tend to be very open and I say what I think and I say how I feel and it sometimes frightens people or they are not prepared for me to be as prepared for death as I am, or to accept myself as much as I do.… Sometimes I wish they would just sit and talk and they would really learn a lot. Sometimes I just wish people weren't quite so frightened of facing their own death and facing the feelings they have, because it really helps you a lot when you do. Sometimes you have to make yourself, but it does help."*

I pressed my lips together and tensed every muscle in my body, holding on for dear life as she made her closing comments, anticipating heaven as a place of rest, smiling self-consciously. The camera faded out, the music swelled, the screen went to credits and then to blue. Pam hopped up, flipped on the lights, and turned to face me expectantly.

"Well, what did you think?"

I wanted to cry, I wanted to dissolve into a flood of tears that would carry us both out the door and down the hall and away from the reality we faced, but I choked them back.

"I'm very proud of you."

Her fists flew to her mouth, her eyes danced, and she just beamed.

"I have a dream, a song to sing, to help me cope, with anything... I believe in angels, when I know the time is right for me I'll cross the stream, I have a dream..."

Abba, one of Pam's favorite groups, blared out of the window and across my patch of carrots, beets, and green beans. On my knees between the rows, I stopped yanking weeds to listen, and then bawled into the dirt and thought about catching the 11 a.m. train to Toronto.

Pam had been in nearly twenty days, but had shown little improvement.

And my destination makes it worth the while, pushing through the darkness still another mile...

Pam was having her own share of bad moments. The longer she languished, the more prickly she became. Her illness had stripped away any pretension she might have left. She told and demanded the truth. Rather than waste a breath suffering the fool she thought you were in a given moment, she simply cut you dead with a look, if she thought that's all it might take.

"Don't tell me I look good if I look shitty," she barked to her friend and favorite physio, Inese. "I know what I look like!"

"You don't know what you're doing, do you?" she blasted a young intern.

"Get out of here and leave me alone," she screeched at a technician. "You're not taking any more blood out of me. What are you, a vampire?"

"I'm uncomfortable," she complained to me imperiously. "Fix my bed."

I did my best to make the demanded adjustments. In disgust, she shoved her oxygen mask off over the top of her head and sat up weakly, fighting with the pillows behind her to prop herself up. I stepped in to assist.

"Never mind, I'll do it," she barked. She struggled down off the mattress and cranked the bed, then fluffed and arranged the pillows more to her satisfaction before climbing back up and sighing deeply. Only then would she deign to reach her spidery arm out for a hug. I finger-combed her soft, sweaty hair as she sat back.

"Don't!" she snapped, jerking her head away and running her own fingers through her bangs.

It was possible to mollify her with a massage. She liked cocoa butter. I bought it cheap at the drugstore in big fat jars.

She lay face down on her hospital bed. I shimmied her top up over her shoulders, dipped my fingers into the pale yellow, mocha-smelling cream, rubbed my hands together, and pushed gently into the glowing white flesh of her back. Her muscles were ropey, tough and lean, steel cables supporting her rib cage, tempered by hard coughing a hundred times a day for over twenty years.

She moaned as I dug my greasy fingers between her ribs, into the intercostal muscles. I had learned about expanding and contracting the intercostals in my voice training at theatre school. I knew how to support my breath, how to hold extra air in my back. I had taught this to Pam. Her intercostals and her diaphragm were strong. It was just her lungs that wouldn't work.

Since relaxation facilitates speaking and emotional response, I had been taught the art of massage in the same class.

I worked my fingers up and down Pam's spine between her vertebrae. I made long sweeping strokes from her shoulders to her lower back. Her breathing slowed. She got a dreamy look on her face. Her eyes closed. I massaged her legs. Her muscles lay thin and fleshless along the bones. She had long toes, and giggled as I plied her feet. I rubbed her skinny arms. I pulled each finger, slowly, firmly, to their clubbed and purple tips. She smiled.

"Thanks," she sighed.

"You're welcome. Maybe you'll sleep better tonight."

It was not enough. Nothing was. Cards and poems and gifts and books were not enough, nor platitudes, nor all the hours in a day. Telephones were not enough. African violets were not enough. Licorice All-Sorts and coconut macaroons and home-made butter tarts were not enough. Pluckiness and backbone and the best of heartfelt intentions were not enough.

There was no comfort, none to give and none to be taken. Coffee and cigarettes and the tears that spilled on the kitchen tables of my friends were not enough. The trains that carried me there and back, the trees and fields, the sky, the rumbling of the wheels and gentle rocking to and fro were not enough. The love my husband made to me was not enough. Sleep was not enough. I stopped sleeping. Food was not enough. I stopped eating. Hurting was not enough either, it did nothing, but I hurt any-way. I lost my temper and shouted at store clerks. I yelled at bank tellers and fought with my husband in the street. Anger was not enough. Apologies and sorrow were not enough.

We were only human.

It was not enough.

On July 4th, the day prior to her release, Pam wrote to herself.

I don't know why I am feeling depressed today, but I can't fight it. It's overwhelming me. Everyone here is trying so hard to cheer me, help feel better, and even understand my tears. It's hard to explain, I sometimes feel so close to God that I get scared. Life is very important to me; but more and more I need so much energy to stay well. Sometimes I try so hard and I don't know if I'm going to have it there next time I'm down.

My spirit in my inner heart, I know will always be strong

and hopeful. My body, though is wearing out. All the people around me, they try so hard to encourage and support, they are desperately trying to feel and understand my feelings. Somehow, they can get close, but never really know...I love them so much. They're all so beautiful in their giving. When they each look at me, I can see in their faces the inner desire to share what I feel...Sometimes I feel such a peace, a real happiness for having lived. I feel so loved, a feeling some people can never find satisfaction with in 60 years.

Suddenly though, I become depressed, like my insides are mixed up and in a state of turmoil. I find it hard to handle then, because my attitude and desire is always to be positive.

My life's end is soon to come. Somehow I know I can cope and accept this. What I am unsure of is how those I love and cherish will? I still have so much I want to give them. Guess there is never enough time!

Pam used her time to drive down to visit us in Stratford as soon as she was able, the big oxygen tank strapped into the passenger seat next to her, the plastic tubing draped over the seat, around her ears and up her nose. She stayed with us twice that summer, in late July and again in early August.

Brenda Devine brought her sister Carol down from Toronto for a couple of days, and the four of us languished on the back porch in the summer heat, making fun of doctors and hospitals, laughing and eating crisp peas fresh from my garden. Pam told us about the earnest new intern at heart clinic who'd placed his stethoscope on the left side of her chest, listened, and heard nothing.

"You should have seen the look on his face as he kept moving the stethoscope around without finding a heartbeat! Then he left the room and brought back the resident, and the resident said, 'Shall I tell him Pam, or do you just want to show him?' so I grabbed the stethoscope and put it way over here on my right side. His jaw dropped and his eyes popped right out of their sockets!"

We all guffawed, holding our sides. Later, we strolled down by the Avon River and twiddled our toes in the water in the shade of a weeping willow. We fed the swans. Pam brought along her oxygen port-a-pak, slung over her shoulder.

She was back in hospital for eight days in late September, came home in early October for Thanksgiving, and went in again for thirteen days at the end of October into early November.

- *I know where I stand – heart failure gradually increasing*
- *pulmonary & circulatory problems severe*
- *can't stop it – nobody can*
- *angers me not 'cause afraid of death – just have to leave so much behind*
- *want to kick, throw, scream, hit table*
- *used to keep feelings to self*
- *think I shouldn't show them*
- *know it's right and normal*
- *need to express it*
- *find a way*

If I had known she wanted to scream, I would have screamed with her. I'd have bought a set of cheap dishes for us to smash together. I'd have kicked and cried and stomped with her, had a big pillow fight, come unglued until our grief was purged and we laughed like we'd never laughed before. If only I'd known. Why didn't I know?

She was trying to protect me, as she tried to protect all of us. We had put so much into her, and given up so much on her behalf, she didn't want to let us down. I think in many ways she was living for us, compelled to stay alive because that's what we wanted her to do. I wonder how much that effort cost her, and how much of it facilitated her own will to survive?

My mother had started her second year of nursing school. She struggled to get up to Toronto as much as possible. I continued taking the train into Sick Kids most days, fitting my married life in and around my sojourns, auditions, and acting classes, and both Rick's and my performance schedule at the theatre.

I soon discovered that Rick was seeing someone—a girl who worked in the box office at the Festival Theatre. "Girl" being the operative word; she was all of eighteen and lived with her parents on our street. I caught them walking arm and arm together, canoodling as I passed by in a cab on the way home from the train station. We had it out. I sought counseling. Rick promised not to see the girl again.

At the Stratford closing night party the girl stood on the edge of the dance floor, staring me down as I danced with my husband. Rick and I moved together in a self-conscious frenzy, sweating, thirsty, tired, but I refused to stop and allow him to leave the dance floor, to leave me.

Finally the girl disappeared. Shortly after, Rick excused himself to the men's room. I drank a glass of wine; I smiled at my friends and cruised the dark room, threading a path between carousing bodies, looking for my husband. He'd been gone a long time. I passed the door to the hallway and glanced out. My gaze fell on a couple huddled together in a corner at the far end. My stomach turned sour.

I stepped to the edge of the precipice between the party and the bright saffron light of the corridor, lined with swords and photos of historic stage fights. I walked toward them, glass of wine in hand. I was going to be gracious. I was going to say a sweet hello and wrap my arm around my husband like a smiling vixen in a soap opera.

Rick looked up as I approached. His lips opened and closed

wordlessly like a fish gasping for breath on dry land. I had the sensation of stepping out of my body, but observing as the rest of me kept going.

"How's tricks?" I heard myself shout. My right hand swept back and then forward, splashing the wine squarely in Rick's face.

"And you," I snapped at the girl, "can fuck off!" I turned and ran. Downstairs in the dark, empty green room, I crumpled sobbing into a chair, sick with fear, certain I had just destroyed my marriage.

We had another, less dramatic scene hours later, at home, in the dead of night and the darkness of our living room.

"Are we through?" I whispered tearfully, heart pounding.

"I don't know," he sighed. "I don't know anything anymore. I don't know what I feel, or why, about anything."

I apologized for my outrageous behavior. I told him I was sorry that he wasn't getting enough attention from me, but what was I to do? "My sister is dying."

"Goddam it, Heather, I know your sister's dying! Don't you think I know that? How could I not know that?"

He was tired of my sister's dying. He caught himself before he said it right out, but I could see the truth glittering in the beautiful green eyes I had loved for so long. He was twenty-eight, he wanted to buy a shiny new motorcycle and take off into the blue. He wanted to laugh and dance at parties and make love to young girls. He did not want to be tethered to a grief-stricken and angry woman, no matter how much she loved him, no matter how hard she tried, no matter what she might have to offer him when the dying was through.

In the morning I got up and showered, sobbing in the hot water until a profound clarity and calm descended upon me. I dressed and came downstairs, where Rick was preparing to leave for a planned week's vacation with a buddy.

"Listen," I said, as straightforward but as tenderly as I knew how. "I have one hell of a year ahead of me. Pam is going to die, and I have to spend as much time with her as I can. I have no other choice. Once she's gone, you and I will have the rest of our lives together. Pam always says she can face anything as long as she knows the truth. Well I can too, so I'm asking you for the truth. If you can't wait, or if it's more than you bargained for and you haven't got it in you, I need to know now."

Rick looked down at his long, elegant fingers. His eyelashes fluttered as tears rolled onto his cheeks. "I don't know, I don't know…"

"Well, okay then," I said, on the edge of losing my patience and resolve. "If you want, we can separate for the year. You can screw your way from one end of Canada to the other, if that's what you need to do, and I'll go home and live with Pam until she dies. When it's all over, we can get back together and see if there's anything left between us we want to salvage."

"What will people think if I leave you now?"

"Who cares what people think? If you want to leave me, do it now, right now, when I know what's ahead of me and I'm prepared to deal with it. I don't want you staying with me out of obligation and then leaving me after she dies. I won't survive that. For God's sake, Rick, I'm begging you, don't do that to me."

I went home to be with Pam, who had just been released from the hospital. With Mom and Dad's help, she had packed up her little apartment, said good-bye to her brief, cherished independence, and moved her things back to the house on Highway 24. My parents hung a door to close off the dining room from the kitchen, and removed their furniture so as to create a private living quarters out of the dining and living rooms for Pam.

My sister and I sat at Mom's kitchen table sipping tea, mourning the loss of Pam's hard-fought autonomy, and the possible demise of my marriage.

"Look," she said, "he didn't say it was over. He just said he needed some time. Don't give up on him."

I nodded glumly.

"Hey, I know it's only the first week of November," she smiled, "but we both need something to cheer us up, so what the heck, let's do the Christmas baking!"

Mom helped us set everything up. Pam sat at the end of the kitchen table, tethered to the ever-present oxygen tank. The plastic oxygen mask covered her nose and mouth. Her shoulders rounded forward, rising and falling with the tide of her breath, riding an ocean of fatigue. She was tired, so tired, tired of breathing, tired of hoping, but not yet tired of living, so she dragged hope along on the end of every labored breath.

Before her lay a cutting board and a faded blue Pyrex bowl full of dates. The bowl was one of a set of four. Like her, I thought. Like me. One of a set of four. The smallest, a green one, which for the moment held two cups of walnuts, sat next to the one with the dates.

We'd grown up with these bowls. The biggest, the one we called the flour bowl, used to be a bright, sunny yellow, but after all the years, and the birthday cakes and oatmeal cookies and brownies that had been mixed in it, and all the washings in my mother's soapy hands, and Pam's, and mine, it had aged to a pale saffron. It sat in the middle of the table now, brimming with flour, while I creamed the butter for shortbreads in the medium-sized bowl that used to be red but had paled to pink.

We had begun this tradition in childhood. Every year we dug out the Christmas music and played it all day long while we chopped and mixed and measured. We sang carols and fueled ourselves with raw cookie dough and tea. We licked our fingers, green and red from sugar sprinkles, sticky with icing, and we laughed.

It was hard to laugh now. My mother furtively drew me aside near the stove. She stared toward Pam and whispered to me.

"Look at her, look at her..."

"I know," I nodded softly, not knowing what to do with the panic in my mother's eyes. "I know."

Pam held a small paring knife in one hand, and steadied each date in the other as she chopped, slowly, methodically. Every few minutes, she put the knife down to rest. Her chest heaved, her shoulders slumped. I came and sat down across from her at the opposite end of the table to roll out the dough, flashing her a smile of encouragement. She gave me a weak half-grin, marshaled her forces, picked up the knife again, and began to chop.

Don't cry, I told myself, *you mustn't cry.* "If I trace the liners for the cake pans, will you cut them out? You are always so much better with a pair of scissors than me."

Pam nodded yes, and then giggled. "God forbid anyone should ever let you near a pair of scissors or a knife, or one of these days your going to kill yourself."

It hurt to laugh, but I did, unfolding the brown paper grocery bags that Pam would cut and I would butter (buttering being the safer of the two tasks), to line the pans for fruit cake.

"Remember that year you had the mumps," Pam asked, "and you insisted on making the shortbreads anyway?"

"Gawd, I remember that," my mother chimed in. "You were about fourteen, I think. And you were in agony, and I had your poor neck tied up to the top of your head with a scarf to hold in the swelling."

"And you kept mixing and rolling," laughed Pam, "and it seemed like it would never end, you made so much dough!"

We all laughed together. It felt warm and good. Then Pam laid down her knife and looked away, as if she was gazing far off somewhere in the distance, to the past, maybe, or to next

Christmas, wondering what it would be like here without her, as I was doing.

Later, Mom gave Pam her treatment in the den while I finished tidying the kitchen. The tins of cookies and fruitcake had been labeled as to what was what, and whose was whose. The bowls stood clean on the counter, empty but for the memories they held. There was nothing else to be done.

Pam coughed. "We're finished here," my mother called to me. "You look tired. I think you should go to bed."

We kissed each other good-night. I climbed into the foldout couch in the family room. A few hours later I woke to the soft sound of sobbing. I lay for a moment and listened in the dark. It was coming from the living room. I got up and tiptoed through the front hall toward the sound. The half-light shining through the bay window fell on a small figure curled fetally on the floor.

"Pammy?" I whispered. "Pam?" There was no response except the quiet sobbing. I knelt down and gently touched her shoulder. She sat up, looking at me with embarrassment and longing. She removed a set of earphones from her head, the ones we had given her for Christmas the year before.

"What's the matter?" I asked her.

"Listen." Pam slipped the earphones gently onto my head. They were damp with her tears. She reached over to the stereo, reset the record, took my hand in hers, and lay down again on the carpet, gazing into my eyes as I listened to Debbie Boone sing the words of Joe Brooks:

"I used to think I could stop the earth, and hold time in my hands. But I watched as it raced on by me, heading for tomorrow. And I hadn't the power to say, we can save today. For a little while longer. Just one tomorrow. Can't I save today? It's been such a good day..."

- *S.O.B., frothy fluid in lungs, general edema, blueness, sleeping, liver pain*
- *insidiously filling up as fast as clear out, respiratory distress, pneumonia*
- *liver scan, ECG, x-ray, exam*
- *O2, Lasix (3 times), antibiotics IV (hypokalemia)*
- *feeling – heart at peace – accept and live with it*
- *advice given early in life – happiness – Follow your heart!*
- *Become closer to love & life!*

In early December, Pam spent eleven more days in Sick Kids. I awoke Christmas morning throwing up, knowing in my gut it would be my sister's last. The dark edge of the storm was upon us.

I ran to the bathroom and knelt before the toilet on the cold linoleum floor, spitting up bile, my eyes wet with fear, and the flowered wallpaper was spinning around me. I sobbed and dry-heaved as I got dressed, and Rick loaded the presents into the car. Gently, he led me trembling out the door and down the sidewalk through a dusting of fresh snow. The cold air smacked me in the face and made me want to throw up again. I crumpled into the front seat, hugging a pillow to my stomach. The countryside between Stratford and Brantford was frozen white, the fields and farmhouses sparkling and utterly still. I was frozen too, frozen with dread and sick with envy for the carefree families I imagined waking with anticipation and joy in those sweet, still houses.

My mother took one look at me when we arrived and said, "What's the matter? You look like death warmed over."

Pam was stretched out on the couch, a festively dressed pile of bones. She waved me over and made room. I collapsed beside her. We lay on the couch together all day, wearing paper party hats. Dad took our picture with the famous Polaroid.

"C'mon," he cajoled me, "where's that wonderful smile?"

Just days before, my smile had been triumphant indeed as I burst into Pam's hospital room late at night (against the rules, but Pam was so sick and the nurses knew me so well), clutching a copy of Anne Morrow Lindbergh's *A Gift from the Sea*. Pam had wanted it to give to her secret love, Fred Tapping, for Christmas.

"Hey," I burbled merrily, "I had to search every bookstore in Toronto, but look, I found it!"

Her room was pitch black. The tiny colored lights of a plastic tabletop Christmas tree blinked on and off, on and off. My sister sat huddled in an overstuffed chair in the corner. Through the dark, her eyes shone wide and desperate.

"It's too late," she said flatly.

"What do you mean?"

"Listen."

I stood still and heard the deep, raw gasping coming through the wall, a rasping, rattling sound of death that rooted me to the floor and stilled my own breath. It was Fred.

"Get me out of here," she said, half-pleading, half-ordering me.

At first the nurses were reluctant to call the attending physician. I demanded, begged, and finally I threatened to kidnap Pam without anyone's permission if they did not comply with our request. While they paged the doctor on call, I ran downstairs to tell Rick, who'd been waiting patiently in the car.

"I'm sorry, I don't know how long this will take," I apologized.

"Don't worry, you and Pammy take all the time you need."

Back upstairs, my sister quietly packed her small suitcase by the intermittent light of the Christmas tree. When she was finished, I pulled the plug. The darkness swallowed us whole. I stuffed the tree in a big green garbage bag.

"Wait here," Pam said, and went into Fred's room. The empty hallway was unlit except for the red exit sign over the door at one end, and a murky pool of light over the nurses' station.

"Fred," I heard my sister's voice. "Fred, it's Pam."

"Pam...," Fred moaned. His chest heaved with effort as he sucked the still, stale air of the hospital into his watery lungs.

"I've come to say good-bye," Pam said tenderly.

I could hardly stand to listen; I tried not to, pacing restlessly to and fro.

"I love you." My sister's voice, gentle as a leaf drifting to earth, floated through the doorway. I knew she had wanted to say those words to him for a long, long time, but had held them in her heart, silent and unrequited. He replied, sounding already as if he were speaking from another place, and I could not make out what he said.

Rick arrived on the ward with a comforter from the back seat of the car.

"I phoned your folks to let them know we're coming," he whispered. I nodded silently.

Suddenly Pam reappeared, her face white and pleading. Rick gently wrapped the comforter around her thin, tired body then lifted her up, cradling her in his arms as we walked to the elevator. I followed, carrying her suitcase and the plastic garbage bag that held the tree.

The car was warmed up and running in front of the hospital. Rick laid Pam gently in the back seat. I climbed in the front and turned Pam's favorite station on the radio. The three of us drove off into the cold, starry night, Helen Reddy's voice crooning softly.

"*...Keep holding on, you'll make it, here's my hand so take it, look for me reaching out to show, as sure as rivers flow, I'll never let you go...I'll never let you go...I'll never let you go.*"

CHAPTER TWENTY-ONE

"I live with the word incurable by overcoming the fear. It is controllable to some extent. Why worry about it? While we are here we must make the best of what we have and where we are. Soon my purpose will end, and I will leave the world bodily, but whatever I have given to anyone, that will remain. I've been thinking about eternal life a lot. I'm grow-ing so much spiritually. We leave and go to heaven, but I don't know what happens – it is a continuing existence with God. Yes, I will be with God. Heaven is not silver or gold – just beautiful. I don't even have visions of being cured in heaven, but just having rest."
— Interview with Pam, April 1980,
The Canadian Baptist Newsletter

Death peeked in at the windows of our house; it stood off behind the trees, laughing. We barricaded ourselves with hope-ful philosophies. It banged on the door and rattled the windows, demanding entry. Death ate our food and slept in our beds, making itself at home like a long-lost member of the family. It went to work, wearing down our spirits like a carpenter's blade planing our souls. Our hopes curled into thin shavings that piled up around our feet.

Days of fury and determination. Nights of despair. The high adrenalin rush of crisis. The exhilaration and perfect clarity of fear. The fatigue of chronic mourning.

It took energy to feed sorrow and anger. It took energy to cast it off. Hospital smells, corridors, beds, tubes, coughing, blood, antiseptic, mucus, salt, tears, tears, tears. It took courage to be happy.

Pam was now in hospital more than she was out. While she was in, Jenny Corey, the miracle CF gymnast whose performance at the Telethon three years earlier had so delighted viewers, died. A raging staph infection claimed her overnight. She was nine years old. At the same time David Bunyan, older brother of Pam's late friend Darlene, lingered like an empty husk in a room down the hall from Pam, until he, too, succumbed.

Pam created what she called a "Madstick" made from a couple yards of green plastic tubing that connected her inhalation therapy mask to the compressor. After folding the tubing in three, she bound it neatly with masking tape. The Madstick lay beside her on her bed, and when she wanted to rage, she picked it up and gave it a few good whacks on the mattress. It was all she could do.

A hard March rain fell the day before her twenty-sixth birthday party. Wet and aching, I tramped the streets of Stratford, in and out of every gift store and card shop, trying to find what I knew would be the last birthday present I would ever buy her.

I stared blankly at the cheery cards that read "Happy Birthday Sister," all of them wishing many happy years ahead. I stared at clothes she would never wear, books she would never read, keepsakes she could never keep. I stood helpless on the street corners, weeping, waiting for the lights to change, hoping the rain and my umbrella would shield me from passersby. The only thing I wanted to give Pam was my life, but even if I could have, she wouldn't have taken it. Pam wanted her own life, such as it was, and she wanted me to have mine.

The next day we had a small party at Mom and Dad's. Mom did up a roast and Grandma Birdsell brought a cake from

White's bakery where she was working part-time. Mom and I found a quiet corner to discuss the candles. Should we put on all twenty-six, or would it be too hard for Pam to blow them all out? Twenty-six, we decided.

We offered a chorus of "Happy Birthday," singing densely through the hard lumps in our throats as I carried the cake into the den, candles ablaze, and placed it ceremoniously on the twig-thin thighs of my sister's lap.

"Make a wish, Pam," said my mother cheerily.

Pam sat for a moment considering us thoughtfully with her gaze, and then she wheezed in as much air as possible and blew. She got the last few candles with a second smaller breath quickly tacked on to the first.

"It's okay," I said. "That counts."

Ten days later, I sat once again in the confines of her tiny hospital room, small as a monk's cell, a jail cell, the bright chaos of spring taunting us from the outside, Death standing nearby, patiently, complacently, staring out the window into the dusty sunlight.

For three days my sister lay in a semi-coma, her temperature spiking and her lungs filling with infection from a terrible flu. I sat by her bed and watched. My mother was away writing nursing exams. Gregg, Jan, and my father each had responsibilities to their own work and could take only limited time off unless Pam took a turn for the worse. Jeff would not be caught dead in this place. Rick was in rehearsal for his new season at Stratford. I watched alone and waited, waited with Death, thinking of my own offer from Stratford and how I'd turned it down for this, turned down any and all work for the coming year or however long it would take, to be the one with Pam, to sit fingering the dimes in my pocket for the telephone call that would alert my family to drop whatever they were doing and *get here.*

I passed the hours wrestling with the choice I'd made, weighing the consequences. I'd been given the opportunity to understudy a major star in a cast of only four actors, with the very real possibility of getting to go on. I was twenty-eight, a crucial age in show business.

This is the choice I made. Personal, not professional. Pam wheezed and tossed and sweated. I pulled my chair closer to her, murmuring that everything was okay. *I was Pam's Protector. I had promised.*

But the promise made by a six year old conflicted with the realities and necessities of the grown woman I had become. The irrationality of that conflict threatened to almost drive me crazy. I couldn't die with my sister. Or could I? *Was this a way to kill myself, by giving up such an important part of who I was? Was this the only way I could assuage my guilt?*

I wiped her face with a cool, damp cloth and suddenly felt the depth and liberation, the kind of love, trust, and selflessness that is possible to experience when someone you love is dying. You lose yourself and find yourself in that love. It is exceptional. Never mind Stratford. Never mind an acting career. This, here and now, being with her, was the greatest privilege I might ever know.

Nurses came and went like moths fluttering around a porch light. I grabbed a quick cup of coffee from the cafeteria and brought it back. I stood by the window and made Death take a walk in the hall, putting it on notice that Pam wasn't the only one putting up a fight.

Pam's chest fluttered up and down with shallow breaths. *Why hadn't I gone to see her plays at Crippled Children's Camp? What could I have been doing that was so damn important? Why weren't there more pictures of us together?*

And on the third day, she rose. She sat up and shook the mist from her eyes.

"Wash my hair," she demanded.

Flush with joy, I leapt out of my chair, walked her over from the bed, and held her up to the sink. She bent her head under the high curved silver neck of the tap. Her face was as white as the porcelain bowl. I tested the water first, the way a mother tests milk for her infant, making sure it wouldn't scald. The water flowed over her short, honeyed hair, sluicing off the grease and sweat of three days and nights' hard struggle to remain in the world.

I held her up with one arm, massaging her soapy scalp with the other, and I loved her so much.

"You're not doing it right!" she yelped in a tone of voice that sounded like she meant my whole life. She reared her head up, gesturing wildly, foam flying and incomprehensible fury spitting from her mouth.

"I have sat next to your bed for three solid days and half the nights," I shouted back at her, "and I don't deserve this. Besides, if you've got enough energy to get this angry, you've got enough energy to get better! Now I'm going down to the cafeteria to get myself a coffee, and when I come back I expect you to be in a better frame of mind!"

When I returned she was perched on the bed, her hair still damp and soapy, her face contrite. We tried again. I rinsed and toweled off her hair, gave her a sponge bath, and helped her into fresh pajamas.

"I'm sorry," I apologized, tenderly combing her hair into place. "You have the right to be angry when you need to, and I shouldn't have taken it so personally."

"No," she said, "I'm sorry. I don't have the right to treat you badly just because I'm sick."

"Wanna' talk about it? What's got you so mad?"

Pam's jaw jutted forward and her steely eyes slid sideways to the window.

"I'm angry that I didn't die. I've done everything I can to prepare for it. I was ready for it. Now I'm mad that I'll have to go through it all again, and everyone else will too."

Looking in her sad, glistening eyes, how was I to say I was

glad Death hadn't taken her this time, that I'd go through it all again on her account, a thousand times if the outcome was the same? But who was I to ask her to prolong her suffering on my account?

She had developed a relationship with Death that was mysterious to me, seductive. The two had grown to share an intimacy apart from her and me, an insidious bond that threatened to shut me out, and continued to flourish in spite of anyone's efforts to dissolve it. She read about Death, talked about it. There were moments in that hospital room I could swear she was looking it straight in the eye.

"I love my earthly life," she said to me one day, almost casually. "But I'm looking forward to finally meeting God."

Later that week Pam dictated specific instructions for her funeral to my mother. She wanted John Denver's song "When the River Meets the Sea" and Debbie Boone's songs "When You're Loved" and "It's Been Such a Good Day." She wanted readings from the Bible. Isaiah 40:25–30, Romans 8:18–39, and the 23rd Psalm. She wanted to wear her blue floral chiffon birthday dress, and to be buried between her two grandfathers, beneath the tree, on the edge of the hill overlooking the city.

I practiced the moment of loss sometimes when I was alone, rehearsing it in my imagination, letting myself feel for a few fleeting seconds what it might be like: the initial shock, the empty, sinking feeling of knowing that she was forever gone. I would not be able to jump down into the roiling linoleum waters of our childhood and save her from drowning, pulling her back safe and sound into the world the way I had in our bedroom at 16 Brier Crescent, when we played The Rescue Game. So I imagined, and rehearsed, and tried to teach myself how to survive the moment of her death.

Saturday afternoons at home, I watched old movies on TV. I was June Allyson as Jo in *Little Women*, wanting to be a writer and move to New York, while Pam was Beth, telling me not to be afraid that she was dying. I was Jane Eyre, screaming and fainting when she knew her little friend Helen was dead.

I played John Denver singing "Sunshine on My Shoulders" on the stereo while I lay on the carpet pretending that Pam was already dead, so I'd know what it would be like to hear her favorite song when she was no longer in the world.

In June, my mother graduated from nursing school. It was our last outing as a complete family. Pam wore the damn blue floral chiffon dress I hated now that I knew she was going to be buried in it. It hung from her like limp curtains on a broken rod. She looked ninety years old, she looked ten, her hair close-cropped, her once-stylish square eyeglasses now too big for her gaunt, shrunken face. They slid down her cheeks where they sat propped by the white nosepiece of her oxygen tubing.

My mother won first prize for nursing proficiency. The instant her name was called we leapt to our feet, clapping, laughing, and hooting. My mother walked bashfully to the podium, her face blushing carnelian red. This was the moment Pam had lived for. There wasn't anything to hold her here now.

In early June, when I'd come up from Stratford for an overnight, Pam awoke at three in the morning coughing explosively, spewing mucus and vomit on her bed. There was a commotion as lights went on and my parents rushed across the hall. I leapt up and ran to the doorway of Pam's room to see Mom pounding my sister's back as Pam retched into the kidney basin she held shakily below her own chin.

"This is the third night in a row," my mother murmured anxiously, accepting the used kidney basin from Pam.

Dad wiped up the mess and stripped the sheets. Jeff stumbled out of his room, bleary-eyed, and stood in the corner of the hall staring at me with a knowing look on his face.

"What can I do?" I asked Mom.

"Go and make some tea."

I turned again to Jeff but he'd already gone back to his room and closed the door.

While I filled the kettle, Pam, wearing fresh pajamas, appeared in the kitchen. Silently and perfunctorily, she went about the business of making a mask while Mom and Dad got dressed.

As if she were pregnant and about to deliver, Pam had packed a "hospital suitcase" to take back and forth to clinic, just in case she was admitted. It stood at the ready in the back of her closet, neatly crammed with pajamas, T-shirts, jeans, socks, and underwear, a couple of favorite books, along with some candy and trail mix. Mom brought the suitcase out to the kitchen and set it by the back door.

We gathered around the table and sipped the tea in silence.

"Better take the station wagon," said Mom quietly and matter-of-factly. "It has more gas."

A final, quick swallow of tea.

"We'll call from the hospital when she's settled."

I stood in the carport, the misty dawn swallowing them up as they departed for Toronto and hospital, my father clamped fiercely behind the wheel, Pam cradled in the backseat, in my mother's arms.

They were greeted in Emergency by Dr. Turner, head of the Chest Department, who noticed golf socks on Pam's feet, the kind with little pom-poms attached to the back of the ankle.

"Planning to play a few holes later?" he teased.

"I may seem down for the moment," she coughed. "But don't kid yourself; I'm still in the game and good for another round."

Her electrolytes were dangerously out of whack. A Brantford doctor had tested them three days earlier, but failed to report the results. While Pam waited to hear from him, patiently and in vain, she had endured seventy-two hours of severe nausea and cramps. The result was life-threatening. Her extreme retching and coughing had resulted in a partially collapsed left lung.

Pam unpacked her suitcase and settled into "her" room next to the nurses' station. She pinned a poem she had copied down in her own hand next to her bed where she could read it.

I asked God for strength, that I might achieve
I was made weak, that I might learn humbly to obey...
I asked for health, that I might do greater things,
I was given infirmity, that I might do better things...
I asked for riches, that I might be happy,
I was given poverty, that I might be wise...
I asked for power, that I might have the praise of men,
I was given weakness, that I might feel the need of God...
I asked for all things, that I might enjoy life,
I was given life, that I might enjoy all things...
I got nothing that I asked for, but everything I had hoped for.
Almost despite myself, my unspoken prayers are answered.
I am among all men, most richly blessed.

During her seventeen-day stay, as often as she felt up to it, she gave cheese fondue parties for the staff and adult patients in an empty conference room, roguishly adding the white wine I smuggled in, while sipping some as cook's nips on the side. On the days when she could not get out of bed, the little ones spontaneously gathered in her room. They knew she had wisdom and insights to share, and were not threatened by the knowledge that she was dying.

In openly sharing her views and experience, Pam was able to maintain an acceptance of herself as a uniquely valuable human being, and to preserve a sense of self-determination and self-esteem in the face of increasing debilitation. It also helped her to overcome the sense of isolation many people feel when others are afraid to see them letting go of life.

She had grown more tolerant now of our grief, and gave us tacit permission to be afraid and to mourn a little ahead of time. It was good for her to witness that our grief was somewhat bearable. Still, she helped me to put my grief in context with hers.

"You are only losing me, but I am losing *all* of my friends and *all* of my family…"

In the same breath, however, she quoted Elisabeth Kubler-Ross, saying she thought it would be better for us not to think of her as dying, but as living until she died.

As if to prove this active connection with life, she continued to take a vital, often vehement, role in decisions about her treatment. She agreed to tolerate several bronchoscopes without anesthetic, for example, but would not allow technicians to take blood unnecessarily, or to schedule x-rays or pulmonary function tests without first consulting her. She accepted hyperalimentation briefly and only when she absolutely had to. The tube that carried the nutrients through her nose and down the back of her throat into her stomach caused more discomfort than it was worth to gain the extra half-pound she was bound to lose again anyway.

By now the entire family, including Pam, had reached a point where we were fighting to hold on and disengage at the same time.

No matter what language Pam used attempting to reframe the experience in a positive light, it was still her task in dying to let go. In that regard she had her own very definite ideas about how and where she wished to die. She made it clear she wanted to be at home.

My parents invited me to join them in a meeting with Dr. Levison, the new head of the clinic since Dr. Crozier's recent retirement.

"I need to warn you," Dr. Levison said, "that if you take on the task of a home death and panic halfway through and then bring her in by ambulance, we'll have no choice but to put her on a respirator and prolong her agony."

Pam had complained to me that Dr. Levison had no bedside manner, but I found him as compassionate as he was direct.

"Well," my mother said. "I think we're all agreed that what's best is whatever Pam wants. Can we do this?" She looked to my father and then to me. My father and I exchanged glances.

"Yes."

"Okay. All I need to do is talk it over with Pam and make sure she's clear on the parameters."

My sister fully understood the ramifications, and told Mom she did not want to be treated aggressively in the final stages. My mother conveyed Pam's wishes to Gregg and Jan, as I did to Rick.

"You mean we'll have to be there?" he whimpered.

"Of course. That's the whole idea. We can't leave it all up to Mom and Dad. It's our final gift to her."

He looked unsure, but nodded as if he understood.

I gave him a big hug and a kiss. "I know you're scared. We all are."

Pam came home July 8th and was readmitted five days later. In the interim, she said good-bye to Jeff. He had just graduated from high school, but caught up as we were in Pam's illness, we had failed to make much, if anything, of the occasion. When he announced that he was leaving for a summer job at a resort in Edmonton, Alberta, however, we all stood at attention, exhorting him not to go.

"What have I got to stick around here for?" he asked me bitterly. "You're all into your own lives and stuff, and there isn't any work around here that can make me the kind of money I can make in Edmonton."

"What about Pam?"

"What about her? Heather, I've got the same disease she has, and if what she's going through right now says anything, I don't have a lot of time. I have to get on with my own life!"

My eighteen-year-old brother stood tall and lanky like his

dad, a halo of fuzzy, sand-colored hair framing earnest blue eyes and thick eyebrows knit with the intense frown of an old man with the weight of the world on his thin shoulders. Where had the joyful little diapered baby who called himself "Duffy" gone? I couldn't see even a hint in his mournful face.

They said what they had to say to each other privately in her room. It took more courage for him to walk out that door than any of us knew. Except, of course, for Pam. She stood by the back door, staring out the window at the empty driveway for hours after he'd gone.

Less than a week after Jeff's departure, she suffered another pneumothorax, a partial collapse of her only functioning lung, and returned to Sick Kids. The appointment calendar I kept that summer catalogued the rent, electricity, and long-distance bills that needed to be paid, the birthdays that needed to be remembered, my father's fiftieth included, the friends I wanted to invite to dinner, and the theatre openings I had to attend. It reflected the awful certitude of life moving forward in spite of itself, filling itself up with the most ordinary details and mundane obligations. What my appointment calendar did not record were the moments when I wished it would all just end and she would die and get it over with, or the seconds that came a heartbeat later, when the thought of her leaving was more than I could bear.

In the empty spaces between Union Gas–$59.11 and YPT Audition–4:40 p.m. were the hours I spent by Pam's hospital bed, serving up the Swiss Chalet chicken she adored, the Chinese honey-garlic spareribs that she loved, and her favorite frozen sweet vanilla yoghurt, though she'd take only two bites and say, "I've lost my appetite. You eat."

"Get me out of here," she said one day. "I need some fresh air."

I helped dress her for the outing, the Heparin lock around her wrist and the Independence badge on her collar her only jewelry.

She climbed into the abhorred wheelchair. Carol Sheppard, head nurse for the ward, called a warning to me down the hall, "You know she's in no condition to go outside the hospital..."

I held my hand up and waved understanding without pausing to turn around, pushing Pam forward down the hall. We rode the elevator to the 11th floor, where we could hang out on the cool and shady patio. Noise echoed up from the street below. Life. There was a look in my sister's eyes. I knew what she was thinking, what she longed for.

"Let's break the rules," I said.

We got back on the elevator and rode to the ground floor, lips pursed conspiratorially. I negotiated the winding halls until we found a back door. When I wheeled her out, we found ourselves on the sidewalk of a dusty downtown side street.

It was not beautiful, but it was free. The sun was warm on our faces.

We strolled around the perimeter of Sick Kids Hospital, past the student nurses' residence, and new construction, and the smokestack of the incinerator where hospital refuse burned. We turned the corner onto University Avenue, pausing to stare with longing up the street toward the lush green and gently waving trees of Queen's Park.

"Better not," Pam smiled.

The wheelchair went bumpety-bump over the cracks in the sidewalk in front of the main entrance. Coming down off a curb to cross the driveway, I lost control of the chair and almost tipped my sister into the street. She laughed.

We went once again around the block.

Later, we made supper together on the 11th floor, where a tiny kitchen sat off to the side of the games room. It held a sink, two burners, and a microwave.

We made wieners and Kraft Dinner. Pam chopped the wieners while I boiled the water. We filled the silence with awkward, menial conversation connected to the task at hand. We set the small table neatly, folding paper towels for napkins, and sat down to eat.

The sharp popping sounds of ping-pong in the next room annoyed me. I was aware, so aware. Pam's wheezing breath, her bony fingers lifting the red plastic ketchup bottle from the fake wood laminate table. The green plastic oxygen tube snaking from her nose down alongside her wheelchair. Her orange-sandaled feet, her long, skinny toes, nails unpolished and purple-tinged. The cracks in the dingy beige linoleum floor. The hum and ghostly glow of the florescent lights. The soft smile on her white face. The hands on my watch, ticking off the precious, lost-forever moments. It was hard to swallow my food.

We made tea and drank it strong.

I wheeled Pam back to her room.

In mid-August my sister went home again, briefly. She bought a new pair of shoes and had barely time to wear them, only four days, before her left lung went again. This time they sliced a hole between her ribs and inserted a chest tube to reinflate it.

"I'm not giving up," she told me. She said she wanted to see Uncle Doug. Grandma called him, and he came to the hospital. Afterward, Pam refused to say much about their visit, but I could sense she was disappointed.

After five days they sent her home, the chest tube still dangling from her side.

"How long will the tube have to stay in there?" I asked my mother.

She shrugged her shoulders, crossed her arms, and shook her head with an unfamiliar resignation that frightened me. "They can't take it out or her lung will deflate again."

"What does that mean?"

"Don't ask me what it means, Heather. You know what it means. They can't leave it there indefinitely."

Back in Stratford, I stopped into St. Patrick's and sat bereft in a back pew, not knowing how to pray, or what to pray for. Then suddenly I knew where God was. He was waiting for Pam. *Thy Will Be Done*, I whispered to the empty, vaulted ceiling. Into Thy Hands I commend her soul.

My mother called to tell me that Pam had asked to go outside for a while that day, so she had carried my sister down the front lawn to the stream and laid her on a blanket on the soft grass.

"It was the way she asked," my mother said. "There was something in her voice, and something about the way she sat once we got out there."

My mother described the scene for me, the shards of sunlight sifting through the tall trees. Pam raised one hand to shield her eyes. I knew her arm lifted against the sun would seem transparent as fine old porcelain.

The trees breathed easily in and out around her. Pam's shoulders, the right one slung lower than the left because of her caved-in, long-collapsed right lung, rocked gently to and fro as her own short, labored breaths fluttered her body.

The day was green and full. Butterflies skimmed the tops of wildflowers bordering the stream. Sparrows and squirrels and bees chirped, swooped, scooted, and buzzed. The distant highway droned with the sound of passing cars. Children were playing somewhere, laughing.

Pam sat, and looked, and tried to breathe. She leaned into the sounds of the world with great longing.

"There was something about the way she drank it all in," my mother told me. "And then she said she couldn't go long without her oxygen, and I asked her if she wanted to go back in, but she said no, she wanted just another minute."

Pam gazed out to the horizon once more, across the fields ripe with corn, and up through the trees into the blue, unfettered sky. Then she nodded to my mother, who bent down and took her baby girl into her arms, cradling her as she walked slowly up toward the house.

"It broke my heart," she said, "how she just stared back over my shoulder."

Back toward the trees, and the sunlight, and the laughter of distant children.

A couple of days later, two women from the Brantford Homecare Unit came out to the house to discuss Homecare's role in continuing to care for Pam.

Throughout the previous months, whenever Pam was at home, a Red Cross homemaker had stayed with her for the few hours a day that my mother or father worked. The arrangement had gone quite well. However, now that Pam had the chest tube, they explained, there were "concerns."

The conversation was tense, difficult, and ultimately unsatisfactory. Having aired their apprehensions and opinions, the women left. My mother had barely closed the door behind them before Pam spoke.

"That's it, Mom. I'm tired. I've had enough."

My sister turned her back, walked slowly down the hall, and disappeared into her room.

CHAPTER TWENTY-TWO

*"The song of the river ends not at her banks but in
the hearts of those who have loved her."* — Buffalo Joe

How do we know when something is over? When a love affair or
a marriage ends? When it's time to move on from a dream that
isn't coming true? When you've given all you can to something
or someone, and taken all that's going to be offered, and there
isn't any more? What instinct tells us that it's time to stop fighting? What kind of courage does it take to face that truth?

When the river meets the sea, it broadens, and slows. Rivers
like the Mississippi have deltas, muddy fingers fanning out,
reaching for the open water beyond. The Hudson River expands,
surrendering wholly to the embrace of the Atlantic Ocean, waiting just beyond the Verrazano Narrows Bridge.

Pam was ready to surrender. But not ready, no, never ready to
give up. She understood the difference, as I am only beginning
to understand.

Giving up implies there's still some fight left, some unfinished business, or unrealized potential that's being tossed aside.
It's a closing off of the heart and mind, a shrinking of the soul.
Giving up takes back all we have given, and fashions a vessel in
which to carry regret.

Surrendering means we know we have done all we can do.
There is compassion in surrender, both for ourselves, and for the

thing we leave behind. It is an offering, a gift. There is forward movement in surrender, an opening of the heart and mind, an expanding of the soul. We broaden, and slow, fingers fan out, reaching for the open water, and the embrace of the unknown.

Giving up is an act of anger or despair. Surrender cannot be accomplished without love.

The house lay dark beneath the heavy, starless sky as we pulled into the driveway. I thought again of Pam's phone call to me the night before.

"I need to see you tonight," she had begged, tearfully. "Please come home."

"I have to waitress tonight," I explained. "I'm coming home to see you Saturday. It's only a couple of days away."

"Saturday will be too late," she said sobbing, and hung up the phone.

I discussed the situation with Rick. He'd been very patient with the amount of time I'd spent with Pam in recent weeks, and I didn't want to take advantage of that forbearance. On the other hand, I told him I remembered the day Grandpa Birdsell died, how he'd called up and asked me to come and see him and I'd said no.

"Call your mother and ask her what she thinks."

I did as he suggested, asking if I should indeed come that night.

"No," said my mother. "She's just upset about something that happened today. The Red Cross homemakers are here and we had a...discussion. I'll tell you about it when you visit on Saturday."

But there we were, before midnight Friday. I'd ignored my instincts, and now my mother had called us to come.

The teapot sat cold on the table in the company of two half-empty cups. The table was built against the wall so you could only sit at it on three sides. It was positioned between the back entrance and the den, so you had to walk past it on your way to or from. It was covered with a white vinyl tablecloth, patterned with orange and green baskets of fruit. Over the next few days, when we weren't sitting at my sister's bed, we sat there, drinking lukewarm tea with too much sugar, our eyes puffed and our hands shaking, bathed in the amber glow of a hanging lamp shaped like a bunch of grapes made of orange plastic globes, with a green vine snaking up the chain.

My mother's silhouette appeared like an apparition at the far end of the family room, beckoning. Rick hung back in the kitchen like a stranger while I headed straight to Pam's room at the far end of the house. She lay in bed in the dark, propped up by several pillows to a sitting position. She could not breathe lying down.

I sat next to her on the bed and took her hand.

"Pammy," I spoke softly, urgently. "It's me, I'm here."

Her eyes fluttered open and attempted to focus, dulled by the task of dying. She stared at me earnestly and squeezed my hand. She knew me.

My mother had set up a TV table near the bed on which she laid out Pam's medicine, a stethoscope, and a kidney basin into which Pam could cough. Her lungs were likely to hemorrhage. There was also a hospital table on wheels to place across her bed so she could lay a pillow on it and sleep sitting forward, a position that could help her breathe better.

Sometime during the night it began to rain. My mother, my father, and I took turns sleeping, and watching Pam. On Saturday morning Gregg and Jan arrived from Toronto. Rick went back to Stratford to perform, with promises to return later that night.

"Should we call Jeff?" I asked my mother.

"I don't know. I don't think he wants to be called. Let's just wait awhile and see how it goes."

Jan and I sent my parents out for a drive to get some fresh air. We set up a lawn chaise in the empty dining room, padding it with pillows and blankets. Together we brought Pam out, made her comfortable.

She gazed out the window. She did not want to lie down and simply be lulled away by the song of the rain, ferried across to the other side on its music, swept into infinity on the soft rush of water dropping down from heaven, her soul traveling deeper into the luscious sound, deeper, until the wistful sigh of falling rain is all that's left of her breath.

The rain was alive to her; the sound was life itself, beckoning fierce and sweet, the urgent thrum a call to stay in the world. The heavy rustle of water through the leaves on the swaying trees is life, the joyous splatting sounds on the front porch, and she wanted to be out there in it, she wanted to run and dance in it, to twirl her feet on the slick cold grass while wet autumn leaves clung to her ankles and mud from the flower bed spattered her legs. She wanted to grab the rain in her fists with her clubbed purple fingertips, to raise her head to the rain laughing, to catch the sweet water with her tongue and not have anyone call from the doorway, "Come inside, you'll catch your death."

She lay on a garden chaise in the empty dining room, watching silver threads of rain lace their way down through the drooping branches of a double birch tree growing just beyond the window. I knelt on one side of her, our sister-in-law Jan on the other.

"C'mon Pam, one more spoonful, just try."

Tenderly, Jan held a spoon of soup below Pam's mouth. Pam stared at it for a moment as if making a hard choice, then lifted her head. She accepted three spoonfuls and lay back, her chest heaving.

"I can't," she whispered. "No more."

Jan perched the spoon in the bowl. We sighed collectively and turned our gaze toward the double birch, its two slim trunks rooted deeply together in the ground yet leaning softly in opposite directions, helpless as the rain stripped it of leaves.

"Oh, I'm glad to see you up and about," my father said to Pam when he and my mother returned. A few minutes later the phone rang in the kitchen.

"Oh ya, ya, she's home," my father answered. "Oh yes, she's doing terrific. Ya, ya, well, I don't know, why don't you ask her yourself, she's right here?…Pam, there's someone on the phone here who wants to talk to you…"

Pam rolled her eyes.

"Dad," I called out, "Pam can't come to the phone right now, she's having her lunch."

"Well that's fine, but this will only take a minute."

I got up and went out to the kitchen. My father stood with his hand over the receiver.

"It's…"

"I don't care who it is," I whispered fiercely, "Pam can't talk to anyone. She can barely talk, period. Hell, she can barely breathe. What's the matter with you?"

My father looked baffled.

"Well," he said into the phone as I returned to Pam, "her sister says Pam's too busy to come to the phone right now, but maybe she can call you back later…Oh no, no, nothing like that, she's doing great."

Pam gazed at me, pleading. "What are we going to do with him?"

"I know," I said, "I know."

Jan offered up the unfinished bowl of soup.

My sister closed her weary eyes.

Rain poured down. Birch leaves fell.

"Let's get her back into her room," I said to Jan.

We did not know what might be happening in the news. Our world was defined by one dark bedroom, a teapot, a clock, a telephone, and the curtain of rain that fell around the house.

My mother taped a chart to the back of Pam's door where she could note my sister's pulse and respirations hourly. Joyce Jellis, Pam's favorite VON (and sister of my old high school boyfriend Jerry) came to the house early on Saturday afternoon to do a treatment. Once she saw Pam, she conceded there was no point.

"Have you called Dr. MacDonald?" she asked my mother.

"He's away for the weekend. The doctor on call thinks we should take her to Toronto. He thinks it's a mistake to let her stay here. I told him this was Pam's choice—that we have discussed it all with Dr. MacDonald and with Dr. Levinson at Sick Kids, but he's not convinced. He said he won't come out here to the house."

"Will you be all right on your own?"

"I think so. I'm in touch with the clinic every couple of hours, and they know what's going on here. They said they'll be there for me if I need anything. I've got Gregg and Jan and Heather here, and Doug of course. We're trying to get in touch with Carol Sheppard and ask her to come. She's Pam's head nurse from the CF ward."

After Joyce left, my mother made tea, took off her glasses, and rubbed the dark circles around her eyes.

"Pam's struggling," my mother told him. "I don't know that we might need something to help settle her down."

"Is there anything we can give her?"

"Well, yes. She told me that when she's been in when other kids are dying that the nurses give them something to help them through. Bromptman's Cocktail, it's called. Morphine. You mix it up with a little milk and maybe some brandy. I know they sometimes give it to cancer patients. She made me promise to get her some."

My mother picked up the phone. Our family physician was away for the weekend, and the doctor substituting for him refused to prescribe the medication. Next she called Sick Kids and spoke to the doctor on call for the CF ward, reporting Pam's pulse and respiration, describing the quality of her breathing, the sound of her chest. Reluctantly, the doctor said he'd phone in a prescription for the morphine to our local pharmacy.

She hung up the phone and sipped some tea. Her face crumpled and dissolved. She took off her glasses and cradled her head in her arms face down on the table. Her shoulders heaved quietly for a moment. She sat up, took a deep breath, grabbed a Kleenex, blew her nose, put on her glasses and sighed. Her eyes drifted up toward the clock. She stood and strode back to my sister's room, to her untimely business.

"Pam," she said softly, "I've spoken with Dr. Levinson, and he says he'd like to try you on some morphine. The only thing is, he says it might repress your breathing. Do you understand what this means?"

Pam nodded yes.

"Do you want to go ahead and do this?"

Pam nodded again in the affirmative.

I ran to the kitchen to answer the phone.

"Mom," I reported back to Pam's room, "it's Grandma Birdsell. She wants to come out here and help."

Pam had already made it clear to us that she didn't want either of the grandmothers with us. "It will be too hard on them," she insisted.

My mother went to the telephone and listened, her face crumpling as her mother carried on at the other end of the line.

"Her own grandmother and you don't want me there!" Grandma's voice was so loud I could hear her through the receiver clear on the other side of the kitchen.

"It's not me that doesn't want you here, Mother. It's not that anybody doesn't want you here. Pam just thinks it would be best."

"Well, if that's the way you want it. But I don't believe Pammy would say a thing like that."

After Grandma slammed her phone down in my mother's ear, she sat stewing in her screened porch, weeping and wringing her hands, wondering how her daughter could be so cruel. I knew this because I knew my grandmother.

My mother sat at the kitchen table in despair.

"I'll pay for this someday," she murmured, tears brimming.

An antique wooden clock hung dutifully on the wall over the kitchen table. Its time-worn hands gathered up the fading hours of my sister's life as we bustled in and out, making tea, weeping, or staring out the window lost in memory.

Pam had baked some squares earlier in the week, before she told my mother she was tired and had had enough, and went into her room to die. We didn't know whether to eat them or not. They were chocolate and coconut and shortbread. They stuck in our throats as we tried to swallow them with our tears. I wrapped the uneaten ones and put them in the freezer, thinking I'd save them forever.

My father went out to pick up the morphine. My sister slept fitfully, moaning. The afternoon turned swiftly from gray to black. We were cocooned by death and the sound of falling rain.

My mother called me back into Pam's room.

"Pam wants to talk to you," she said evenly.

I went in and stood at the foot of her bed, knowing that our words would be the last we'd share.

She sat upright, propped by pillows, her fragile arms stretched forward and up over the hospital table so she could breathe easier. She wheezed, the humidity of August a granite slab weighing on her chest. Her gaze was fiery, direct, and intense. She began to speak, her words coming hard, slowly, punctuated by long, trembling, tortuous breaths that she drew from the center of the Earth. Her bony fingers, clubbed and purple at the tips, clenched the sides of the hospital table as she struggled to get out everything she had to say.

"Heather…"

"Yes Pam."

"Don't…leave…Rick…alone."

"I won't."

"Don't…leave…him."

"No, Pam, I won't leave him alone."

She gasped for breath and raised her hand to indicate there was more. "You aren't…meant to…stay in…acting. You won't find…what your spirit…needs. You won't find…the people…to support you. You must write…write…and teach…"

Pam was so close to whatever lay beyond, the barrier so transparent, that I believed I felt a Divine presence. My sister was doing the talking, but I was certain I was hearing God's intentions for me.

"Write…write our story…what we…lived through…together…promise!"

A soft roar filled my ears, the hiss of teeming rain, the whoosh of my own blood racing. For a moment I was drowning, picked up and carried along in a swift current of cold, dark water, my ears throbbing with the deafening rush of oblivion.

Pam sat before me as if on a far shore, panting, her eyes expectant, waiting for my reply.

"Yes Pammy, I promise."

She closed her eyes and sat briefly, just breathing, in and out, in and out. Then she grabbed my hand.

"I want you…to remember…something."

"Okay."

"If you can get through this weekend with me...you can get through anything."

"I'll remember."

"Good. I need...to talk...to Mom."

I fled the room.

My father stood in the kitchen, wearing a rain-flecked over-coat and an air of breathless confusion.

"What happened while I was gone?" he asked.

"Pam and I just had our last talk."

"Oh," he breathed, as if I'd shot him softly in the heart with a small pellet. He put his damp arms around me.

Mom came out from Pam's room, wiping her eyes and blowing her nose.

"Did you get the stuff?" she asked, as if being succinct was the best way to ask a distasteful question.

My father pulled a small brown bottle from a paper bag and sat it on the kitchen table. We stared at it, feeling illicit in its presence. My mother shrieked softly, steadied herself on the back of a chair, and wept. My father still hoped for a miracle.

"Let's not give it to her right away," my mother said. "We'll wait first and see how she does tonight."

"Oh wait, I forgot something." He dashed out to the car and back again. "I stopped in at Mother's on the way home, and she sent these for Pam."

Peach-colored roses, from Grandma Bill's garden. We placed the bouquet in a vase next to Pam's bed. Almost immediately one dewy petal dropped, and a short while later, another.

Through the dark hours that followed, the fresh roses wept their soft petals. A puddle, a stream, a river.

I took another shift with Pam. She tried so hard to breathe. Her chest heaved in short bursts, followed by long-drawn-out moments of utter stillness, each one longer than the last. My heart jumped before she breathed again. Her lips were blue.

They fluttered almost imperceptibly. Fluid gurgled in her lungs. Even so, she struggled to stay in charge of her situation, constantly fighting to rouse herself enough to give precise instructions as to how her pillows should be placed, what items she wanted close by, how the oxygen tubing was to be draped. She spoke up sharply with one-word demands if things weren't done just so.

"No!" "There!" "Lift!" "Stop!"

When she lay quiet I held her tiny hand. She stared at me unblinking, cherishing my face until her eyelids closed against their will. My breath came hard against the pain of losing her. The rain catapulted against her window.

Jeff called. He had been sitting with friends in a bar in Jasper Park, Alberta, rock music pounding in his ears, when he felt struck by lightning.

"I have to call home, now," he told his buddies, and took off to find a payphone.

Pam had begun to ask for him, and we had been debating whether or not to call him when the phone rang.

"Should I come home?" he asked.

"It's up to you," my mother whispered.

Inese Krastins, Pam's favorite physio and my own close friend, arrived from Stratford late in the evening. She sat with Pam through the night while the rest of us tried to sleep.

Sunday morning brought more rain. Pam had spent a restless night. My mother agonized over giving her the morphine.

"Let me call Peter Quinlan first, and ask his advice," she said. "He'll know what to do."

Peter, my cousin Gail's husband, was a lawyer. Mother explained the situation to him over the phone, and asked him if there was anything we hadn't thought of.

A Will. Pam had to sign a Will before taking the Bromptman's Cocktail or her final wishes would be invalid.

My father haltingly wrote down Peter's instructions. Meanwhile my mother went in to ask Pam how she wanted to disburse what little she possessed, and then sat at the kitchen table and scrupulously, in her elegant hand, wrote out two copies of the final document.

"Oh my God," she said quietly when she finished. "C'mon Doug, let's get this over with."

They disappeared into my sister's room to get Pam's signature.

"That was the hardest thing I'd ever had to do," my mother cried when she and my father emerged a short time later.

Steeled with her newly won authority as a registered nurse, my mother mixed a small amount of morphine in a little snifter with some milk and Pam's favorite Peach Schnapps.

"I wish someone else could do this," she said, quietly frantic. "I wish Carol Sheppard were here. She's done this sort of thing before…"

I followed my mother back to Pam's dark bedroom and sat close by. My mother slid her arm around Pam's back and helped her sit up to receive the drink. She was terrified that it might be too strong.

My sister took the glass with both her hands and sipped the potion through a straw, her eyes open and determined. She stopped between each sip to breathe. She knew what she was doing.

"There," my mother said. "We'll see how that does."

Later that afternoon Joyce Jellis dropped by. By this time, Pam had reacted favorably to the Bromptman's Cocktail and drifted comfortably somewhere into the netherworld between sleep and semi-coma. Joyce gave her a sponge bath and a light massage.

"How long do you think she can hold on?" my mother asked.

"It's hard to say. It might only be a matter of hours, but knowing Pam, it could go on this way for days."

My mother was upset because the local doctor disagreed with our decision to let Pam die at home and would not come out to attend.

"Doctors!" Joyce said, rolling her eyes. "They're always afraid of this kind of thing. That's why God made nurses. Will you be all right on your own?"

"I think so. I'm in touch with the clinic every couple of hours, and they know what's going on here. They said I could call them for anything right up to the end."

Jeff telephoned from the Jasper Park Lodge resort to say he was on his way, but it would take time. He had to take a bus into Edmonton, and then see what he could get flying standby.

"Grandma Bill has paid for your ticket," Dad told him. "Travel safely."

Again we took turns watching her through the night, Mom and Dad, Jan and Gregg, and me. Rick didn't have much stomach for it and mostly hung out in the kitchen, good for a hug when I needed it.

Several times in those small, dark hours Pam stepped to the precipice of death, only to retreat.

"She's waiting for Jeff," my mother whispered.

At Monday's dawn, the clouds hung low and dense, a grim, gray shroud outside the house. Pam was far enough along that she spoke out loud to those she saw on the Other Side.

"Which door? Which door?" she asked anxiously of someone not within our realm, and then called again for Jeff.

"He's coming Pam, he's on his way. Hold on."

Early in the evening, Rick and Jan drove off in a violent rain to fetch Jeff from the airport in Toronto.

In the interim Carol Sheppard arrived, to my mother's great relief. Carol and Pam had become precious friends, breaking the conventional bounds of the nurse/patient relationship. Now that she was with us, my mother could stop being a nurse, and just be a mom. Medically, Carol would handle the rest.

"It won't be long now," she said after examining Pam. "Sometime tonight."

I sat with my sister while Mom and Carol shared a cup of tea out in the kitchen. Out of nowhere, Pam opened her eyes and startled me by sitting up. With a burst of energy she swung her legs over the side of the bed and furiously began pushing the buttons on her clock radio, huffing and murmuring in frustration.

"What is it, Pam? What are you trying to do?"

She spoke firmly, without panting for breath. "I need to set the alarm for tomorrow morning."

"Okay, okay, I'll do it. What time do you want it set?"

"For 7:30. Set it for the music to come on and not the alarm."

"Okay, 7:30 a.m. There, it's done."

She frowned uncertainly at the clock radio as I pushed the buttons to prove I had set it correctly. Then she pulled herself back under the covers, draped her oxygen tubing just so, and closed her eyes.

Throughout the evening she called for Jeff in earnest.

"He's coming, he's on his way. Rick and Jan are bringing him from the airport."

We looked at our watches and prayed under our breath. Around eleven we heard tires brake in the wet gravel outside, and the sound of commotion at the back door. I went out to greet Jeff and then followed him back to Pam's room.

Seeing her, my brother caught his breath.

"Hold me," she begged him.

Jeff climbed up on the bed behind her, so she could rest her head on his chest. He wrapped his arms and legs around her, embracing her entire form with his long, sinewy limbs. She relaxed.

"It's all right Pammy," he whispered. "I'm here, I love you, it's all right."

Rain fell in thick curtains around the house.

I fled to the kitchen, craving the safety of my husband's arms. Rick paced the floor, car keys in hand.

"What's going on?" I asked.

"Come outside with me for a minute."

I followed him out the door into the garage. The air was damp and chill. I began to shiver. He looked at me strangely and took a deep breath.

"I'm not staying."

My heart exploded like buckshot in my chest.

"What do you mean?"

"I'm not needed here. I've got a show tomorrow. I've got to get a good night's sleep. You can call me if anything happens and I'll come right back."

I struggled to make sense of his words.

"What do you mean if anything happens? She's going to die tonight. Carol said it's only a matter of hours. By the time you make it home you'll only have to turn around again...I don't understand...you won't be doing a show tomorrow, Pam's going to die tonight..."

Rick sucked in his breath, shifting his long, blue-jeaned legs in restless circles, jingling the car keys. The garage was thick with the sweet smell of motor oil, wet earth, and rain. My stomach pitched as if on a rough sea.

"I need you," I said, through chattering teeth.

"You don't need me. You've got your whole family in there."

"You're my family," I cried out.

"I'm sorry," he said, but there was no sorrow in his voice, or in his flickering green eyes.

I fell to my knees and threw my arms around his waist, burying my face in the rough blue cotton of his jeans.

"Please, please don't leave me."

He reached down with his slender arms, took hold of me with

both hands, and peeled himself away. I tumbled to the garage floor, my gaze scraping the handprint left by my sister in the cement when the house was first built.

"I'm sorry," he said again.

I staggered to my feet, staring past the shovels, hoes, rakes, and hammers hanging mute along the walls. Dark trees foamed in the wind beyond the wide mouth of the garage door. His feet crunched on the gravel drive. The car door shut with a sharp thud.

I did not run after him.

The engine turned. The car disappeared into the rain-lashed night.

I stumbled back inside the house, and the death room, and my patient, grieving mother. We sat together in the dark, listening to the rain, watching my sister's chest rise and fall.

Hours later, claiming to have heard Pam's voice calling him back, my husband returned. We lay together on a mattress in the empty dining room, fitful, the miles he'd driven still between us.

The rain ended suddenly. Silence. Stillness deep as a clock that had stopped ticking. The faint, gray light of dawn crept in. My mother appeared in the doorway and called to us softly.

"Come," she said. "It's time."

We gathered as a family around her. Pam roused herself, sat up, and looked around the room. Her gaze lingered briefly on each face, calling our names one by one, as if in prayer.

My mother lay down beside her. She whispered, "It's okay Pammy, you can go now."

"I'm not giving up," Pam replied, defiant.

She lay back, and closed her eyes.

I held my sister's hand and began to recite the 23rd Psalm. The others joined me.

Before we said *Amen*, she was gone.

SPIRITUM EX MACHINA
(The Ghost in the Machine)

"There's a river somewhere that runs through the lives of everyone." — ROBERTA FLACK

Is the end of a life the end of the story?

In grief, I climbed from moment to moment, hand over hand, as if up a slippery wet rope, from the bottom of a dark well, toward a vague light that some days I only half-heartedly aspired to. Some days I slipped back again, almost to the depths. Then, with cold, raw hands, I began once more to climb.

I had no hunger. I ate dark chocolate, smoked mentholated cigarettes, drank more cheap red wine than was good for me. I sat wide awake in the middle of the night without the lights on. I wanted to learn how to breathe without weeping.

I had no words then, for my grief, but I do now. Still, they are only words for the memory of it.

Grief weighed heavy. I sighed deeply, compulsively, constantly, but I couldn't relieve the pressure that felt like an axe in the middle of my chest. Electric currents buzzed through my heart. My eyelids burned red hot. I wanted to close them. I wanted the world to go away, the traffic sounds and the stray voices of people on the street; I wanted it all to just melt away. Fatigue overtook me. I didn't have the energy to stand up, or even to sit, but I couldn't lie down because it was like being drunk, when lying down makes it worse. I closed my eyes and everything spun. I was dizzy with sorrow.

Tears betrayed me at will.

I underestimated the anger grief clutches in its gnarly fist. Everyone on the street made me mad, just because they were there. They were walking along, laughing, and Pam wasn't, and these people didn't know and couldn't care less. I wanted to shout at them, and sometimes, I did.

Grief emptied my marriage of what little there was left. Rick found someone else. Of course, I should have seen it coming.

My body reduced itself to a stick drawing. I slept for hours, waking only to cry or to watch TV Evangelist Tammy Faye Bakker at two in the morning. I related to Tammy Faye—she was the only person I knew who cried more than I did.

One day I saw blueberries on sale and remembered how Pam had loved them, and thought how I would probably have baked a nice cobbler if only there was somebody there to make it for. Then I asked myself if I was somebody. I bought the blueberries, made a huge dessert, and ate the whole thing myself. *I'm not giving up.*

A few weeks later I borrowed a thousand dollars from my mother and signed up for a ten-day all-women whitewater rafting school.

That September, just over a year to the week Pam died, I found myself floundering in the cold, speeding rapids of Oregon's Rogue River, wondering what I'd gotten myself into.

"We need a volunteer so you can learn how to run a rapid in your life jacket," explained Janet, our river guide. "At some point in the trip you're bound to be dumped from the raft, and you have to know how to save your own life."

My hand shot up. So what if I couldn't swim? I hadn't traveled three thousand lonely miles to sit back and not have a Total Experience. And I had nothing left to lose.

I swung my legs into the water and clung to the side of the

raft, heart pounding, staring up at Janet as she spoke. She was everything I aspired to: tall, bronzed, sleek-haired, and muscular. Her voice was calm and confident.

"Rapids are rated in classes one through six, according to their difficulty," she said. "Sixes are unrunnable; they must be portaged. The one you're running this morning is just a riffle, so you should be okay. Relax and let the water carry you. At the end of any rapid, you pass through a series of standing waves. When you see one coming, hold your breath. You'll go under for a moment and pop back out. Look up, and when you see the next wave cresting, hold your breath again, and so on until you're through the standing waves and into the eddy. Then we'll pick you up in the crew boat."

I took a deep breath and pushed off. The river grabbed my legs with startling force. The current was icy and swift. I struggled to stick my feet out in front of me, but the river would not let go. I panicked, flailing my arms in the water, instinctively trying to swim for shore.

"No! No!" I heard Janet yell.

"I don't want to go," I shouted back, gulping a mouthful of water.

"You have no choice," she called out.

The river sucked me right down the chute of a Class Two rapid. I had no control. For a long moment I thought of letting myself go and slipping under, of ending the pain in my chest that had suffocated me since my sister died and my husband walked out. Then I pictured my mother standing over my coffin, weeping on my father's shoulder.

"If only I hadn't lent her the money..."

I stuck my feet out hard in front of me. Within seconds I saw the standing waves. I held my breath, went under, popped up, opened my eyes, held my breath, went under, and popped up again—until, miraculously, I was in the eddy, treading water.

Upstream, the crew boat pulled hard on their oars, trying to reach me.

"Are you all right?" they asked, pulling me aboard.

"I'm great," I grinned, shivering, "just great." *I'm not giving up.*

Five days and several adventures later I awoke in the night, crawled out of my tent, and looked up at the stars. The sky stretched above me like a great veil of mourning. I thought of Pam. *If you can get through this weekend with me you can get through anything.* How many times had I already harkened back to these words, spoken to me two days before she died? They had almost become a mantra.

Sitting in that deep, dark Oregon valley in the cool hush of an autumn night in 1981, I knew that I faced an uncertain future. Being Pam's sister, I also knew that the boundaries of my life were not determined by my circumstance or past, but by my choices and my possibilities.

When each of her CF friends died, I remembered, she had chosen the qualities that she admired in them, that gave her strength. Then she adapted them as her own, so the best part of the people she loved could live on in her. These very qualities had become the guiding principles of her life: temerity, kindness, honesty, forgiveness, patience, generosity, and love. Through the conscious practice of those principles in my own life, I hoped that part of my sister would now live on through me.

Pam had set an example of such courage for me, that I would never fail to be inspired by it. She had taught me to acknowledge fear, and then move past it. As I had done in the rapids that week. As I did sitting on a riverbank in the Oregon wildnerness, facing my future. I could almost hear her laughing in the stars.

*"Life must be understood backwards; but it must
be lived forward."* — SOREN KIERKEGAARD

I know now that had I died ten times over, I would not have been able to subtract the tiniest fragment from Pam's fate.

The days trickle by, flowing into weeks and months. One year, then the next, and the next, a river of time growing deeper, wider. I used to count by how long she lived. Now I count by how long I have outlived her.

The poet Mary Oliver says, "A lifetime isn't long enough for the beauty of this world / And the responsibilities of your life."

Pam saw the beauty of this world, despite its tragedy, and she knew its responsibilities. She taught me to do the same. Now, I can't tell if I see the world through her eyes, or if she is seeing it through mine.

Rain teeming on the Hudson. Windshield wipers humming on the bus along Boulevard East. Hot pea soup from the Greek deli. Sheets warm from the dryer. So much to celebrate. So much to take for granted.

I long to see her in the doorway. I long to gaze into her placid hazel eyes, to feel her knobby fingers clasp my own, to taste the salt on my palms, warm, after she has held my hand. I want her to know me as I am now, to know who I am becoming. I want my me to be a constant good gift to her, to the memory of her.

My family is intact. But surviving intact, and becoming healed and whole, are two different things. It is no one's fault. Loss is irrevocable. Pam's death has torn a hole in the fabric of our family.

"And you keep trying to sew it up," my mother says. "It can't be mended. We just have to accept it as part of who we are now, as a family."

The boys don't talk about Pam, and rarely to each other. Gregg and Jeff are grown men, but my parents and I still refer to them as "the boys." Maybe that is one reason why I seldom hear from them. Their silences wound me. Especially their silence about Pam. I want to talk with them about her, share what we remember. Because if she doesn't live on in us, in our conversations as well as our silent memories, then I fear she really dies.

The loss of our sister stands in the way of our deeper intimacy with each other. How close can we afford to get before that loss becomes too painful? We are each the harbinger of pain's memory and herald of future pain. When we are together all these years later, our loss is still palpable, and encompasses far more than just Pam's death.

Gregg continues his work as a police officer and remains married to Jan. True to his word, my brother is a devoted family man. Together, they are raising four healthy, strapping sons. They hold their family tight as a clenched fist, and hold the past the same way. I am never sure whether their boundaries are meant to keep us from intruding, or keep them from disintegrating. Perhaps Gregg's answer to the chaos he experienced in our family is to keep strict control of his.

My brother's brow is creased; his hairline, like both his grandfathers before him, quickly receding. His blue eyes flicker with worry, and mischief. I see in Gregg both the strong savior and defender of the right, and the small boy humiliated by Mrs. Patyk, his Grade Four teacher. My nephews tell me that their dad is very funny. Gregg doesn't let my parents or Jeff and me see that side of him. He employs a gruffness with us that is hard to get past. I stifle the urge to joke with him and ask if he's going to arrest me. But there are rare, precious moments when he smiles and hugs me tightly in his arms, and my heart falls to its knees in gratitude for his love.

He cannot mention Pam without weeping.

Yet in the way he has committed himself to his job, and to his own little family, his circle of light, I know he has a spirit that refuses to give up.

Jeff lives alone with his dog Cougar in a very small town, laughing when he observes that if he'd known he was going to live this long, he'd have taken better care of himself. He has walked a crooked path, first practicing a trade as a blacksmith, then falling into despair, drug use, and a brush with the law. Single-handedly, he rehabilitated himself, got a job on the line at Ford, and on the side, owned, trained, and rode horses, show jumpers. An industrial accident at Ford further damaged his lungs, and the horses became too expensive. In his mid-thirties, he got his certification as an expert in whitewater kayaking, canoeing, and rafting.

We have often questioned Jeff's choices. This has hurt him, and left him lonely and distrustful. I have learned that's the trouble with many parents and siblings—we so often feel our other family members should be making different choices, and tell them so, when it is really none of our business. Our business is not to judge, but simply to love each other.

Now he spends his days on the river, as often as he is able, sometimes as a guide and teacher, sometimes just to feed his soul. Lacking a car, he bikes around town. He lives life on his own terms, partly in rebellion against his disease, and partly to give himself a sense of control over the uncontrollable. Now one of the few Cystics in North America alive past the age of forty, he is sinewy and strong as the bands of steel that hold up the George Washington Bridge, yet he weighs only 140 pounds soaking wet, on a six-foot frame. He has only 50 percent lung capacity, though on a good day he can kayak with me for several hours and still drag his boat uphill to the road, laughing, leaving me in the dust. On bad days, it's all he can do to get out of bed. The bad days are starting to edge out over the good.

When Pam's name is mentioned, he leaves the room.

Yet with every stroke of his paddle, every pedal of his cycle, he is fighting, he is fighting; he refuses to give up.

My parents have been awarded the Order of Canada for their work with the CF Foundation. Not content to lie on a beach following retirement, they have traveled to Third World countries volunteering their skills. My father has helped businessmen from formerly Communist countries set up marketing plans so they can become good capitalists. My mother has brought her nursing skills to undeveloped cultures. She has also been a parish nurse in her own community, working through First Baptist Church to care for members of the congregation.

They rarely speak of the loss they try to hide, cry through, let go of, hang on to, bury, live in the silences with beneath the porch light on summer nights, moths fluttering, or on cold winter nights, snow piling up softly in the backyard. There are no words.

Looking back, I now cherish the small graces my parents offered that I took so much for granted when I was focused on nothing but my own needs, or what I thought they'd failed to do.

My mother, always bucking up and trying to be cheerful in the face of every difficult hour, leaving notes in my lunch box, offering helpful suggestions, teaching me with a patience of which I wasn't then aware. Taking me in with her blue eyes, full of more compassion than I knew for the tangle of emotions I was.

My father, out there fighting to give us the world, when it was really only him we wanted. My mother laughs and calls him

Don Quixote. Her "Man of La Mancha." There is so much of my father in each of us. We are fighters, and survivors, because of him.

My parents believed in the power of one, the ability of solitary people to manifest great change in the world. This belief was not flimsy philosophy, but gut-felt emotion, doing, as my father said, what they had to do. That day when my mother came into our room, gathered Pam and me up onto our pink chenille bedspreads, and told us my sister was sick to death, she vowed that she and my father would never give up. They never have. They never will.

What I took to be my father's foolish denial was no Pollyanna vision of the world. He is simply a man who sees invincible summer in the midst of every winter. His unshakable optimism, and innate belief in a brighter future, are a gift to us all. In that respect Pam was her father's daughter, and as it turns out, so am I.

My parents taught us love, perseverance, honesty, courage, and faith. The tears they shed, they shed for us. The battles they fought, they fought for us. When their hearts broke, they broke for us. If I didn't see it then, I do now.

"We made too many mistakes," they chastise themselves.

But even their mistakes were made on our behalf. Perhaps they didn't always do or say the right thing, or make the right choice, but they did and said what they thought was right at the time. What I find breathtaking is how willing they were to shed the tears, fight the fight, have their hearts broken, and make the mistakes that made a difference in me, and in the world.

"And where was God in the matter?" my mother sometimes asks.

I tell her God was there in her tender, caring hands, and in my father's brave heart. God was there in my anger, and in Pam's faith, and in the way we kept trying to come through for each other.

Still, I've had to ask myself: do we forgive God for the pain visited on us? For the sick child, the flood, the famine, the war? Does God have the power to stop these things, or does He simply have grace?

Pam always said there was no one to blame. She accepted His grace.

So holding God responsible may only be a way to avoid the real question. Can I forgive myself? Is survival a sin, or just a painful destiny?

Pam said, "Please don't continue to punish yourself."

But there are promises that can't be broken. Mustn't be.

I will be your Protector, and we will die together.

There are words that can't be spoken. Mustn't be. Or even thought.

I'm glad it was her and not me.

There is the unalterable fact that sits like a hard pit in the middle of my heart.

She died and I'm alive.

The grace I seek comes through forgiveness. The forgiveness I seek is my own.

I know I can't make up for anything. The life my sister didn't live. The love my mother didn't get from her mother. I cannot save my father from his regrets, or my brothers from their private heartaches. I can only live my own life fully. I can only love them as I do.

I have not lost entirely the sense of danger, damage, and possible death that was ever present in my early years, but I have learned how to comfort myself, and to consciously choose faith over fear. I fill my life with what I love, the people, music, images, and words that give me inspiration, pleasure, and sustenance. I cry hard, though not often, anymore. I find good reasons to laugh, and when I do, I laugh out loud. I remind myself that the attention I need most is my own, that my soul is struggling to be visible to *itself.*

Like Pam, like my parents and my brothers, I refuse to give up.

Yet what does it mean to not give up? We could have just lain down in exhaustion and pain after she died, and said okay, that's enough. We could have allowed our grieving spirits to shrivel. We could have given up on each other, and there have been times, believe me, when we almost have. Yet in giving up we would be choosing a minimal existence, and that is no way to honor all that we have loved and lost. Pam continues to inspire us to live on the edge of our potential. We do not retreat from life. She would be appalled if we did. So there is nothing left but to attack it. All the energy we used to keep Pam alive, we are using to keep ourselves, and each other, alive. Using your life energy to its fullest capacity, whatever that may be in any given moment—that's what it means not to give up.

Now I live where the river meets the sea, married to the love of my life—a man who by his mere presence blesses me every day. Because I have loved and lost, because I love now, and because I know that loss is part of life, the taste of truth is bittersweet: there is no happy ending.

But there is the day. The sun, the rain. The chance to say I love you. The willingness to forgive. The courage to remember. The opportunity to be kind. The ability to laugh and to be generous. The fact that we can choose our joy in each moment, no matter what. This, in itself, is the miracle.

Pam said, tell our story. Mother said, tell the truth. The story I have told lies somewhere between truth and memory.

Pam survives through the telling. So do I.

I enjoyed most every moment of my life, whether it was up or down… there was always something to learn from, and there was always something in the world that was beautiful that you could take from, and every experience could mean something if you looked at it that way.

If we take the chance and opportunity of seeking out beauty in the world about us, every moment of every day can be treasured. I have learned that no matter what misfortunes or joys one may be faced with— life will surely go on…with love.

Pamela Gaye Summerhayes
1954–1980

ACKNOWLEDGEMENTS

Although, like every writer, I did much of the work on this book in solitude, I did not write it alone. Pam, of course, was always there with me in spirit; but there were many other voices and faces that kept vigil with me, urging me on, coming to me out of the darkness even as I felt this task was beyond me.

The women of the International Women's Writing Guild are chief among these. I owe this book, and my life as a writer, to them. Hannelore Hahn, founder of the I.W.W.G., holocaust survivor, single working mother, and champion of any woman with a story to tell, has created a singular, remarkable place in the world where books like this one can be nurtured. My first mentor, June Gould (in whose workshop I began this work), and those that followed: Eunice Scarfe, Susan Tiberghien, Maureen Murdock, Pat Carr, Jan Phillips, Myra Shapiro, and Alice Orr, are extraordinary women who lovingly gave of their expertise, patience, and faith so that my story, and my gift for telling it, could be served. I also thank the thousands of women writers who have found their way to Skidmore College and the annual Remember the Magic Summer Conference hosted by the Guild. You have fed me with your words, inspired me with your sacrifices, and lifted me up with your joy. You are my tribe.

There is another group of women (and men!) without whom I could not have lived through the last thirty-four years, much less written this book. Laura Press, Angie Gei, Brenda Devine,

Rosemary Dunsmore, Peter Van Wart, Marie-Hélène Fontaine, Inese Krastins, Katia de Pena, Jacquie Presely, Diana Reis, Kerrie Keane, Elisabeth Nordquist, June, Sonny, Megan and Mitchell Van Dusen, Judy Kaye Green, David Green, Suzanne McKenney, Alan Royal, Deborah Burgess, Marlene Moore, Laura Kieley, Pat Burdett, Gary, Kyle, and Tess-Marie Beechey, Glynis Davies, Roberta Maxwell, Bonnie Sweeney, and Rhonda Hayter. I am truly blessed by your love, forbearance, and support: it gives me immense joy to share my love for you in return, and my deepest gratitude for your friendship, in print.

I am indebted to Ms. Céline Dion for her patronage, her support of this book and the cause of Cystic Fibrosis, and I am also beholden to the Canadian Cystic Fibrosis Foundation, particularly June Pierotti, Cathleen Morrison, and Laura Broger.

My enduring appreciation to Ted Conover, Sally Bingham, D.M. Thomas, John de Groot, Joyce Engelson, Phylis Fleiss, Bruce Bauman, Amy Friedman, and Leah Komaiko for your invaluable contributions and assistance; to the late Nancy Wilson, and to Dr. Mary Ann Feldstein, for the healing you brought me; and to the late Mrs. Hagey, the grade school teacher whom I carry always in my heart, because she was the first to believe in me.

Affection and thanks to the members of the Galaxy Writers Group, who for three years have offered me incisive critique and valued friendship.

To Jennifer Adamowsky of Sylar Media, who designed my website: you are a brilliant and beautiful angel.

To Mel Ryane and William Yeh: the generosity of your talent and friendship will always be remembered, and cherished.

Scott Rozman, dear, unexpected friend, who has coached me, encouraged me, and bugged the hell out of me. :) I wish for you someday what you have helped me to achieve.

It is an actual dream come true to have the incomparable Anne McDermid as my agent, along with her wonderful cohorts, Jane Warren and Martha Magor, taking such good care of the book, and me. (I'll never forget chocolate cookies and tea on a rainy spring afternoon.) To Bethany Gibson, who edited a pivotal draft of the manuscript with such wisdom and compassion, I offer my admiration along with my thanks.

Words are not enough to thank the irrepressible and astonishing Kim McArthur, my publisher and final editor, and her merry band, Janet Harron, Ann Ledden, and Taryn Manias, along with book designer Tania Craan, and copy-editor Pamela Erlichman: your passion for what you do, and your belief in this book, have given me the gift of a lifetime.

To my glorious family in Winnipeg: the Carious, Harrises, Mills, et al. You are a wonder to me, a gift and a blessing, especially my precious Laurel, Brian, Alanna, and Garrett Repski.

Deborah Grover, soul-sister and light of my life. You've held me up for so long. God knows where I'd be, or who I'd be, without you.

To my brothers, Gregg and Jeff: we have endured together. Let us go forward now, not with tears and silence, but hand in hand, bound by the knowledge that life is too short for anything but love.

Mom and Dad, you are my heroes. It is a privilege to be your daughter. I will forever aspire to the depths of your love, steadfastness, compassion, and integrity. I could not have done this work without your blessing and encouragement. I pray every night that God grants you the peace and joy you both so deserve.

And to my beloved Len, my heart, who has so amazingly changed my life, changed *me*: you are the one who leaves me speechless—but meet me on our balcony every night at sunset, and I'll try to find the words.